A FREELANCE LAWYER'S GUIDE TO FINANCIAL SUCCESS

H. NICOLE WERKMEISTER

AMERICANBARASSOCIATION

Solo, Small Firm and
General Practice Division

Cover design by Mary Anne Kulchawik/ABA Design

Printed in the United States of America.

28 27 26 25 24   5 4 3 2 1

ISBN: 978-1-63905-487-9
e-ISBN: 978-1-63905-488-6

Discounts are available for books ordered in bulk. Special consideration is given to state bars, CLE programs, and other bar-related organizations. Inquire at Book Publishing, ABA Publishing, American Bar Association, 321 N. Clark Street, Chicago, Illinois 60654–7598.

www.shopABA.org

For my parents. May their memories continue to be a blessing.

Contents

Part V
Avoiding Pitfalls   143

Part VI
Striking a Work-Life Balance   169

Preface

"Every accomplishment starts with the decision to try."
—John F. Kennedy

This book is based not only on the accounts of countless lawyers I have interacted with over the years but also on my own experiences as a lawyer with more than 30 years of litigation experience who, one day, out of circumstance and necessity rather than choice, started freelancing.

When I started freelancing, the practice of law was on paper and in person. Lawyers did not participate in depositions or court hearings via Zoom, court filings were not electronic, and document management software did not exist. The advent of technology and remote work necessitated by the 2020 COVID-19 pandemic changed the practice of law. It also made freelancing more accessible, manageable, and profitable.

Becoming a freelance lawyer need not be a matter of trial and error like it was for me. There are many resources now about how to build a law practice that identify the tools for success. However, freelancing is unique and requires different considerations than a traditional law practice. While starting a freelance law practice can be an exciting, rewarding, and lucrative career path, it is not without challenges. This book highlights the approaches that are particularly relevant to maximizing income as a freelance lawyer and to achieving a work-life balance as a solopreneur. In the words of Kalpana Chawla, an Indian-born American astronaut and aerospace engineer who was the first woman of Indian origin to fly to space, "The path from dreams to success does exist. May you have the vision to find it, the courage to get on to it, and the perseverance to follow it."

About the Author

H. Nicole Werkmeister lives in Albuquerque, New Mexico, with her family and special needs dog. She became a lawyer in 1992, practicing primarily in the area of civil defense litigation for most of her career. She worked for law firms of all sizes, large, medium, and small, in addition to working in the public sector as a special prosecutor, hearing officer, and arbitrator presiding over municipal labor disputes, before starting her freelance law practice in 2012. For more information about the author, visit www.werkmeisterconsulting.com.

Introduction

"Absorb what is useful, reject what is useless, add what is specifically your own."

—Bruce Lee

True story. When Elena was faced with a very sudden move across the country because her husband had to relocate for his job, she already had decades of experience practicing law. She knew the ins and outs of a large law firm practice, had built a network of professional colleagues and clients, and had established a very successful career. Moving to a new state where she had no friends or family and where she had no professional contacts changed everything.

Restarting a career from scratch seemed unimaginable. Elena was not interested in studying for and taking another bar exam, searching for a job, or spending the time and effort it would take to rebuild her professional network, especially with young children and elderly parents to care for. Luckily, Elena had some time to figure out a new career path. Her former law firm needed her help to wrap up her cases and transition clients due to her sudden and unexpected move. Elena agreed to assist her old firm remotely after she moved. So started Elena's career as a freelance attorney.

Freelancing was very different when Elena started down that path. There was no ability to file documents with the court electronically and law firms still relied on paper files. Elena's law firm would fax documents to her for review based on what they thought was important without Elena being able to look at the entire file herself. There was no model for Elena or her law firm to follow regarding how to structure her remote work. Would Elena just research and ghost write? She was unable to sign and file her own briefs from a different state. Would she travel back for court appearances? Videoconferencing was not an option at the time. If so, would the firm reimburse her for travel expenses? Discussion about what she would do and the appropriate compensation and reimbursement ensued without much guidance to inform a resolution. Elena and her former law firm finally came to a mutually beneficial arrangement through trial and error.

When Elena's relationship with her law firm ended once she brought all her cases to a resolution and transitioned her clients to new lawyers, Elena was back to square one. She still did not want to study for another bar or try to recreate a law career in a new state and really liked the idea of continuing to freelance. However, Elena did not know how she would generate work, what sort of compensation model to pursue, the type of resources that would streamline her work, or how to begin to manage the administrative side of a law practice.

Overwhelmed, Elena decided to approach her career the same way somebody starting a small business would begin. Elena studied the type of corporate entity to form for her freelancing business that would best suit her needs, explored the options of freelancing from an office she could rent locally versus working from home, evaluated different types of compensation models, assessed her technological needs, devised strategies for generating work, and became familiar with ways to promote herself.

Trying to wrap her head around a staggering amount of information, Elena decided to create a business plan, which she modified over the years as her wants, needs, and circumstances changed. In fewer than 10 years, Elena's freelancing law practice quadrupled in revenue. She makes more money now than she ever made working at a law firm, works less, and has achieved a balance in life that she could once only dream about.

Lawyers just starting out, lawyers tired of the daily grind of working for a law firm, lawyers looking for more flexibility and autonomy in a legal career, or even lawyers at the end of their careers who want to partially retire can all find a freelance law practice to be the perfect option. Freelancing in the legal profession is becoming an increasingly popular choice for lawyers who want more control over their work schedule, who want to choose their own clients, and who want the ability to work where and how they desire. However, starting a freelance law practice can be intimidating, especially for those used to a traditional law firm environment.

There is an abundance of information available today on every subject imaginable, including starting and building a successful law practice. This book distills that resource material into a helpful guide specific to a freelance law practice, by simplifying complex topics related to running and marketing a business and by outlining the critical factors to consider in making freelance work profitable. Nothing in this book is meant to constitute legal or professional advice and the information put forth is not a substitute for independent analysis. There are so many variables related to a freelance law practice, which can vary tremendously among jurisdictions and from person to person based on needs, preferences, and individual circumstance, that being overly specific becomes challenging. However, understanding how to navigate common challenges will go a long way to setting a freelancer on the path to success.

From crafting a business plan to drumming up clients, managing finances, or understanding technological needs, this book strives to provide a comprehensive guide to starting and building a successful freelance law practice, while also aiming to address some of the more common pitfalls, so that a freelancer can create a profitable freelance law practice while still maintaining a work-life balance. Whether a seasoned lawyer looking to retire and work part time on the side, a new law school graduate exploring job options, or an experienced lawyer looking to change things up, this book is designed to help practitioners at all stages of their careers build a successful, sustainable, and rewarding freelance law practice. Legal freelancing can be an exciting and very lucrative career path where lawyers can attain both personal and professional wealth. This book aims to steer lawyers who want to explore freelancing in the right direction toward attaining that wealth.

PART I

An Introduction to Freelancing

CHAPTER 1

Demystifying the World of Freelancing

"The changing face of the legal profession is something that should be embraced. It is an opportunity to create something new and be a part of the future of law."

—Julie Houth, Esq.

Lawyers reading this book have probably been thinking about a way to practice law outside of the traditional law firm model. Welcome to the world of freelancing. Regardless of the reasons for considering a freelancing career in the law, whether it is a desire for more flexibility or mobility, a wish to be self-employed as opposed to working for somebody else, a need to inject more control over time and workload, or a longing for more balance in life, know that freelancing comes with a lot of freedom and many rewards. However, freelancing also brings a unique set of challenges. Before considering a freelancing career, it is important to first understand exactly what freelancing is in the context of practicing law.

To start, there are different ways to refer to a freelance lawyer. Another common name for a freelancer is a contract attorney. In the past, a contract lawyer referred to somebody who worked for a legal services agency that provided help on a project basis to law firms. The legal services agency, not the law firm, would pay the contract lawyer. In other words, the legal services agency was the intermediary to connect a lawyer and a law firm. A contract lawyer would typically work on one project at a time through the legal services agency. Freelancers, on the other hand, are paid by the hiring lawyer or law firm directly and can work for multiple lawyers or law firms and on many different projects at the same time. The distinction today between a freelancer and a contract attorney has largely been lost and the two terms are often used interchangeably.

The same is true regarding use of the term "consultant" in referring to a lawyer who freelances. Consultants can be independent contractors or can be employees of a company in a particular field. Consultants were traditionally involved in strategic decision making rather than providing a specific work product. For example, a marketing consultant might assist a law firm with putting into place a campaign involving branding, digital advertising, and social media promotion. In other words, the consultant would be involved in the planning process of a marketing campaign. A freelancer, on the other hand, is responsible for delivering a specific work product. For a freelance lawyer, that could be a memorandum of law setting forth a legal analysis of a particular issue, a draft of a contract or motion, a record review, or an appearance at a deposition or trial. However, because a consultant is simply a professional who provides expert advice or services, which is exactly what a freelance lawyer does, the distinction between a freelancer and a consultant has all but disappeared.

This book uses the term "freelancer." However, whether called a freelance lawyer, a contract lawyer, or a consultant, a freelancer is different from a solo practitioner and a freelance law practice is different from a solo or small firm practice. While a freelancer and a solo practitioner share similarities, there are key differences. With a solo law practice, a lawyer represents clients directly, handling all aspects of the required legal work. A freelancer, on the other hand, is a lawyer who provides legal services to other lawyers or law firms. Therefore, the lawyers and law firms are a freelancer's clients.

The freelancer operates as an independent contractor to provide support or expertise in specific areas of the law or regarding specific tasks or cases. Therefore, while a solo practitioner works directly with clients throughout the entire legal process and has direct communication and interaction with clients, a freelancer's client is the hiring lawyer or law firm. Although some freelancers will directly interact with the ultimate clients depending on the assignment, many do not and instead focus on the specific tasks or projects assigned to them, communicating only with the hiring lawyer or law firm.

The primary difference between a freelancer and a solo practitioner is that because for a freelancer, the hiring lawyer or law firm is the actual client who engages and pays the freelancer as an independent contractor, the hiring lawyer or law firm bears the ultimate responsibility to the end client for the work product. Freelancers are generally not directly liable to the ultimate client because they are working under the supervision of the hiring lawyer or law firm. Therefore, whereas solo practitioners bear the responsibility for their work and are directly obligated to their end clients, typically, freelancers are answerable only to the hiring lawyer or law firm. Therefore, the hiring lawyer or law firm pays the freelancer, not the ultimate client.

A freelance law practice can look very different for different lawyers. For example, a freelance lawyer can work on an hourly basis for one or more different lawyers or law firms. While many freelance lawyers work for a single law firm, providing specific services on an as-needed basis, others work for multiple lawyers at the same time. This flexibility allows freelancers to build a broad network of lawyer or law firm clients and to establish themselves as experts in their chosen practice areas. It also offers the prospect of diverse revenue streams, reducing the risk of financial distress from the loss of a client. For example, a freelancer might have two different established law firms as clients to provide a steady and reliable income stream by affording a base amount of legal work while also providing advice to a start-up law firm in the hope that once the business grows, it will need more legal advice and will look to the freelancer for additional help.

There are also many variations in the type of work a freelancer can do. Some freelancers only provide written work and will not do appearance work. Those freelance lawyers might help with legal research and writing or drafting motions but would not appear for a deposition or in court. Other freelancers are eager to appear in court and might assist a hiring lawyer or law firm with covering hearings or even trying cases. A freelancer interested in transactional work could limit work to only the preparation of draft documents, could also assist with due diligence and document review in the context of negotiating a purchase and sale transaction or some other type of deal, or could even help with the contract negotiation itself.

Compensation schemes for freelance lawyers are as varied as the practice structure and type of work a freelancer can engage in. Some freelance lawyers choose to work on specific projects at a flat- or fixed-fee rate rather than providing services reimbursed on an hourly basis. If a freelance lawyer is working on a plaintiff's case, perhaps a contingency compensation arrangement exists, with a law firm paying the freelancer a percentage of the contingency fee the law firm would receive upon successful resolution of a lawsuit. Still other freelancers work on a subscription basis pursuant to which a law firm pays the freelancer a recurring monthly or annual fee in exchange for providing legal services. Some freelancers combine the different compensation schemes, using different fee arrangements for different lawyer or law firm clients or combining fees structures into a hybrid arrangement.

There are even various pay structures within the same category of compensation. For example, there are many ways to pay a freelance lawyer working on an hourly basis. The simplest is payment pursuant to a straight hourly rate. Take Andres for example. If he worked 30 hours a week at an hourly rate of $70, he would earn $2,100 per week. However, Andres could have a different type of hourly compensation agreement to work a certain number of hours at one rate, but upon exceeding those hours, the hiring law firm would bump up his compensation to a higher hourly rate. In that scenario, if Andres agreed to work 100 hours per month at $70 per hour with the hourly rate increasing to $85 an hour above the 100-hour threshold, the hiring law firm would pay him $11,250 for working 150 hours in a month (100 hours at $70 per hour, or $7,000, plus 50 hours at $85 an hour, or $4,250).

Regardless of how a client compensates a freelancer, it is by far not the only factor that impacts income. In addition to how a freelancer is paid and the amount of revenue a freelancer can generate, expenses are also an important factor. The availability of or need to pay for the resources necessary to build a freelance law practice will impact expenses. The higher the expenses, the lower the net income.

If, for example, Andres worked from home using his own resources, his net income would be reduced by the cost of the resources he needed to establish a home practice, such as the expense of a legal research software license or case management software. However, suppose Andres had an office at the law firm that he freelanced for and assume he used the law firm's resources. For example, maybe the client law firm allowed Andres to use its computers to do his work, provided him with access to the firm's legal research software, and gave him the leeway to use the firm's legal assistants to format his written product. In that case, Andres could keep most of what he earned because his operational overhead would be minimal.

However, the hiring law firm might also deduct overhead from the amount it paid Andres for his freelance work. One scenario might be that in return for being able to access the firm's resources, Andres must work 20 hours before receiving compensation to account for the firm's overhead. If he worked 150 hours a month under that compensation arrangement, Andres would earn $5,600 for the first 100 hours worked (80 hours over the 20 "overhead" hours at $70 per hour). He would earn the same $4,250 for the remaining 50 hours worked over the 100-hour threshold, for a total of $9,850.

While the compensation would be $1,400 less than Andres would have earned by working at home and not using the firm's resources, it is impossible to assess whether the lesser compensation in exchange for access to firm resources makes sense without considering work preferences and the cost of resources. For example, many lawyers can format their own documents and do not require help from a legal assistant. Transactional lawyers might not need access to legal research software. Most lawyers today have their own computers. Because the freelancers in those situations do not have a significant need for access to a law firm's resources, they might not want their compensation reduced for overhead expenses.

Andres, however, only has a laptop at home. He likes using a desktop at the law firm with dual monitors for his legal drafting work. He also knows he would have to pay more than $2,500 a year for a legal research software license, which he needs for his litigation practice. In addition, Andres has never been adept with technology and needs computer help, especially when it comes to formatting letters to clients and federal court briefs. He knows he could not hire even a part-time legal assistant for less than $20,000 a year.

Because of Andres' work preferences and the cost of the resources he needs to practice law, it makes sense for him to use the hiring law firm's resources in exchange for lower compensation. If he did not use the firm's resources, he would have to buy a desktop computer and monitors, a significant start-up cost. He would also have to spend at least $22,500 annually, or over $1,875 monthly, on overhead for part-time help and a legal research software subscription, which amounts to more than the $1,400 monthly compensation deduction for using the law firm's resources.

In addition to expenses, different billing models will also have an impact on net income. Suppose Andres charged a flat fee for his legal work. For example, assume he charged $500 for preparing a state court brief that did not involve a dispositive motion. He charged $750 for dispositive motion briefs in state court. He doubled those amounts for federal court briefs because of the added complexity of federal law. However, after a short time of doing flat-fee work, Andres found that he was unable to make a reasonable amount of money because of his lack of technological expertise, which made him inefficient at completing assignments.

Freelance attorneys who bill on a flat-fee basis are rewarded for their technological know-how. Automating routine tasks through technology makes any lawyer more productive and is essential for flat-fee work. For example, programming a computer with macros to create headings or signature blocks with a few keystrokes saves a lot of time in completing repetitive tasks that involve multipart and time-consuming formatting. Contract templates avoid the need to recreate standard contract provisions. Document automation also allows for the optimization of a lawyer's time.

Realizing he was not adept with technology, Andres understood he was lacking a competitive advantage in taking on flat-fee work and made the change to hourly billing. After switching from a flat-fee arrangement to an hourly fee compensation scheme, Andres realized he needed to do something about the fact that he hated the administrative work necessary to accurately capture and bill for his time. He did not like billing in six-minute increments and never felt like recording his time at the end of the day, finding himself at the end of every month trying to recreate the time he had spent doing legal work. He wound up forgetting a lot of what he had done in the prior month and, therefore, not billing for it.

Because Andres primarily provided legal services to one law firm, he was able to offer his services on a subscription basis. The law firm paid him a recurring, flat, monthly fee in exchange for Andres agreeing to provide up to 100 hours of legal services per month. Andres, then, did not have to keep track of his time or invoice the law firm. The law firm was thrilled because the subscription-fee billing gave it predictability in terms of its legal costs, and Andres was happy to avoid the administrative obligations of recording his time.

Through trial and error, Andres combined different types of freelancing work and billing models so he could reach his goal of earning $10,000 per month while cutting back as much as possible on the administrative work necessary to bill clients. Following is the hybrid work arrangement Andres came to that was sustainable for him.

A law firm paid him a subscription rate of $7,000 per month for a maximum of 100 hours. One of the many online legal services platforms matched Andres with a solo practitioner who wanted to hire a freelance attorney at $80 per hour to provide up to 10 hours a week of discovery-related work, such as drafting and responding to written discovery requests. Those 10 hours would result in up to $3,200 per month, bringing total compensation to just over Andres' goal of $10,000 a month. However, because the hiring lawyer from the online legal services platform did not guarantee 10 hours per month, Andres decided to hedge his bets by entering into a contingency-fee compensation arrangement with a lawyer he knew who was going to trial and needed somebody as a second chair. Andres agreed to second chair the trial in exchange for either $25,000 or 10 percent of the hiring lawyer's recovery, whichever was greater.

With these different work arrangements and fee structures, at worst, if Andres and the trial lawyer did not prevail and if the online legal services arrangement did not result in 10 hours of legal work a week for Andres, he would still earn $7,000 per month from his subscription-fee arrangement with the law firm. However, the potential upside if he received even some work through the online legal services platform or if he prevailed at trial was well over his $10,000 per month goal.

What a freelance practice looks like is limited only by imagination. No matter what shape a freelance practice takes, one of its main advantages is flexibility. Not only do freelance lawyers have the flexibility to enter into different billing arrangements, but they can work from anywhere. Many freelancers work from a home office. However, freelancers can also rent an office for themselves or rent a shared or joint office space. Freelancers have the option to work any place with a reliable internet connection, whether from a local café, by a hotel pool, or from a boat in the middle of the Pacific.

Another benefit of freelancing is the ability to choose the type of legal work to do. At a traditional law firm, a lawyer typically works on the matters assigned or that come in. As a freelancer, however, a lawyer can choose to only do transactional work and not litigate. A litigator can choose to only work on certain types of matters, such as legal research and writing, but not do appearance work. Or, a freelancer can decide to build expertise in a specific area of the law, like intellectual property or estate planning, and only work on matters in that field. The flexibility of freelancing allows lawyers to build diverse and interesting practices that align with their interests and passions.

Regardless of the name by which a freelance lawyer is referenced, the practice structure, the type of work a freelance lawyer engages in, or the nature of the compensation arrangement, the common thread is that freelancing is self-employment and that a freelancer works for another lawyer or law firm. Therefore, freelance attorneys are independent contractors, providing legal services to other lawyers, not to the ultimate client.

While this type of arrangement has many benefits, it is not without challenges. For example, because freelancers are self-employed, they pay their own taxes and are responsible for securing their own benefits, such as health insurance or retirement plans. This is one of the downsides to freelance work. Another challenge for freelancers is finding clients. Unlike traditional law firms that have established referral networks and client bases, freelance lawyers must develop their own client network and market themselves and their services to generate clients. In addition, freelance lawyers sometimes have difficulty managing workloads when there are periods of high demand for their services followed by periods of little or no work. Freelancers must also be able to manage their finances effectively. As independent contractors, freelancers must track their income and expenses, pay taxes, and budget for contingencies like periods of slow work. However, with good planning, a freelance lawyer can mitigate potential downsides to maximize income and the potential for success.

More and more law firms, whether big or small, as well as solo practitioners, have started to step away from the traditional work model. As a result, they are considering more flexible employment relationships and are outsourcing legal work, causing a rapid expansion in the freelance legal market. Taking advantage of this new, growing market can provide immeasurable rewards in terms of time, freedom, flexibility, and balance. However, understanding the challenges and knowing what pitfalls to avoid is also vital. Thoughtful consideration of the pros and cons of a freelance practice before jumping in will help ensure success in creating a sustainable business model, both from a professional and a personal perspective. So, why would a lawyer want to give up the security of working for a law firm to begin a freelance practice?

CHAPTER 2

Embracing the Freelance Revolution

Unlocking the Benefits of Independent Work

"Never get so busy making a living that you forget to make a life."
—Dolly Parton

Lawyer burnout is an increasing problem. Lawyers put in a lot of time, often working outside of regular business hours. Exhaustion from working excessive hours is compounded by a competitive professional culture that exacerbates stress. According to a 2016 study by the Hazelden Betty Ford Foundation and the American Bar Association Commission on Lawyer Assistance Programs, about a quarter of working lawyers were problem drinkers and suffered from depression. That percentage has undoubtedly grown.[1]

The mental health crisis among lawyers, especially after the COVID-19 pandemic, has turned into a national conversation. Bar associations across the country have started compiling mental health resources for lawyers, providing free lawyer assistance programs to support lawyers who are facing mental health or substance abuse issues, and allowing lawyers to fulfill their continuing education requirements by taking courses on mental health and wellness issues.

A review of Lawline, a popular online provider of continuing education programs, showed 2023 offerings of dozens of substance abuse and mental health continuing education courses for lawyers, including "A Whole New World: The Evolving Mental Health Dialogue in the Legal Profession," "Attorney Wellbeing & Ethics: Taking Care of Ourselves & Our Practice," "Be It Resolved: Striving for a (Realistic) Work/Life Balance for Lawyers," "Depression: An Occupational Hazard of the Legal Profession," "Developing Resilience and Achieving Well-Being in Times of Challenge and Chaos," "Effective and Ethical Management of Work-Related Stress for Attorneys," "Intervention Strategies for Helping Legal Professionals," "Mental Health, Substance Abuse & Competence in the Legal Profession," "Overcoming the

---

1 Patrick R. Krill, Ryan Johnson & Linda Albert, *The Prevalence of Substance Use and Other Mental Health Concerns among American Attorneys*, J. ADDICTION MED., Jan.–Feb. 2016.

Impact of Chronic Stress: How to Successfully Maintain Your Competence and Your Legal Practice," "Strategies for Combating Stress and Substance Abuse for Legal Professionals," "The Impaired Lawyer: A Call for Action," "The Role of Attorney Wellbeing in Your Legal Practice," and many more.

Medical and mental health professionals like Dr. Neil Schamban, MD, from Huntsville, Alabama, are sounding the alarm on the mental health crisis among professionals like lawyers:

> The struggle of professionals in high stress careers like healthcare, emergency services, finance, and the law highlights a growing mental health crisis that requires attention. The incessant pressure to perform at peak levels takes a toll on professionals. The relentless demands, long hours, debt burden from education, responsibility for critical outcomes, and the real risk of malpractice liability can lead to burnout, anxiety, depression, addiction, and other mental health issues.
>
> Addressing the mental health crisis among professionals is not just a matter of personal well-being. It also has much broader implications. When professionals suffer from mental health challenges, the quality of their work, decision-making, and performance can be compromised, negatively impacting those they serve.
>
> By normalizing open discussions about emotional well-being, we can diminish the stigma around mental health challenges. Workplaces can become more supportive and encourage people to seek help without fear of shame or repercussion, creating environments that promote work-life balance. Prioritizing mental health will not only allow us to safeguard the well-being of professionals individually, but will also help fortify the foundation upon which their professions stand, ensuring that we have a workforce of individuals who can navigate the challenges of today's demanding world.[2]

The COVID-19 pandemic completely shifted the way we work. Many law firms were required to shut down partially or entirely. Lawyers began working remotely. Client conferences, depositions, hearings, and even trials were conducted via Zoom. The entire practice of law changed. Law firms had to adapt and transition to remote work to survive. Even now, years after the pandemic has ended, lawyers are still conducting meetings over Zoom rather than traveling to meet personally with clients or witnesses. Remote court appearances still happen regularly. Hybrid meetings with personal and remote participation are the norm. A combination of in-person and remote work has become a part of the professional landscape.

As part of the changing legal landscape, more and more law firms and solo practitioners are engaging freelancers to help them with their law practice.

---

2 N. Schamban, MD, personal communication, Aug. 30, 2023.

Successfully navigating the freelance world provides a way for lawyers to achieve a work-life balance and to minimize stress and burnout. Freelancing has become an increasingly popular career choice for professionals across a wide range of industries for a reason—it allows them to take control over their careers and to work on their own terms.

Ruby found out firsthand the benefits of freelancing when she left her law firm. She began providing legal services to several lawyers, one of whom she had co-counseled with on several complex litigation cases. Although she had never worked for him directly, Ruby was familiar with his work because they had been on the same side of multiparty litigation representing different clients. However, never having worked directly with this lawyer, all Ruby had seen over the years was his final work product, not any of the behind-the-scenes efforts that yielded the result. Ruby was extremely impressed with the lawyer's competence and decided to freelance for him after leaving her own law firm.

Very quickly, his emergencies became Ruby's crises. He would call Ruby late in the afternoon and ask her to prepare a motion to enlarge a deadline that was about to pass the next day. Once, he asked Ruby to prepare a federal appellate brief that had to be filed only two days later. Ruby often had to obtain affidavit testimony from witnesses to support motions when he had forgotten to depose those witnesses prior to the discovery deadline. Ruby even had to respond to a motion for sanctions on his behalf because he had overlooked answering interrogatories and requests for production in one case.

It seemed like Ruby had never left her old law firm. She was still working nights and weekends to deal with the emergencies the hiring lawyer created by not being diligent or organized. Trying to get him out of a potential contempt ruling was nerve-racking. Preparing a well-researched and written federal brief in just two days created more stress than Ruby wanted to deal with. However, because as a freelancer, Ruby could choose who to provide legal services to, she decided to stop freelancing for the lawyer who was constantly creating emergencies for her. Providing legal services to him was hurting her work-life balance, not helping it. As a freelancer, Ruby was able to drop her work with that lawyer and focus on her relationships with other lawyer and law firm clients. Her work life and stress levels immediately improved.

Being able to choose who to work with is one of the major benefits of freelancing. So is the ability to decide what kind of work to do. Another lawyer Ruby freelanced for wanted her to be an appearance lawyer to attend depositions and go to court. Ruby had plenty of experience litigating so being an appearance attorney was right in her wheelhouse. However, a litigation practice is often inconsistent with being able to control when and how much to work. If a judge schedules a trial during the week between Christmas and New Year's, it does not matter that Ruby had planned to spend time with her children that week, who would be out of school on winter break. She would have to find a childcare option so she could go to trial. When one of Ruby's children got sick and was unable to go to school on a day Ruby was scheduled to cover a deposition, her wife had to take off work to care for their child so Ruby could keep her work commitment.

One of the reasons Ruby left her law firm in the first place was so she could spend more time with her family. Freelancing as an appearance lawyer was incompatible with that goal. Although Ruby did not mind appearing for other lawyers occasionally, she started moving away from doing it regularly. As Ruby made court appearances less and less a part of her freelancing practice, she realized how much more flexibility she had with days that remained relatively unscheduled. As a result, Ruby eased away from appearing in court altogether. Now, although Ruby will cover a deposition or a hearing for another lawyer if there is an emergency and nobody else is available, she no longer tries cases, and she makes it clear to hiring lawyers that she is not interested in being an appearance lawyer as part of her freelancing services.

Ruby's experience shows that one of the most significant benefits of freelancing is the flexibility it provides. Not only did Ruby decide who to work for and what type of work she wanted to do, but she could also set her own work schedule and work from home most of the time. When her kids were home from school, she could be with them. When she wanted to plan a vacation, Ruby was able to do so. This flexibility allows freelancers like Ruby to balance work with other important aspects of their life, like family and personal interests.

Increased flexibility leads to a better work-life balance. After Ruby realized that she no longer wanted to do appearance work, she structured her days so that she stopped working when her children came home from school. That way, she could spend time with them, help them with their homework, and attend their practices and games. If there was a project she needed to spend time on, she was willing to work on it after her kids went to bed. Her ability to make decisions about when to work, how to structure her work, and how to manage her time gave her an autonomy she never had when working for a traditional law firm. The autonomy Ruby had as a freelancer led to not just greater job satisfaction than she ever had before but also to a work-life balance that reduced her stress and eliminated burnout.

Because Ruby no longer wanted to do appearance work, she decided to use her litigation experience to generate clients without having to go to court. Ruby started promoting herself as somebody who could provide risk management advice to small businesses and start-ups to avoid costly litigation. One law firm hired her to provide training to one of its clients, a local nonprofit that did not have the financial ability to hire a full-time human resource professional. The law firm engaged Ruby to train the nonprofit's employees on harassment and discrimination issues and to create an employment manual for the organization. That work generated referrals, and Ruby soon established herself as an expert in the area of harassment and discrimination law in the context of helping employers minimize risk and avoid potential employment disputes.

By leveraging her litigation skills, Ruby was able to work on a different aspect of the same practice area. Instead of defending employers in litigation when an employee filed a sexual harassment lawsuit, Ruby was able to instead help law firms who represented employers provide advice to their clients on how to avoid the lawsuit in the first place.

The variety offered by freelancing to work on a wide range of projects with diverse clients is very attractive. It can help keep work interesting and provide opportunities for professional development and growth. Another benefit of freelancing is being able to choose a compensation scheme. While a lot of work, especially in the litigation arena, is still performed on an hourly basis, law firms are increasingly moving to non-hourly billing models. As illustrated in the preceding chapter, freelance lawyers can work on a particular project for a flat or fixed fee, can provide legal services on a subscription-fee basis, or might elect to participate in a case and share the risk of success with a contingency-fee arrangement. Even when a hiring law firm compensates a freelancer according to an hourly rate, there are alternatives to simply paying a freelancer by the number of hours worked times the hourly rate. For example, an hourly billing freelance attorney can agree to work a set number of hours at a lower rate that increases once a threshold is met.

The diverse compensation schemes give freelancers the potential to earn more than they would in a traditional employment arrangement. A freelancer who carefully limits overhead by working from home or who uses a hiring law firm's resources can charge more affordable rates to generate clients and still take home the same amount of compensation. If Ruby decided she only wanted to work 25 hours a week, she could charge $80 per hour and still generate six figures in annual gross revenue, a significant salary for part-time work. By minimizing overhead, Ruby would be able to keep most of that gross revenue as net income. And, unlike a salaried position, Ruby would have the ability to take on more work to increase her net income.

Freelancing is not necessarily a Monday through Friday, nine to five proposition. A freelancer who is a night owl can wake up at 10 a.m. but work late into the evening. On the other hand, a freelancer who needs to care for an aging parent can wake up early and work in the morning and then provide care during the afternoon. Going to a child's soccer game at 3 p.m. no longer presents a problem for a freelancer who can structure the day to finish work on time to cheer on a child. Most lawyers cannot even contemplate taking a three-week vacation. A lawyer who freelances can advise hiring lawyers well in advance of unavailability so that taking a vacation uninterrupted by work becomes possible. Or, a freelancer can work virtually and spend a couple of hours every morning on vacation working from a laptop. Because freelancers can decide if they want to work 50 hours a month or 250 hours a month, they can structure their days to meet their needs and goals in a way that a lawyer who is employed by a law firm cannot.

Freelancing is a wonderful career whether working full time, part time, or using freelance work to supplement income. A law professor who teaches a course on insurance law might also consult with insurance defense law firms as an expert witness in insurance coverage disputes. An appellate lawyer who wants to write fiction instead of legal briefs might freelance to support those ambitions until the lawyer becomes a published author. A retiring lawyer who does not want to get completely out of the game might freelance to keep occupied. A lawyer who no longer wants to practice law can freelance to supplement income while starting a business that is more closely aligned with the lawyer's passions.

One of the most appealing reasons to freelance is the flexibility to work from anywhere. Geographical freedom can provide opportunities for travel and a greater sense of freedom in choosing where to live and work. If freelancing for a law firm, a lawyer might have the option to work from the firm's offices. If that is not an option, there are many office spaces and workspace solutions. Turnkey offices are available to rent that fit all budgets. A turnkey office could be shared office space, could consist of a private office, or may even be an office suite. Many turnkey office spaces offer shared conference rooms, high-speed internet connections, as well as other professional amenities like kitchens or a shared receptionist, minimizing overhead expenses.

Working remotely from home instead of from a rented office is the preferred method for many freelancers. Or, given that the only necessary equipment to do many types of freelance work is a laptop and reliable internet, a freelance lawyer can also work virtually from a coffee shop while enjoying a cappuccino, get in a few hours of work on a plane while traveling to visit family, or work a few hours a day while on an extended vacation in the French Riviera. Mobility is one of the biggest perks of freelancing.

Freelancing provides so many advantages for a lawyer, including flexibility, autonomy, variety, increased earning potential, geographical freedom, and work-life balance. Freelancing can provide a fulfilling, rewarding, and very lucrative career path that can greatly reduce the stress so many lawyers experience in their careers. However, while freelancing may sound like an ideal work arrangement, there are also challenges. A freelancer must be willing to take on not just the rewards of entrepreneurship but also the risks. Planning to maximize the benefits and minimize the risks is essential to becoming a successful freelancer. While the benefits of freelancing sound exciting, understanding the downsides to freelancing is a necessary step in the planning process.

CHAPTER 3

Navigating the Challenges of Freelancing

"The way I see it, if you want the rainbow, you gotta put up with the rain."
—Dolly Parton

While freelancing may sound ideal, there are challenges that cannot be ignored. Before deciding whether to start freelancing, understanding some of the challenges and ways to mitigate them is critical. Although this chapter addresses some of the significant challenges in general terms, subsequent chapters offer specific strategies for dealing with them.

As previously mentioned, flexibility is one of the biggest upsides of freelancing. It can also be one of the biggest pitfalls. Flexibility means freelancers can work from home, can work while having a beer at a local pub, or can work on vacation. It also means freelancers do not have to get dressed to go into the office every day, can start work at noon, or can interrupt the workday to stream a movie on Netflix or to take a nap. There is nobody monitoring a freelancer's performance. Therefore, freelancing requires lawyers to monitor their own performance.

This is easier said than done. Even if there is no formal supervision of a lawyer's performance in the office, there is always informal monitoring. If a lawyer takes frequent breaks in a law office, two-hour lunches, or is constantly on the phone for personal reasons, that does not go unnoticed. Therefore, working in an office setting provides a sort of informal regulation of a lawyer's productivity. Working remotely or virtually, on the other hand, requires self-regulation. Some people are good at self-regulation. Others are not.

Freelancers must be self-motivated and disciplined to succeed. Without the structure and accountability of a traditional workplace, it can be easy to fall into unproductive habits or to lose focus. For those who struggle with self-motivation and discipline, freelancing can be a particularly challenging career path. It takes a high level of self-management to stay productive and focused. Therefore, freelancing is probably not the right career choice for a lawyer who lacks self-motivation.

Working in an office, especially given the competitive culture of the legal profession, can provide its own motivation. For example, many lawyers who work in law firms have a billable hour requirement. Sometimes, salaries or bonuses are dependent on meeting or exceeding that threshold. The expectation to bill a certain number of hours, especially if income is dependent on it, provides the motivation to work efficiently and to stay productive. No lawyer enjoys only billing five hours in a day despite spending eight hours at the office because of a lack of focus.

Law firms also often gather their lawyers for regular meetings to discuss workload, tasks, and outcomes. Those types of meetings can provide informal motivation for a lawyer to move cases along so the lawyer is not in the position of having to explain to colleagues a continued failure to draft a motion, to provide a status update to a client, or to finalize a contract.

On the other hand, working from home without sources of external motivation can be very difficult for some lawyers. Whereas some lawyers find that working from home or working in another setting outside the office increases productivity because of the absence of typical office distractions, like colleagues wanting to chat about what happened over the weekend or the call for everybody to gather in the kitchen for a birthday celebration, other lawyers find that a lack of external motivation adversely impacts their productivity because they cannot keep focused. Those lawyers need to learn self-motivation and how to concentrate on work outside of an office setting or they will never be productive, successful freelancers.

In addition to productivity and motivation issues, lawyers who enjoy working in an office setting often find freelance work isolating. Freelancing can be a lonely profession. Freelancers working by themselves may miss the social interactions and support networks that come with traditional employment, leading to feelings of loneliness, which can negatively impact mental health and well-being. While freelancers can turn to online communities and networking events to connect with other lawyers, those efforts can sometimes feel forced or insufficient, particularly for lawyers who thrive on socializing or crave in-person interactions.

The COVID-19 pandemic resulted in many people working from home. Many found remote work satisfying and reported being more productive. That led to a lot of businesses allowing workers to keep a hybrid schedule of working partially at the office and partially from home, even after the end of the pandemic. However, an observation reiterated by many remote workers was that they missed the social interaction that came with being in an office environment. They found the lack of in-person interactions to be challenging. After a year of Zoom conferences, they started tuning out. While there are many possible ways to complement freelancing with face-to-face interactions, such as attending local bar association events, becoming involved with a legal service nonprofit organization, or seeking out mentoring opportunities, creating personal interactions when working remotely is intentional and means freelancers must extend themselves.

Another significant drawback to freelancing is the lack of access to the same benefits and protections that traditional law firm employees have, such as health care, disability and life insurance, or retirement plans. This can create financial stress and insecurity. One of the biggest expenses to consider before starting to freelance is health insurance. Most law firms pay a large portion, or at least some portion, of their employees' health insurance costs. A freelancer, on the other hand, might have to absorb the entire cost of insurance. Depending on the state, a policy for a single person can easily exceed $20,000 annually before deductibles and copays, with a family policy costing even more. In addition to the cost, the availability of coverage varies greatly depending on locality. A freelancer living in a rural area might have very limited options regarding the types of health insurance policies or coverages available. Even some cities offer much more limited selections for individual plans as opposed to employer health insurance plans.

Therefore, exploring options for health insurance, if necessary, prior to striking out as a freelancer is essential. Under the Affordable Care Act, the federal government's Health Insurance Marketplace allows freelancers, as self-employed individuals, to obtain health-care coverage. States also have health insurance exchanges for their residents. In addition, there are demographic specific plans, such as Medicare for adults 65 and older or TRICARE, which is the government's health-care program for members of the military and their families. Professional organizations often provide group plans for members as well. For example, many bar associations offer group health insurance plans. The good news is that a self-employed freelancer can deduct premiums for health insurance from adjusted gross income as a business expense, which will reduce tax liability. However, the cost of health insurance for a freelancer cannot be ignored.

In addition to no longer having the benefit of an employer's health insurance plan as a freelancer, there are other types of insurance a freelancer will miss out on by not working in a law firm, including professional liability insurance, workers' compensation coverage, life insurance, and disability coverage. A freelancer will also lose the advantage of being able to participate in an employer's pension or 401(k) retirement plan, including receiving an employer match for amounts contributed to a retirement plan. In short, working at a law firm provides many hidden benefits that can often go unnoticed.

One freelancer from Merion, Pennsylvania, was only able to start a freelancing practice because she was married and her husband's job provided most of the necessary employment benefits. Because of their combined income, they could max out his retirement plan and obtain the full employer match so the fact that she did not have a retirement plan of her own was not as impactful. In addition, because of his income, she had the chance to build her freelancing practice without worrying about the lack of enough work at first. Her husband's job also provided coverage for medical and dental care. Although she has a thriving freelancing practice now and can afford the necessary and desired employment benefits for her family, which has allowed her husband to retire, starting the practice when she had a spouse with a job that provided employment benefits and a steady income stream gave her the cushion to build her freelancing practice without a lot of stress or worry.

A freelancer who does not have the luxury of a partner who can provide employment benefits or income that allows for a cushion can start building a freelancing practice by working part time for a law firm, which will provide steady income and employment benefits. Or, a freelancer can convert a traditional job at a law firm into freelance work. For example, a freelancer could negotiate a different payment structure at a law firm so that instead of receiving a salary, the law firm could pay the freelancer a small base stipend, which would provide steady income, and then pay the freelancer a certain percentage of amounts billed or collected from clients over a monthly threshold. This type of payment structure would not only provide steady compensation to the freelancer but would also allow the law firm to cover the overhead costs that would include employment benefits like health and professional liability insurance premiums.

Putting numbers to this kind of scenario, assume a law firm paid Max a base stipend of $2,000 per month. If the law firm calculates overhead to be $10,000 per lawyer, then the law firm could also pay Max, in addition to the $2,000 per month, an additional 30 percent of all amounts billed or collected over that $10,000 threshold. If Max billed at an average hourly rate of $200 and if he worked part time and billed 20 hours per week, or 80 hours each month, he would bring in $16,000 per month. The law firm would then pay Max his $2,000 base salary plus 30 percent of $6,000, the amount he brought in over the law firm's $10,000 overhead threshold, which would be $1,800 per month. Adding the base stipend with the additional percentage comes out to $3,800 per month, or $45,600 annually.

This scenario is a win-win for the employer and the freelancer. The law firm is paying Max based on how much he works. If he bills more than 80 hours per month, he will make more. However, if he works less than 80 hours per month, he will make less. The law firm is also covering its overhead, including Max's base salary of $2,000 per month, by only paying Max more than his base salary if he covers the firm's overhead threshold. Therefore, even if Max works more and the law firm pays him more, the firm is still covering its overhead while generating a profit of 70 percent of every dollar Max earns above his overhead threshold. For Max, there is a steady income stream and employment benefits that allow him the cushion to build his freelancing practice.

Starting a freelancing practice with some sort of cushion is advantageous so that a freelancer has time to build a practice that can cover the cost of the employment benefits a freelancer will give up by leaving a traditional law office. However, there are other expenses a freelancer will need to assume when freelancing. Working remotely instead of in an office requires a home office. This requires dedicated hardware such as a desktop or a laptop, fast and reliable internet, a printer and scanner, and office furniture and supplies. A freelancer who works remotely from home should have a dedicated home office space that has a professional feel. Nobody wants to see their lawyer on a Zoom call with a bunch of clutter in the background, and no freelancer wants to be in the middle of talking about the complexities of an assignment with a colleague while a dog can be heard barking in the background. Setting up a home office can be an expensive proposition.

Freelancers might take for granted all the software and databases available when working at a law firm until having to purchase them when striking out on their own. There is word processing software, practice management software, document management software, time tracking and billing software, legal research tools, e-discovery tools, cloud-based storage solutions, videoconferencing software, payment software, client portal software that allows for the secure sharing of information, and much more. Some freelancers can run their practices from an Excel spreadsheet. Some need much more sophisticated management and administrative solutions that cost a lot of money.

Another challenge of freelancing is the need to manage finances. Because freelancers are independent contractors, they are responsible for paying their own taxes, tracking revenue and expenses, and preparing for financial contingencies, which can be daunting for those who have never managed their own business finances or who do not have an interest in managing their own business finances. At least a basic understanding of accounting, cash flow, and other financial concepts are critical for maintaining a successful freelance practice.

While balance is one of the primary reasons many lawyers choose to freelance, finding balance, especially when first starting out, is not easy. When a lawyer works in an office, there are natural boundaries between home life and work life. The most obvious is location. A lawyer must change into business clothes and commute to an office. That signals the start of the workday. Leaving the office signals the end of the workday. While smart phones have clouded the line between work and personal time, leaving home to go to work still creates at least somewhat of a differentiation between work and personal time. Lawyers do not generally watch television in the middle of the day, take their dog for a walk, or nap, if they are in an office setting. People act differently in an office than they do at home.

The problem with not separating work and personal time if working at home or virtually is that it can thwart finding balance. If a lawyer who is working from home takes an hour nap during the middle of the day, that lawyer might have to skip a family dinner to meet the next day's deadline. It is much easier to work another couple of hours in the evening to the exclusion of spending time with family if a lawyer works from home and must only step into the next room to work than it would be if the lawyer had to drive a half an hour into the office. Binging a series on Hulu during the workday means working extra hours another day, either to make up for the time and associated income lost from not working or to complete an assignment by a specific deadline. If a lawyer blurs the lines between work and personal time, never clocking out, finding balance between work life and home life will remain elusive.

Freelancers often struggle with setting boundaries between work and personal life. Without the clear separation provided by a traditional workplace, it can be difficult to switch off from work and to maintain a healthy work-life balance. For example, freelancers may feel pressure to be constantly available to clients and to respond quickly to emails and messages. This can create a sense of always being "on" and can lead to burnout and exhaustion.

Overcommitting is also an obvious detriment to balance. Especially when first starting out as a freelancer, there might be a tendency to take on as many clients or projects as possible to generate an income stream. Some freelancers find it difficult to say no, especially if a client seems desperate for help. This reflexive instinct to take on work is risky. If a freelancer does not have enough time to provide excellent services, the chances of repeat clients or larger projects decline. Too much work means that a freelancer cannot provide the type of quality services that will keep clients coming back. Long-term clients rather than short-term work will make for a much more successful freelancing practice.

In addition, overcommitment leads to a freelancer becoming overwhelmed and burnt out, which is what the lawyer presumably wanted to avoid by becoming a freelancer in the first place. Anxiety and stress resulting from too much work is probably one of the reasons a freelancer said goodbye to a traditional law practice. Saying yes to every opportunity that comes along is not a good strategy for success in the long run. Therefore, time management is an essential component of being a successful freelancer.

The opposite of too much work is not having enough. This is a serious downside of freelancing. There are no guarantees of work. The potential for financial instability necessarily comes with self-employment. Unlike a traditional law job, freelancers do not have a guaranteed salary or a steady stream of work. Instead, they must generate their own clients to maintain a steady income. This can be particularly challenging for lawyers that have never had to find work or promote themselves. Freelancers do not have the same level of job security as traditional employees. A period when work is slow or when a major client decides to end the relationship can have a significant, adverse impact on a freelancer.

A freelancer's ability to generate business and to develop client relationships is essential for success. In other words, in a sense, freelancers must be sales people as well as business people and lawyers, promoting themselves and their ability to deliver value. However, many lawyers do not like the idea of rainmaking. Someone who is not ready to seek out business might find freelancing to be more taxing than rewarding. A freelancer who is not willing to self-promote to stand out in a crowded market place might not be able to generate enough business to stay afloat.

Another very tangible disadvantage to freelancing is the lack of help. At a law firm, there are any number of legal professionals to help with the business of servicing clients. A paralegal provides help with drafting, compiling exhibits for a brief, summarizing a deposition, or reviewing medical records. A legal assistant schedules meetings and depositions, calendars important deadlines, and makes sure digital files stay organized. An intern or summer associate can help with gathering records for due diligence or responding to discovery. Other lawyers at a firm are available to cover hearings or mediations. An office manager sends out bills and takes charge of making sure clients pay them.

Freelancers, however, must do all this work themselves or contract with legal professionals for help. Disorganization in operating a freelance law practice will significantly impair the ability to thrive. For example, although most files today are digital, if a freelancer does not have a system on the computer to organize case material, locating the documents or pleadings necessary to complete an assignment becomes more difficult, which kills productivity. A freelancer who is sloppy about calendaring increases the possibility of forgetting about certain obligations. When a freelancer does not keep track of time regularly, neglects to send out invoices in a timely manner, or fails to track whether clients pay those invoices, there is a negative impact on revenue and cash flow. Organization is critical to a freelancer's success.

Freelancing comes with many challenges that can make it a difficult career path for some lawyers. From financial instability and isolation to the need for self-motivation and discipline, freelancing requires a high level of resilience and adaptability. Understanding the challenges of freelancing is imperative to building a successful practice because it allows freelancers to proactively address and mitigate challenges. By acknowledging and planning for potential obstacles, freelancers can create a more sustainable and resilient business model.

For example, by recognizing the potential financial instability or job insecurity that comes with freelancing, a lawyer can decide to diversify revenue streams by seeking out more clients or longer-term contracts. By addressing isolation through active networking, a freelancer can maintain a level of social interaction. By acknowledging the need for self-motivation and discipline, a freelancer can develop strategies for maintaining productivity and staying focused. By setting clear boundaries, a freelancer can prevent burnout and maintain a healthy work-life balance. In short, understanding the challenges of freelancing allows lawyers to take a proactive approach to addressing them, creating a more sustainable, fulfilling, and lucrative freelance career.

Armed now with a general understanding of many of the pros and cons of starting a freelance law practice, it is time to turn to the nuts and bolts of actually becoming a freelance lawyer. At the end of this book in Appendix A is a checklist enumerating some of the important considerations discussed in detail in subsequent chapters.

PART II

A Lawpreneur's Blueprint

How to Build a Successful Freelance Practice

CHAPTER 4

From Vision to Reality
Creating a Powerful Business Plan

"Some people want it to happen, some wish it would happen, others make it happen."

—Michael Jordan

The first step to building a successful business, whether a freelance law practice or some other type of business, is to have a plan. The purpose of a business plan is to create a roadmap for achieving goals. A good business plan will help a freelancer start, manage, and grow a new business. It is a way to figure out the components necessary to make a freelance law practice successful.

The different components necessary for a successful business will be set out like sub-plans within the overall business plan. For example, while the primary goal set forth in any business plan will be to generate a certain amount of revenue within a set period of time, within the plan will be a section on marketing that sets forth how to structure the advertising and promotion of the legal services to reach revenue goals, a section on rainmaking that will detail how to obtain and retain clients, and a section on finances that will compare revenue generation objectives to anticipated expenses. In addition to goal setting and defining strategies for achieving those goals, a good business plan will also contain ways to measure whether the goals have been met. A business plan should be a living document that is reviewed and revised periodically as goals or as circumstances change.

There is no set way to write a business plan. A simple Google search will reveal numerous templates for writing one and even templates specific to a business plan for freelancers or even for freelance lawyers. The formality of a business plan will also vary depending on its use. If the intent is to try and secure funding like a loan or a line of credit to start a freelancing business, or even to find a family member to invest in the new business venture, the business plan will be more formal. However, if the business plan is for private use only, as a means of establishing goals and strategies to achieve them, then the plan can be more informal. For example, a formal business plan presented to a banker or loan officer would generally have an executive summary and very specific financial forecasts, whereas a business plan for internal use might be more general.

Whether a business plan includes an executive summary or not, all business plans should have sections outlining the services offered, the target market or target clients, the niche the freelancer intends to fill, how to generate clients and the related topic of how to retain clients, marketing strategies, measurable objectives for achieving the goals set forth in the business plan, and a section regarding budgeting and financing. This chapter presents an overview of each of these topics, while later chapters explore them in more detail. Appendix B contains a sample business plan.

Executive Summary

If the need is for a formal business plan, careful thought should be given to the executive summary, which is what will be read first. There are many ways to style an executive summary for a business plan, but the key is to include a hook. A hook is something that will make sure the reader is enticed to examine the rest of the plan with an eye toward investing in the business. Hooks are generally short, concise, and easy to remember.

There is no single formula for creating a hook. A hook could be the factor that sets the proposed freelancing business apart from the competition. For example, Miguel, a former teacher and public school administrator, just passed the bar and received his law license. Although he has no experience as a lawyer, he has a wealth of knowledge regarding legal issues impacting the schools from a staff and faculty perspective.

As a teacher, he was personally involved in the Individualized Educational Plan (IEP) process and the legal requirements involved in the creation and management of IEPs. As an administrator, he dealt with matters that had employment law ramifications, such as hiring, firing, and disciplining employees. In his role as faculty and staff in the public school system, Miguel underwent hundreds of hours of training during his school career regarding Title IX, Section 504 of the Rehabilitation Act, progressive discipline, due process issues, and other laws impacting public schools. He also worked closely with legal counsel who defended lawsuits against the school district. As a lawyer, Miguel is interested in defending schools and school officials in lawsuits brought against them.

Because, as a new lawyer, Miguel cannot create a hook based on his legal expertise, his hook could instead focus on his extensive background as an insider within the school system. His intimate knowledge of the functioning of a public school is what sets Miguel apart from other lawyers who practice school law. In other words, Miguel's background provides a unique niche that will benefit his clients. This niche offers value to prospective clients that his competitors cannot duplicate, despite their greater legal expertise.

A different hook could be a distinctive type of services Miguel is able to provide to prospective clients. States or localities generally have an insurance fund that provides coverage for lawsuits against public school districts and school officials. A public insurance fund typically pays lawyers to defend lawsuits on an hourly basis. Because of Miguel's experience and training within the school system and his knowledge of the different legal aspects informing the delivery of educational services, he can quickly read an IEP and evaluate whether it complies with the law, can scan disciplinary records and immediately understand whether the disciplinary procedures used met due process standards, and can understand the parameters of Title IX well enough to know whether alleged sexual harassment rises to the level of a federal statutory violation.

Due to his in-depth background in the schools and knowledge of the applicable law, even as a nonlawyer, Miguel can offer his services on a flat-fee or project-based basis to a law firm representing the public insurance fund rather than pursuant to an hourly rate and still generate sufficient revenue in relation to the time spent on a particular project. While another lawyer might have to spend hours engaged in legal research to file a summary judgment motion analyzing why the termination of a teacher did not violate the teacher's due process rights, Miguel already understands the nature of the law in that regard without undertaking the legal research. Likewise, while another lawyer might have to spend hours reviewing the teacher's personnel file to compile the evidence necessary to support a summary judgment motion, Miguel knows that a teacher's disciplinary file is kept separately from the remainder of the personnel file and knows exactly where to find and how to access the information he needs to support the motion.

Therefore, if the other lawyer had to spend six hours on background work before drafting a summary judgment motion and 15 hours writing the motion at a rate of $150 per hour, the insurance fund would be paying that lawyer $3,150. However, because Miguel would not have to spend six hours researching the law and reviewing the file but only two hours, even if he spent the same 15 hours preparing the written briefing, he could charge a flat-fee rate of $2,550 for the project and wind up with the same effective hourly rate as the other lawyer. Miguel's hook would be that he can provide the same legal services for about 20 percent less. For the law firm representing the insurance fund who engages Miguel as a freelancer, the flat-fee arrangement provides predictability in terms of legal defense costs, which is particularly important because the law firm is required to provide a detailed litigation defense budget to the insurance fund.

Using the preceding hooks as an example, an executive summary for Miguel's freelancing business could look something like this:

> Miguel began his teaching career in 2001. After 10 years, Miguel obtained his master's degree in educational administration in 2011 and started serving as a vice principal and then principal until 2017, before serving as the

deputy superintendent for the school district from 2017 until 2020. In 2020, Miguel went to law school. Graduating with honors, Miguel became licensed to practice law in 2023. With an extensive background in school administration, which included close collaboration with legal counsel for the school district, Miguel is uniquely qualified to defend lawsuits against public schools and school officials on a flat-fee or project-specific basis, providing law firms representing schools and their insurers with flexibility and predictability regarding legal defense costs.

Services Offered and Pricing Model

The section of the business plan setting forth the type of services offered should be specific. In Miguel's case, he should state more than simply he will be providing litigation services. A more specific description would be representation in civil defense litigation related to lawsuits against public schools and their officials.

The business plan should also set forth how those services will be offered and the specific scope of work. For example, if offering services on a per project basis at a flat-fee rate, the business plan should define whether Miguel intends to simply complete the initial project for the agreed-upon fee or whether he will include revisions for the project in the flat-fee price until the project meets the client's expectations.

Taking a different fixed-fee example, if there is an agreement to provide litigation representation for a fixed fee, the business plan should detail whether the scope of the representation includes the administrative aspects of the claim, such as proceedings before the Equal Employment Opportunity Commission (EEOC), or if the representation also includes dealing with a post-verdict appeal. In other words, Miguel needs to be clear when offering a fixed-fee rate for litigation representation what specific aspects of litigation are covered. If Miguel intends to offer a fixed-fee rate for the proceedings in trial court only, but the hiring law firm assumed the fixed-fee rate included the administrative and appellate phases as well, there will be a misunderstanding that can negatively impact the relationship between Miguel and the law firm hiring him.

Target Market

The business plan should also contain a section identifying the target clients. In Miguel's case, the target clients would be law firms or lawyers representing public insurance funds providing coverage to schools that defend litigation against school districts and school officials. This section could detail the problems facing an insurance fund in defending school litigation and propose how Miguel can offer a solution.

For example, money to fund public lawsuits needs to be accounted for annually within a state or locality's budget. Predictability, therefore, is particularly important. If a locality knows from history that a law firm it engages can defend a case for a reasonable amount, it can come much closer to hitting its annual budget targets than if the defense costs vary considerably. Therefore, the locality might gravitate to hiring law firms that can provide predictability in litigation defense costs. A law firm working with Miguel and paying him on a flat-fee basis rather than on an hourly basis would be better suited to providing that predictability. Identifying a target market or target clients, their problems, and how the freelancer can solve those problems should be set forth in the client section of a business plan.

A business plan should also identify the freelancer's niche and how it applies to the target market. This is not the same as detailing the nature of the services that a freelancer will provide. Describing a niche is more about defining how the services provided will be different than the services other lawyers or law firms can provide. The business plan should pinpoint what makes the freelance services stand out from the competition.

One way to do that is to show how the freelancer can provide more value to a particular client or target market than competitors. Another way is to show the unique benefit brought to clients that competitors cannot offer. Perhaps the freelancing dynamic itself can provide the unique value. One of the benefits of freelancing versus working in a law firm is the possibility of significantly lower overhead. With lower overhead, a freelancer can charge a lower hourly rate and still generate substantial revenue. The lower hourly rate made possible by freelancing is a competitive advantage that creates a niche.

Marketing

One of the most important sections of any business plan involves rainmaking or generating a client base. The main points about how to generate clients are elements to include in a business plan. For example, Miguel, whose plan is to offer services in the civil defense litigation arena, might try to generate clients by joining his local defense lawyer's association or the national Defense Research Institute (DRI) and seek referrals from other civil defense lawyers. Miguel's professional contacts from his teacher and school administration career can provide a nice referral source for him, particularly if those contacts are willing to tell law firms that they want to work with Miguel. Alternatively, Miguel could seek clients from any number of legal freelancing platforms. How Miguel intends to make money through generating clients is one of the most important parts of his business plan.

Related to generating clients is keeping clients. How Miguel proposes to keep clients once he gets them should also be set forth in his business plan. One of the best ways to retain clients is to provide excellent services. If clients are happy with the services provided, they are likely to come back. An important part of keeping clients happy is effective and regular communications with the client. Take, for example, a law firm that hires Miguel to help try a case in which a student was accusing a teacher of sexual harassment. Miguel defends the school on the basis that it took prompt and effective corrective action against the teacher that stopped the harassment. After trial, a six-figure verdict comes back against the school. Miguel has never advised the law firm of the possibility of such a big adverse verdict. The school will predictably be unhappy and the law firm will not likely ask Miguel to assist it with any more cases.

On the other hand, suppose Miguel had advised the law firm that although there was a strong defense to liability, because of the nature of the misconduct that was perpetrated by a teacher against a minor student, a jury might nonetheless emphasize with the student and come back with a large verdict against the school based on the emotional harm suffered by the child. In addition, suppose Miguel had advised the law firm to settle the case and avoid trial because of the possibility of the large adverse verdict. If the school chose instead to roll the dice and go to trial despite Miguel's advice, chances are the law firm representing the school would not be surprised by a six-figure adverse verdict and would not fault Miguel for it.

Another way to retain clients is to reward loyalty. For example, if a law firm consults with Miguel on all school-related lawsuits the insurance fund has assigned the firm, Miguel might drop the hourly rate he charges the law firm by 10 percent. The volume of work the law firm is willing to give Miguel means he does not have to spend so much time trying to generate other clients, which provides value to him. In return, he can offer value to the law firm. Miguel could also offer to conduct free training for school districts, write articles for the insurance fund's quarterly newsletters, or draft sample policies and procedures for school districts to use as a benefit to the hiring law firm and as a reward for giving him so much work.

Marketing strategies help generate and retain clients and are, therefore, essential to identify in a business plan. Even if a freelancer does not intend to engage in formal marketing practices like social media advertising, most lawyers, at a minimum, have a website and a LinkedIn profile. Even this limited online presence presents an opportunity for marketing. For example, a prospective or current law firm client might look at a freelancer's web profile for contact information and notice how professional it looks. While the online profile might not directly generate clients, a sloppy profile will certainly drive away business.

Marketing needs will vary greatly depending on circumstances. A new lawyer who does not have a professional network to generate clients might create a profile on a legal freelancing platform to obtain clients. On the other hand, experienced lawyers can generate clients by asking former colleagues for work and might not have to advertise or market online or through social media. Creating a business plan will allow freelancers to think about and decide what marketing strategies are best suited to their unique circumstances.

To ensure the business plan is a practical document that has more than just theoretical value, it should set forth objective ways to measure the extent to which a freelancer is meeting marketing goals. Therefore, a good business plan will set forth not only the key marketing goals but also the strategies and a time-line for meeting them. For example, a key goal could be the number of new clients to obtain in a certain time period. Maybe Miguel's goal is to obtain one new law firm as a client in a six-month period that does school work, along with two general litigation law firm clients, so he can diversify his revenue streams as he builds his school law practice.

Another goal related to marketing is a revenue target. Perhaps Miguel wants to generate $50,000 in revenue his first year of practice. The business plan should then set forth the strategies for reaching the revenue goal. Miguel could identify how many hours he would need to bill at a certain rate or how many flat-fee projects he would need to take on to reach the revenue projection. Other strategies could focus on sending out a certain number of legal services proposals per month to try and reach the goal of obtaining a certain number of clients, to join specific bar-related organizations to build a professional network to obtain referrals, or to engage in certain marketing or advertising efforts to generate business.

Revenue, Expenses, and Financial Projections

Every business plan needs to address budgeting and finances. Projecting revenue and expenses is critical to measuring success. Normally, law firms have wage and benefit expenses for employees, rent or mortgage expenses for office space, equipment lease costs, subscription expenses for things like legal research licenses or law office management software, the expense of professional liability insurance, advertising and marketing expenses, interest and principal expenses on a line of credit, and various professional fees, such as for a certified professional accountant (CPA) to prepare tax forms.

A freelancer might very well not incur many of those expenses. For example, a freelancer who works from home will not have a rental expense. To the contrary, that freelancer can deduct on tax returns the expenses related to a home office. More specifically, a freelancer can deduct a pro rata share of home mortgage and utility expenses based on the square footage of the home office as compared to the total square footage of the home. Likewise, a freelancer might be covered on a hiring lawyer's legal malpractice policy and, therefore, would not need an independent policy. Joining a professional organization like the American Bar Association (ABA) might eliminate the need to pay for mandatory continuing education classes because the ABA has a resource bank of free continuing education classes for its members.

One of the biggest advantages of freelancing is the ability to generate a net profit without the need to bill high rates or to work long hours. As shown on the sample business plan in Appendix B, by working just an average of 15 hours a week billing at an hourly rate of $100, Carla can generate $72,000 annually. Even without factoring in any additional revenue streams, because the overhead for engaging in freelance work is often much lower than working at a law firm, Carla would be able to keep most of the money she earned as net income. Using the estimated overhead figure of $20,000 in the sample business plan in Appendix B, Carla would net $52,000 by working an average of 15 hours a week.

In sum, a business plan will set forth goals and provide a roadmap for achieving them. It is a way to measure accomplishments, growth, and success, however a freelancer chooses to define those dynamics. Nobody thinking about starting a freelance law practice should begin without a plan. Understanding what is necessary to make a freelance law practice successful, setting goals to accomplish that, and knowing how to measure whether those goals are realized is like having the help of a map or GPS to navigate to an unfamiliar destination. Without that help, it is easy to go off course.

Having now shared some of the general considerations for creating a viable business plan, it is time to turn to specifics. Given that one of the biggest expense considerations a freelancer should address in a business plan is whether to work remotely or virtually versus whether to incur the rental expense of working out of an office, understanding the issues involved in making that decision is important.

CHAPTER 5

Decoding the Brick and Mortar versus Virtual Business Office Dilemma

"We are all now connected by the internet, like neurons in a giant brain."
—Stephen Hawking

There are so many options for a freelancer to choose where, when, and how to work. In the past, most lawyers worked in an office environment. That used to mean one thing—an office away from home with other lawyers and support staff. Today, however, an office could be a traditional law office, a home office or a dedicated workspace at home, a single room that a freelancer rents in an office building, or a shared office suite. Freelancers can also be location independent, working virtually from wherever they happen to be, whether at home, visiting family, or on vacation.

In addition, there are hybrid work arrangements. Some freelancers will work remotely from home for certain clients but go into an office to work for others while bringing a laptop on vacation for a couple hours a day of virtual work. Each type of work arrangement offers distinct advantages and comes with its own challenges. What works best for any individual lawyer will come down to personal habits and preferences.

Remote or Virtual Work

Working remotely or virtually allows a freelancer to work anywhere outside of an office. Typically, a freelancer would work remotely from home. However, with the advent of technology, it is now possible to work virtually from a sailboat in the Gulf of Mexico, from a California beach, or from the Alaskan wilderness. Virtual work provides complete location independence. Some people find themselves more productive when working outside of an office because the distractions commonly found in traditional office settings, like interruptions from colleagues, long breaks, and commuting time, are not present with remote or virtual work.

Working outside of a traditional office setting is much easier now with the advent of technology. A freelancer working remotely or virtually can tap into a pool of clients locally, nationally, and even globally. For example, a freelancer with a home office can connect with lawyers and law firms all over the country who need freelance legal services through legal services platforms like LAWCLERK. Some freelancers make a living solely through work derived from legal services platforms.

Remote or virtual work presents an opportunity for a significant cost savings. It eliminates the need to rent office space or to buy an office, which significantly reduces overhead. In addition, freelancers working remotely or virtually save on commuting and expenses, along with office attire and other office-related expenses.

However, working remotely or virtually also has its challenges. For a lawyer who is used to working in an office environment, working remotely or virtually, even from home, can be an adjustment. Many lawyers are not as productive working away from an office as they are working in a traditional office setting. In addition, it can sometimes be difficult to maintain professionalism when working from home or elsewhere. A lack of productivity and professionalism is one of the primary impediments to a successful remote or virtual law practice.

There are many ways to maintain productivity and professionalism when working outside of an office setting. The best way is to have a dedicated workspace. A home office that a freelancer uses only for work is ideal. For example, a freelancer with a dedicated home office can ensure a professional looking space for the times when there is a need to videoconference and clients, colleagues, or others on the call will be able to see the freelancer's workspace. There are many stories of unprofessional looking backgrounds during videoconferencing calls. If a freelancer is conducting a deposition, appearing at a hearing, or even just communicating via videoconferencing with a colleague, nobody should see an unmade bed or dirty dishes in the background.

A dedicated office with a door that can close will not only maintain a professional looking workspace but will also prevent unwanted sounds as well, like the noise of a television in the background or a dog barking. Again, a freelancer wanting to maintain an air of professionalism is not going to want a client during a videoconferencing call to hear kids fighting in the background or the dishwasher running. Not only will a dedicated office help maintain a professional looking and sounding workspace, but it will also help eliminate distractions, which will enhance productivity while working.

Eliminating distractions can be difficult with the amount of technology that permeates everything these days. When trying to work, one of the biggest killers of productivity is the constant stream of social media notifications popping up on a computer screen or notifications buzzing on a cell phone. Turning off all notifications for email, social medial, and non-work-related apps and checking them only when taking a break from work will help eliminate distractions, which will keep the focus on work.

If a freelancer working remotely or virtually does not have a spare room for an office, there are plenty of creative ways to create a dedicated office space. One of the easiest is by dedicating a portion of a dining room table for work. Remove one of the chairs from the head or foot of the table and replace it with an office chair. Move the replaced chair off to the side and set up a storage basket on top of the replaced chair and under it for office supplies.

Another solution for those without an extra room for a home office is to remove a nightstand from a bedroom and replace it with a small desk. Built-in shelves above the desk will create additional storage space. Working in a bedroom where it is possible to shut the door will have the same effect of creating a noise- and distraction-free work zone that a dedicated home office space would provide. Just make sure the view from a camera is toward a window or wall, as opposed to a bed or the bathroom door.

Unused nooks under stairs or in a corner are also possibilities. Removing a door from a coat closet can create a perfect space for a small desk and office equipment. Think about how hotel rooms take very limited spaces and create dedicated places to sleep, eat, lounge, and work all within the same room.

Whatever the solution is for a home office, the key is to have a dedicated space to work from. Kids should not have an expectation of using a work computer to play games on, and videoconferencing should not occur while sitting in bed or on the couch. A dedicated, distraction-free workspace is critical to maintaining professionalism and productivity.

Rob Krasow is a realtor in Sarasota, Florida. He describes the post-pandemic trend of home offices.

As a residential realtor, it is truly remarkable to witness how the concept of a home has transformed in the post-COVID era. The pandemic has reshaped not only the way we work and live but also the features we now seek in our homes. Clients are increasingly recognizing the value of having a dedicated home office. New builds illustrate that the days when a home office was a mere afterthought are gone. Home offices are now a fundamental consideration in home buying. Builders give a lot of thought to the ideal home office now, strategically positioning them within the layout of the home so they are away from high-traffic areas to minimize distractions.

Of course, not everybody can buy a place to live with a dedicated home office. When I look at houses or apartments that do not have a dedicated home office, I try to engage clients in a creative reimagining of space utilization, helping to find ways to transform spaces into functional office space no matter the size or layout of the property.

When touring homes, I often see spare rooms that have the potential to evolve beyond a guest bedroom. A room with natural light, wall space for storage solutions and shelving, and a layout that can accommodate a desk and chair can be transformed into an inspiring home office. In a small apartment, a closet can be repurposed as office space by installing a fold-down desk, wall-mounted shelves, and a pocket door to close off the space when not in use. Every living space has corners that often go unnoticed. Integrating compact desks and floating shelves into these corners can create a workspace that is functional while still blending in harmoniously with the rest of the room.

Flexibility is key when making an office out of unconventional spaces. Foldable desks and nesting tables have a small footprint. Shelving and wall-mounted storage can make the most of vertical space.

Navigating the demands of a post-COVID world, I have come to see the home office as a reflection of new priorities. It underscores the desire for work-life integration, redefining what people want in their homes.[1]

Creating a functional space at home to work from is only one challenge. Switching off from work can be also be difficult. Having a designated work-space helps create a clear boundary between work life and home life by signaling that the focus is on work when in that space. Being outside the home office space is an indication to switch off from work.

It is easy to check work email at all hours of the day and night or to work long hours without taking breaks. To avoid burnout, it is critical to set clear boundaries between work life and home life. In addition to having a dedicated workspace that is not used for personal interests, another way to create boundaries is to set specific working hours. Decide when to start work and when to finish. Stick to those hours as much as possible. Make sure work colleagues and clients know those working hours, too, so they do not have expectations of availability outside of those times.

One of the reasons productivity can become a problem when working remotely or virtually is due to a lack of these kinds of boundaries. It is easy to stop working and take a nap in the afternoon when working from home, whereas if working from an office, a lawyer would power through afternoon lethargy. When the phone rings, it is very tempting to have a lengthy conversation with a friend or relative when that would not normally happen at the office. Jumping up from a legal project to do laundry or the dishes is easy when working at home, a distraction that does not exist in an office environment.

A freelancer who works remotely or virtually must be disciplined to work during scheduled work hours. Getting dressed and ready for the day helps create a clear boundary between work and home life. When working from home, it can be tempting to stay in pajamas or sweats all day. However, getting dressed and ready for the day can help create a work-centered mindset. Dressing in business attire is not necessary. However, an effort to change out of pajamas

---

1 R. Krasow, personal communication, Aug. 31, 2023.

into something suitable to go out in will foster productivity by signaling it is time to work.

Rented Office Space

If working from home or virtually is not ideal, a freelancer can rent office space instead. Traditionally, a lawyer would rent office space and would have to furnish it and provide the equipment. However, there are many alternatives today to that traditional office rental model. With the current decline in commercial rentals, particularly in downtown office buildings across the country, there are many management companies that have taken over large spaces in commercial buildings and have created custom-designed, turnkey office spaces that come fully serviced, which are available to rent on a short-term or on a long-term basis. These management companies provide a wide choice of different office sizes and layouts, with access to essential equipment and technology like printers, copiers, and high-speed internet. Some of these rental spaces also include the use of a shared conference room or receptionist.

A more cost-effective solution to renting a private office or office suite, even a turnkey one, is to rent a joint workspace. A joint workspace is a shared office that can accommodate multiple people or teams. Joint workspaces also often come with resources like printers, copiers, and high-speed internet that can be costly for freelancers who have to pay out of pocket for that equipment. For a lawyer who cannot avoid distractions working from home, renting a joint workspace can provide an environment that is more conducive to productivity. Working alongside other people who are focused on their own work makes it easier to concentrate. Being able to rent an area in a joint workspace on a short-term basis can provide flexibility and cost savings, particularly for a freelancer who is just starting out.

One of the downsides of freelancing and remote work is the lack of social interaction. This concern remains even if renting a single office space or office suite, as opposed to a shared office space. Joint workspaces can provide opportunities for social interaction like a lawyer would have if working in a traditional law firm environment. This can help combat feelings of isolation that can sometimes accompany freelancing. For freelancers, a joint workspace can provide a sense of structure and community that can be difficult to achieve when working independently or remotely.

Working from a Client's Office

From a cost perspective, being able to freelance from client lawyer's or law firm's office is the most cost-efficient. There is no rental fee and all the furniture, equipment, technology, and other resources are available without cost. For example, while a freelancer who works from home might have to pay for a legal research software license or case management software, a freelancer working out of a client law firm's office can use the firm's technology.

Another advantage of working in the client lawyer's or law firm's office while freelancing is the opportunity to network. Interacting with other lawyers can help with problem-solving. Being in a traditional law office setting can also lead to new professional collaborations and may even help generate more freelancing work.

However, just like some lawyers find working from home to be distracting, others think working in an office is distracting. With more people around, there is more noise and more activity, which can make it difficult to focus or concentrate. It is easy to get sidetracked in conversation getting coffee in the kitchen or grabbing office supplies in the file room.

Traditional law offices also have more bureaucracy and red tape, which can make it difficult to complete work efficiently. For example, copiers, printers, and legal research software might require a lawyer to input a client code, which can be annoying if a freelancer is not used to having to do that when working from home.

Hybrid Work Arrangements

Sam has a freelancing practice that combines three types of work arrangements—working remotely from home, working from the office of a client law firm, and working from an office he rents for himself. He has young children who he needs to care for when they are out of school on break or when they are sick and cannot attend school. During those times, he needs to be able to work from home outside of regular business hours so he can spend most of the day with his kids. To accommodate those needs, Sam set up a home office where he can work remotely in the early mornings and during evenings so he can take care of his kids during the day when they are home from school.

However, because Sam is not particularly productive at home, he also rents office space where he can work when his kids are in school. Because Sam works only part of the time from his rented office, he leased a joint workspace, which is cheaper than leasing a private office. The joint workspace comes with a shared receptionist; conference rooms; high-speed internet access; office equipment like a printer, scanner, and copier; and a stocked kitchen.

Sam only works part time from his joint office space when he is not working from home because his primary client is a local law firm that handles complex business matters and needs his help reviewing documents to conduct due diligence. Sam does the due diligence work at the offices of the law firm where he can access the law firm's server and document management system.

In sum, Sam works from a rented office, works remotely from home when necessary to fulfill his childcare obligations, and works at his primary client's law offices. Each type of work arrangement has its pros and cons.

The rise of remote or virtual work and hybrid work arrangements has revolutionized the traditional workplace dynamic. There are many options now regarding different types of office environments. A freelancer can work from a client law firm's office. Working remotely or virtually, on the other hand, provides location independence. However, remote or virtual work requires strong self-discipline and self-motivation and can lead to feelings of isolation. In addition, the blurred boundaries between work and personal life and the difficulties in maintaining productivity can be downsides of remote or virtual work. Renting shared or joint office space is an alternative to both a traditional office setting and to working remotely or virtually. It combines the flexibility of remote or virtual work with the benefits of in-person interaction.

Deciding what type of work environment is best or whether to have a hybrid work arrangement requires weighing the pros and cons of each, including cost, the availability of space, access to resources, the opportunity to interact with other lawyers, and distractions. Ultimately, the decision involving where and how to work depends on personal preferences, money, and the availability of workspace options. Flexible approaches to work and leveraging technology will create a thriving work environment that is best suited to a freelancer's individual needs.

Flexibility is a theme that runs through all the different considerations important to building a sustainable and profitable freelance law practice. The same flexibility in determining the most suitable work environment also applies to generating revenue—how should a freelancer charge for legal services?

CHAPTER 6

Beyond the Billable Hour

Unlocking Profitability with Innovative Billing Models

"If you stop at general math, you're only going to make general math money."
—Snoop Dogg

As with any professional service, billing models for freelancers can vary greatly. Understanding the different types of billing models and the pros and cons of each can help a freelancer make an informed choice about how to charge client attorneys or client law firms.

Hourly Billing

Hourly billing is still the most traditional billing model used by lawyers outside the context of contingency fee arrangements for representing a plaintiff in litigation and it is still the most common way to charge for legal services. With hourly billing, a freelancer would charge a client a certain hourly rate for the time spent working on a project. Typically, a lawyer charges in increments of one-tenth of an hour or in six-minute increments. Therefore, if a freelancer spent 30 minutes working on a project, the time billed would be 0.5 hours.

Setting an hourly billing rate can be tricky. When working directly for a client, rates can be set based on the level of experience and expertise of the lawyer, a client can fix rates, a billable rate can result from a combination of the two, or a lawyer can negotiate a billable rate. For example, an insurance company paying a law firm to represent its insureds in vehicle accident cases might pay paralegals a certain hourly rate, lawyers with up to 10 years of experience a higher hourly rate, and more experienced lawyers the highest hourly rate. That might look like hourly rates of $70 for a paralegal, $150 for a less experienced lawyer, and $225 for a more experienced lawyer.

Insurance companies generally pay lower hourly rates than non-insurance work generates. For example, an hourly rate for a highly specialized and experienced lawyer, such as a 25-year, intellectual property lawyer with a PhD in chemistry, might be $450.

In addition, hourly rates vary by jurisdiction. Lawyers at large law firms in San Francisco might have an $800 hourly rate while a high hourly rate for a lawyer in a small firm or in a smaller city might only be $175 for the same type of matter.

The hourly rate for freelancers will nearly always be less than what the hourly rate is for the lawyers they work for. Therefore, if a lawyer bills a client an hourly rate of $200, that lawyer might only pay a freelancer an hourly rate of $100. This is one of the reasons freelancing is such a growing area of the law. The client lawyer or law firm makes money off a freelancer's work.

Taking the preceding example, a law firm billing a client an hourly rate of $200 for 10 hours of work by a freelancer would collect $2,000 from the client but only pay the freelancer $1,000, keeping $1,000. The law firm does not have to provide employment benefits to the freelancer or account for the freelancer's overhead, so there are no expenses that would eat into the $1,000 the law firm would make off the freelancer's work.

Sometimes a freelancer cannot choose the hourly rate to bill. For example, a freelancer performing hourly work generated on a legal services platform will not be able to choose the hourly rate. Instead, that freelancer agrees to do work for the hourly rate proposed by the hiring lawyer or law firm. Hourly rates dictated by lawyers seeking freelancers through legal services platforms are generally lower because there are so many freelancers on those platforms looking for work. Rarely will a freelancer make $100 per hour through a legal services platform.

Even if freelancing for a law firm that was not sourced from a legal services platform, freelancers still cannot always set their hourly rates. Using the example of an insurance company paying $150 for a less experienced lawyer, a freelancer who is fresh out of law school would never be able to charge more than that, regardless of the circumstances. No lawyer or law firm is going to pay a freelancer more than it can bill the ultimate client.

Because hourly rates vary depending on the type of work, level of experience, and jurisdiction, setting an hourly rate requires knowledge of the legal market in which a freelancer is providing services. Some research will go a long way in helping to determine an appropriate hourly rate. For example, while insurance companies are known for paying lower hourly rates, just because a client is not an insurance company does not necessarily mean a freelancer can charge a higher billable rate. Some of the largest corporations in the country pay very low effective hourly rates because they can find any number of lawyers to do their work.

Hourly rates do not need to be static. A freelancer can set different hourly rates for different clients. If working for a law firm that does insurance defense work that pays $200 per hour, for example, a freelancer can set an hourly rate of $80 to $120 depending on experience, while charging more for work on a matter for one of the law firm's business clients who pays $300 per hour.

Hourly billing is the most common billing method for a reason. It is transparent. Clients can see exactly how much time a freelancer is spending on a project. However, hourly billing is not always predictable and can lead to disputes because a law firm does not know how much a freelancer will bill until the freelancer completes the work.

For example, if a freelancer is preparing a contract and the lawyer who assigned the work thinks it will take three hours to draft the contract but receives a bill from the freelancer for five hours, the lawyer will not be pleased. Communication is the key to avoiding this type of quandary. A freelancer who begins a project can ask what the expectation is regarding the amount of time the assigning lawyer thinks it will take to complete the project. If the freelancer starts work and realizes it will be impossible to complete the project in the expected time, that should prompt a conversation.

With hourly billing comes the risk of unintentional overbilling. Hourly billing rewards inefficiency because if a freelancer took five hours to complete a project that could have been completed in four hours had the freelancer been working more efficiently, the freelancer will still charge for the five hours worked. However, that is not the way to retain clients. Providing efficient and cost-effective services is how a freelancer will keep assigning lawyers or law firms happy and ensure future work.

Hourly billing is not for every lawyer, and some lawyers hate keeping track of their time in six-minute increments so much that they have left the practice of law altogether or sought a different type of legal job where they do not have to keep track of their time, such as an in-house counsel position. Janae, for example, was always so busy working that she never stopped during the day to record her time. Every morning, Janae told herself she would enter her time after she had finished all her work for the day. However, the end of the day would come and she was always too tired to record her time. The next morning, Janae would start in on her work and the end of the day would come again without her entering her time.

By the end of the month, Janae was in the position of spending many uncompensated hours trying to recreate her time by going back and looking through her emails, cell phone logs, and work files to try and remember what she had done. However, it was impossible to capture all her time doing that and she lost countless hours she could have billed for had she kept track of her time as she was working.

Without the discipline to systematically record time, hourly billing will be a difficult model for a freelancer to use. Flat- or fixed-fee billing is an alternative model to hourly billing.

Fixed- or Flat-Fee Billing

With flat-fee billing, a freelancer charges a set fee for a specific service regardless of the amount of time it takes to complete the work. Fixed fees can be for a specific task, such as drafting a contract, can be project based, such as reviewing a document production and evaluating the necessity for a motion to compel, or a fixed fee can be for an entire case, such as handling a divorce proceeding or an administrative discrimination claim before the Equal Employment Opportunity Commission (EEOC).

Unlike hourly billing, fixed-fee billing is predictable. Clients and freelancers both know exactly how much the charge will be for a specific service. Therefore, fixed-fee billing allows not just clients but also freelancers to budget accurately. Freelancers know exactly how much they will charge and can make accurate revenue projections, and the hiring lawyer or law firm will know exactly how much they will spend.

In addition, fixed-fee billing incentivizes efficiency. The more quickly a freelancer can complete a task, the better able that freelancer is to maximize revenue. Using technology to enhance productivity, such as legal research software or document management platforms, can help a freelancer work more efficiently.

Lawyers have started turning to fixed-fee billing more and more to attract clients.

Kerline Jean-Louis, Esq. is a lawyer from Sommerville, Massachusetts who explains why she uses fixed-fee billing:

> Greater time spent billing does not necessarily confer the greatest benefit to the client. I have left hourly billing behind and now offer clients value-based billing. This means I provide legal services on a flat-fee basis so clients know the cost of the services they have chosen upfront. No hidden fees. No extra costs. No surprises.[1]

To provide flat-fee rates, Kerline uses cutting-edge technology and proprietary systems to efficiently deliver legal services without compromising quality. She also tries to offer legal services in other, nontraditional ways that will benefit her clients. For example, she has created templates her clients can purchase inexpensively if they want to try and handle their own legal needs.

The biggest risk for a freelancer with a fixed-fee billing arrangement is the possibility of underbilling. For example, if a freelancer charges a fixed fee of $2,000 to draft a motion for summary judgment but ends up spending 50 hours on the project, that equates to an effective hourly rate of only $40.

Organization is critical to mitigating the risk of underbilling in a fixed-fee situation. There are many ways organizations can result in efficiencies. A freelancer who litigates can create a library of state and federal summary judgment standards so that when preparing a motion for summary judgment, the freelancer can just cut and paste those standards into the summary judgment motion, rather than looking up case law and drafting the standard each time there is a need to

1 K. Jean-Louis, Esq., personal communication, Sept. 21, 2023.

prepare a summary judgment motion. A transactional lawyer can have a form residential lease and only need to insert the transaction-specific details, rather than starting from scratch each time an assigning lawyer asks for a draft lease. An estate planning lawyer can have form powers of attorney and health-care directives ready to go so only a little time is needed to customize those forms for a particular client. Flat-fee billing rewards freelancers who are organized and who can leverage technology to minimize the time spent on projects.

Contingency-Fee Billing

Another type of billing model is a contingency-fee arrangement. Contingency-fee billing is often used by plaintiffs' lawyers in litigation. The lawyer is paid a percentage of the resolution amount—a settlement amount or the judgment amount obtained after a trial. The risk is that if the lawsuit is not resolved favorably, the lawyer does not earn a fee. Therefore, if a lawyer goes to trial and loses, despite all the work spent preparing the case for trial and trying it, under a contingency fee arrangement, the lawyer would not be paid.

If a freelancer wants to help with a contingency-fee case, the amount and details of the work should be agreed upon with the assigning lawyer or law firm in advance. For example, if the assigning lawyer has a 40 percent contingency-fee arrangement and agrees to pay the freelancer 10 percent upon resolution of the litigation, but the freelancer ends up doing most of the work on the case, that might not be such a fair agreement.

One way to eliminate the risk of doing most of the work but receiving only a small payout on a contingency-fee matter would be to come to an agreement on the amount of work the freelancer will do. For example, if the freelancer came to a 10 percent contingency-fee arrangement, which equates to one-quarter of a 40 percent total contingency fee, there could be an agreement that the freelancer would only do approximately 25 percent of the work.

To accomplish that in a trial situation, there could be an agreement that the freelancer will only be responsible for the direct or cross-examinations of two of the eight total witnesses who are testifying at trial. Alternatively, the freelancer could take responsibility for the written trial work, like the preparation of jury instructions, motions in limine, or post-trial motions, but would not participate in the trial itself.

The freelancer takes the same risk with these examples as the freelancer would when agreeing to a contingency payment—that there is a successful resolution of the case. However, by agreeing to the specific details of the contingency work expected, the freelancer minimizes the risk of doing 90 percent of the work on a contingency fee case but only being compensated with 10 percent of the contingency fee.

A freelancer should carefully think about balancing risk and reward when negotiating a contingency-fee arrangement as compensation. The reward can be substantial. A 10 percent contingency fee of the amount a law firm receives as compensation in a case that is settled for a million dollars, where the hiring law firm receives 40 percent or $400,000, would amount to $40,000. The risk, however, is that the freelancer does significant work without any payment.

Subscription Fees

Payment for work can also be on a subscription basis. A subscription-fee payment is a billing model that is becoming increasingly popular for freelancers. Many legal freelancing platforms have lawyers or law firms wanting to pay lawyers on a subscription basis. Under this model, a lawyer or law firm will pay a freelancer a monthly or an annual fee in exchange for access to legal services in the same way somebody pays a monthly fee for a gym membership or for access to a community center's facilities.

For a subscription-fee model to work, it should be based on a predetermined level of service. For example, it could be based on a set number of hours of legal work per month. It could also be based on access to certain types of legal services, such as a subscription fee for working on discovery or for preparing estate planning documents. Or, a subscription fee could be based on a freelancer's general availability to provide ongoing advice of a varying nature regardless of the number of hours spent.

Subscription-fee models can also be tiered so clients can choose different levels of service based on their needs. For example, if a law firm is defending an employment discrimination claim, a subscription fee service could be built on a fee for handling the administrative claim, which is a prerequisite to suing, and then offering a different fee if the claim is ultimately litigated.

Once a law firm has subscribed to a particular level of service with a freelancer, it can access the freelancer's legal services as needed. This can include phone consultations, document drafting, legal research, or representation in court. The exact services included in the subscription fee will depend on the level of services negotiated. For example, if a freelancer does not want to appear in court, that type of service should be excluded from the subscription-fee agreement.

Again, a subscription-fee agreement offers a freelancer predictability. The freelancer will know exactly how much revenue will be generated each month from the subscription agreement, which will help with budgeting. Also, for the same reasons as with a fixed-fee billing model, a subscription-fee agreement provides an incentive to work efficiently. The less time it takes to complete a project, the greater the effective compensation rate.

However, it can be difficult for a freelancer to plan and manage workload effectively with a subscription-based billing model because it is unclear how much time will be necessary to complete the services requested. For example, if a freelancer agrees to handle discovery in a litigation case on a subscription-fee basis, and there are motions to compel, motions for protective orders, and motions for orders to show cause filed, the time the freelancer will spend dealing with discovery will be very different than if it is possible to just answer written discovery requests without the necessity of seeking court intervention.

Hybrid or Blended Billing Arrangements

A freelancer need not be tied to only one type of billing model. Andres, from Chapter 1, combined different types of billing models based on his work preferences and the sources available to him for generating clients. He worked on a subscription basis for a law firm that paid him $7,000 monthly. He agreed to provide up to 10 hours a week of work at an hourly rate of $80 for a lawyer he connected with through a legal services freelancing platform. And, he also entered into a contingency-fee arrangement in a case going to trial, which, if successful, would provide compensation in exchange for second chairing the trial.

Another example of using different billing models is set forth in the sample business plan in Appendix B, pursuant to which Carla works not just on an hourly basis but also offers document templates to clients as a source of income. The flexibility of freelance work in terms of multiple possible billing models is one of its greatest advantages.

In addition to using different types of billing models, a freelancer can blend them. Blended billing combines the elements of different billing models. A blended billing model might combine elements of hourly billing and flat-fee billing. A freelancer would charge a fixed fee for a particular service but with an hourly rate component for any additional work required. For example, a freelancer could charge a fixed fee for drafting a contract but an hourly rate for any subsequent revisions to the contract resulting from further negotiation.

One of the primary benefits of blended billing for the client lawyers or law firms is that it provides predictability regarding the cost of a specific legal service while still allowing for flexibility if additional work is needed. On the other side, blended billing can be beneficial for freelancers by allowing them to manage risk while still providing clients with certainty in terms of the fee structure.

Another example of a blended billing arrangement can bring certainty to a contingency-fee agreement. A freelancer can agree to a contingency-fee payment and take the risk of a successful resolution of the matter, but the payment would equate to the freelancer's hourly rate for the time spent working on the case rather than a percentage, which would minimize the risk of being underpaid if the resolution generated less income than expected.

Take, for example, an agreement to pay a freelancer $100 per hour contingent upon the successful resolution of a plaintiff's case. If the freelancer worked 100 hours getting ready for trial and if the case settled, regardless of the settlement amount, the freelancer's compensation would be $10,000. This reduces the risk of under-compensation. However, it also reduces the possibility of a big reward if the case is settled for a large amount where a 10 percent contingency compensation would far surpass the hourly rate equivalent of the work done.

There are advantages and disadvantages to the various types of billing models. Hourly billing allows for flexibility and accurate tracking of time spent providing legal services. However, unintentional overbilling is a concern. Flat-fee billing provides clients with a predictable fee structure and a freelancer with a more certain revenue stream. On the flip side, an inefficient lawyer will not receive a reasonable effective compensation rate with a flat-fee arrangement. Subscription billing allows for the development of long-term client relationships by providing general access to legal advice but, like flat-fee billing, rewards efficiency. Lawyers who do not have the discipline or know-how to be productive in shorter amounts of time will not benefit from a subscription-fee model.

Fee arrangements are limited only by imagination. Ultimately, freelancers should consider their own business objectives and preferences in addition to their clients' needs when selecting the type of billing model to use. Understanding business needs and preferences will allow freelancers to choose sustainable billing models. Understanding those needs and preferences is also critical to another important aspect of starting a freelance law practice—choosing what type of corporate entity to establish.

CHAPTER 7

Building Your Legal Fortress

Choosing the Right Corporate Entity for Success as a Freelancer

"If you have built castles in the air, your work need not be lost; that is where they should be. Now put the foundations under them."

—Henry David Thoreau

The foundation of any law practice is the corporate structure of the business. This will be one of the first decisions a freelancer makes in starting a practice. The business structure influences law firm administration and how much time is spent dealing with corporate formalities. It also has ramifications for both tax and personal liability.

There are pros and cons to any corporate structure. None are perfect. The goal should be to choose a corporate entity that provides the best balance of advantages and drawbacks to meet a freelancer's goals, which will vary from person to person. For example, freelancers who have no need for financing and who do not contract with vendors for resources because they can use another lawyer's or law firm's legal research and document management tools might not have a strong need for liability protection.

Other freelancers, on the other hand, who need to lease office equipment and rent office space might want a corporate structure that provides more personal protection from liability. After going through the exercise of creating a business plan, these kinds of considerations should be well-defined, which will make it easier to choose the best business structure for a freelance law practice.

With wants and needs in mind, choosing the right corporate entity becomes much simpler. The most important question to ask, because state laws vary tremendously, is what kinds of corporate entities are allowed for law practices in a particular state. Most states, but not all, allow law practices to operate as limited liability companies (LLCs) or professional limited liability companies (PLLCs). Some states require law firms to operate as a professional entity, such as a professional corporation (PC) or a professional association (PA), meaning that other types of corporate structures cannot even be considered. Still other states define a particular type of corporate structure for law firms that might not exist in other states.

Keep in mind that whatever the corporate structure, Model Rule of Professional Conduct 5.4, promulgated by the American Bar Association (ABA), prohibits nonlawyer ownership of law firms. Under the ABA's Model Rule 5.4, legal services must be provided only by a law firm that is owned, managed, and financed exclusively by lawyers. Model Rule 5.4's purpose is to ensure the professional independence of lawyers. While certain states have whittled away at or eliminated Model Rule 5.4's requirements and although there are proponents of nonlawyer ownership and operation of law firms, as it stands as of the date of publication of this book, only lawyers can own and operate law firms in most states.

This chapter is not state specific and it discusses the most common corporate structures for freelance law practices: sole proprietorships, partnerships, LLCs, and corporations. Professional entities like PLLCs, PAs, or PCs generally follow the same rules as their nonprofessional companion structures but have special formalities that professionals must adhere to. For example, a PLLC would operate like an LLC, and a PA or PC would operate like a corporation. While picking which corporate form is most suitable may seem daunting, it usually comes down to only a handful of considerations.

Ownership

One of the considerations in choosing a corporate structure is the number of owners. Certain corporate structures are suitable for a single owner, some work with either one or more owners, and others can only exist with multiple owners. A sole proprietorship, for example, has only one owner. Partnerships, on the other hand, have multiple owners. An LLC can have a single owner, called a member, or multiple members. Corporations can also have one or more owners, called shareholders. Therefore, a freelancer who is not planning on starting a business with another lawyer would not consider a partnership as a corporate structure even though a limited liability partnership (LLP) and a professional limited liability partnership (PLLP) are some of the most common corporate structures for law firms, large and small.

Liability Protection

Another principal consideration in choosing the right corporate structure is to what extent a corporate entity can provide insulation from liability. Importantly, while different corporate structures come with different levels of liability protection, liability protection that exists because of the nature of a corporate entity is distinct from professional liability protection for legal malpractice. In other words, even with the highest level of liability protection, because of the type of business structure, the form of a corporate entity will not protect a lawyer from a legal malpractice claim.

Therefore, obtaining a professional liability policy or making sure that another lawyer's or law firm's professional liability policy provides coverage for freelancing work is critical. Corporate structures only provide protection from the normal types of corporate, rather than professional, liability to varying degrees. For example, if a law firm has a contract with a third-party information technology (IT) firm but stops paying its monthly invoices, with some corporate entities, the IT company would only be allowed to collect its debt against the corporate entity, not against the individual assets of the lawyer owner of the company.

Each type of corporate structure has a different level of liability protection. A sole proprietorship does not provide any personal liability protection because it is not incorporated as a separate business entity. That means the law firm's assets and liabilities are the same as a freelancer's personal assets and liabilities. Therefore, in the preceding example, an IT company that is owed a balance for the services it provided could come after a freelancer's personal assets to satisfy the debt, if the freelancer was operating as a sole proprietorship.

An LLC, on the other hand, protects its members from personal liability in most cases. Therefore, LLC members would not normally be personally liable for any debt to the IT vendor. Limited liability protection, sometimes called the limited liability shield, is one of the main reasons why many entrepreneurs, including freelancers, choose to structure their business as an LLC. By forming an LLC, freelancers can separate their personal finances and assets from those of the business, which reduces the risk of personal financial loss in the event of a business failure or legal disputes.

However, while an LLC generally provides protection from personal liability, it will not shield a freelancer from all forms of liability, such as a member's own intentional acts or personal guarantees on business debts. In addition, an LLC's liability protection can be pierced if the business was not properly formed or maintained or if a member engages in fraudulent or illegal activity.

Partnerships, such as limited partnerships (LPs), LLPs, and PLLPs, provide a mix of liability protection. In an LP, there is a single general partner with unlimited liability and multiple limited partners with limited liability. The limited partners are only liable for debts incurred by the partnership up to the extent of their investment. Therefore, they do not have personal liability to third parties, and their risk is limited to the amount they invested in the LP. With an LLP, all the partners have this limited liability. State laws differ as to whether partners in an LLP are liable for the contractual debts of the partnership, but generally, partners in an LLP are not liable for the misconduct or tortious acts of other partners. This is why so many law firms incorporate as LLPs or PLLPs.

Corporations are entities that are wholly separate and distinct from their owners. Therefore, corporations offer the strongest liability protection. The liability protection offered by corporations is known as the corporate veil. Corporations are typically C corporations or S corporations, known as

C-Corps or S-Corps. The primary difference between the two is how they are taxed. Both provide liability protection to their shareholders so that owners are not typically responsible personally for the business debts or liabilities of the corporation. However, like LLCs, a corporation's liability protection can be pierced if the company was not properly formed or maintained or if shareholders engage in fraudulent or illegal activities. Likewise, shareholders can still be held liable for their own acts, such as intentional wrongdoing and personal guarantees.

In sum, sole proprietorships have unlimited personal liability, the personal liability with partnerships varies, and owner members of an LLC or owner shareholders of a corporation are not personally liable as a general matter. While at first glance it would seem like a corporate structure that almost completely limits liability would be the right one to choose, there are other considerations that might take away from that conclusion. An important one is how each type of entity is taxed.

Tax Treatment

Because a sole proprietorship is not considered an entity separate or apart from its owner, it is considered as a disregarded entity for tax purposes. That means a sole proprietor would document business taxes on personal tax returns. On the other hand, a C-Corp's profits are taxed at the corporate tax rate before being distributed to the owner shareholders, who then must pay their own taxes on those profits. This is known as double taxation. Many consider it a big downside of a corporation. An S-Corp, however, avoids the double taxation drawback.

An S-Corp is not really a separate type of corporation from a C-Corp. Rather, it is an election for tax purposes that a C-Corp or an LLC can make regarding its tax treatment. If, for example, there is an S-Corp election, owner shareholders of a corporation can avoid the double taxation so that profits and some losses are passed through directly to the shareholder owners and are not first subject to corporate taxes. LLCs can also operate as pass-through entities, or as a disregarded entity in the case of a single member LLC. With partnerships, profits and some losses are also passed through to the partners. Therefore, while a corporation offers the greatest liability protection, there are drawbacks to how it is taxed.

Corporate Formalities

Another consideration in deciding which business structure to use is the operational costs of different corporate entities in terms of not only money but also, especially, in terms of time. Different states have different requirements in terms of filing and registration fees for corporate entities. In addition, businesses that are taxed as separate entities will require tax returns distinct from the lawyer's personal returns. The time and organization necessary to adhere to the required corporate formalities can be a significant factor in deciding what type of corporate entity to use.

Corporations, for example, require the holding of annual meetings and the keeping of meeting minutes, conditions that a sole proprietorship does not have to adhere to. Similarly, while the formation of a corporation requires articles of incorporation, bylaws, the appointment of a registered agent, the formation of a board of directors, the election of officers, and ongoing record-keeping and reporting requirements, a sole proprietorship requires none of these formalities. Sole proprietorships and partnerships generally have lower operational costs, both in terms of time and money, because there are no filing fees to establish them, no separate tax returns, and far fewer requirements to adhere to corporate formalities. LLCs fall somewhere in the middle between the extensive formalities necessitated by a corporation and the lack of nearly any such formalities required of a sole proprietorship.

The factors just discussed are distilled into a chart that can be found in Appendix C. Understanding the needs that come with starting a freelance practice, as well as preferences, is critical to choosing an appropriate corporate entity based on those factors.

For example, take a lawyer who decided to leave a traditional law practice to create more flexible time to care for an elderly parent. That lawyer's former firm agreed to work with him on a freelance basis to maintain client relationships and because the firm valued his work. Because of the freelancer's established professional network over decades of practicing law, other law firm clients were not hard to attract.

Because the freelancer will start with a steady income stream, paying vendors is not a concern. However, with the desire for more time, the freelancer was not interested in devoting much effort to corporate management issues, such as opening separate bank accounts, state filings, or preparing separate tax returns. Given this freelancer's particular wants and needs, a sole proprietorship might be the best corporate structure. On the other hand, a corporation with all the reporting and management requirements would probably not be the most suitable corporate entity to choose, given the reasons for leaving a traditional law practice in the first place.

However, assume the freelancer was recently graduated from law school with a need to obtain financing to start a law firm. For example, the freelancer needed funding to buy subscriptions for the technology and software platforms necessary to practice, to lease office equipment, and to rent an office. This would present a riskier business model from a financial standpoint, so perhaps the freelancer would want the additional liability protection that an entity such as an LLC or corporation could provide. Because the freelancer is very organized and does not consider it a big deal to manage all the corporate formalities, the operational cost in terms of time to manage a more formal business structure would not present a significant downside.

Choosing the right business entity for a freelance law practice should not be an afterthought. It is an important decision that has legal, financial, and operational implications. Making an informed choice requires knowledge of the common business structures available to law practices in a particular state, an evaluation of liability protection needs and risk tolerance, taxation considerations, compliance requirements like state-specific rules for law entities, governance obligations and operational flexibility, and administrative requirements. Only after evaluating these factors can there be an informed decision made on the most suitable business entity for a freelance law practice.

There is no right or wrong answer when choosing a type of corporate entity. There is also no perfect answer. Each entity has its advantages and drawbacks. While consulting with a lawyer or tax professional can prove helpful in navigating state laws impacting different types of entities and in evaluating the pros and cons of each, determining the desired scope of liability protection, the type of tax treatment desired, and operational or management needs will go a long way toward helping a choice become apparent as to the type of business structure that can best meet the requirements and preferences of a particular freelancer. Some of these same considerations also apply to understanding start-up needs in terms of the financial commitments necessary to start a freelance law practice.

CHAPTER 8

Dollars and Sense

Mastering the Financial Landscape of Starting a Freelance Practice

"You are the storyteller of your own life, and you can create your own legend, or not."

—Isabel Allende

Starting a freelancing practice is a serious undertaking that requires careful planning and an understanding of many financial considerations, the first of which is start-up costs. Awareness of the necessary start-up costs will provide a realistic foundation for creating a comprehensive financial plan. By estimating initial expenses, a freelancer will be able to determine the amount of funding required to launch a law practice and sustain it until it becomes profitable.

Whether there is a need for financing or whether a freelancer will be self-funding a new law practice, knowing the start-up costs is critical to being able to prioritize expenses, to exploring cost saving measures, and to setting realistic expectations about revenue generation. Setting realistic expectations will negate surprises and unexpected financial strain in the early stages of starting a law practice.

Initial Capital Outlay

First and foremost, a freelancer must understand the capital requirement to start a practice. Starting any business usually requires an initial investment to cover various expenses like office space, equipment, and technology. Knowing the financial requirements for these kinds of necessities will help determine the amount of funding that is necessary to launch a practice and whether a freelancer can self-fund a new practice or whether there will be a need to borrow money. If seeking financing, an accurate estimate of costs will enhance credibility when approaching a lender, increasing the chance of securing the necessary funding.

One of the reasons why freelancing can be so lucrative is because many of the start-up costs a lawyer would be forced to incur when starting a traditional law business can be minimized or eliminated with a freelancing practice. For example, the cost of renting or purchasing office space is typically one of the most significant expenses associated with starting any law practice. However, as set forth in Chapter 5, there are many ways to minimize the cost of office space as a freelancer. Working virtually or remotely from home negates the need to rent or purchase office space altogether. Freelancing for a law firm and using its space also avoids the need to spend money on an office rental. If renting office space is necessary, joint workspace can be a cost-efficient alternative to renting traditional office space.

Furniture, equipment, and supplies are also essential start-up costs. While working remotely from home will avoid the cost of renting office space, to set up a successful practice, a freelancer will still need a desk, chair, a desktop or laptop, monitors, a copier and scanner, high-speed internet, and videoconferencing equipment. However, working from a client's law firm or renting joint workspace will likely avoid or at least significantly minimize these costs. Therefore, while working remotely from home will eliminate office space rental costs, there will be furniture, equipment, and supply costs that a freelancer will likely not incur by working from someone else's office or renting a joint workspace.

Marketing and advertising costs are also important for a freelancer to account for when looking to start a practice. To attract clients and establish a law practice, a freelancer typically needs to invest in some type of marketing and advertising efforts. A freelancer should have a website, will need business cards, and might also want a social media presence. In addition, professional branding might be a cost to help set a freelancer apart from competition. Some freelancers are able to do basic or even highly developed marketing and advertising themselves. However, even for freelancers who spend their own time marketing and advertising, that time eats into the time they can spend working and generating revenue.

A time-cost analysis is important to determine whether it is worth paying a third party to do any necessary marketing and advertising. For example, if a freelancer spends 10 hours creating a website and a few hours to establish a social media presence, that adds up to 13 hours in the first month, which, if spent working, could equate to $1,000 or more in revenue. If the cost to pay a third-party to do the work is under $1,000, that cost might be worth paying.

Any freelancer will need access to specialized legal software to manage client information, billing, digital storage needs, and case management. These software packages can be expensive. Ongoing support costs must also be considered. There are many different categories of software to consider. Case management software will help a freelancer manage files, track deadlines, and share information. Practice management software will help a freelancer manage daily operations, including time tracking, billing, and accounting. Document management software will help a freelancer manage and organize documents such as contracts, legal briefs, records, and correspondence. E-discovery software helps in managing the discovery process, including data collection, processing, review, and production. Legal research software provides access to legal databases, cases law, statutes, rules, treatises, and other legal resources. Contract management software can help a freelancer organize and draft contracts. Document assembly software automates the creation of legal documents.

Although expensive, legal specialization software will help a freelancer manage work and increase efficiency. By leveraging technology, a freelancer can streamline operations to avoid unnecessary time spent on practice management and focus instead on servicing clients and generating revenue. The type of software a freelancer needs will depend on many factors. A litigator will probably not need contract management software or document assembly software, and a transactional lawyer will likely not need e-discovery software and maybe not even access to legal research databases.

A freelancer with only one or two clients might not need sophisticated practice management or accounting software and can instead pay a very low monthly subscription rate for software like FreshBooks, which is intuitive accounting software for small businesses that allows individuals to generate invoices and track accounts receivable and payable, and which provides various kinds of financial reporting. A freelancer's type of practice, needs, and preferences will dictate what type of software is necessary to start a practice, which can vary greatly from practitioner to practitioner.

Some freelancers will not even need to account for the costs of technology when starting a practice if there is access to technology through the client law firms. For example, some law firms engaging a freelancer will allow the freelancer to have access to Westlaw or Lexis for legal research and will encourage the freelancer to use the firm's case management software to schedule deadlines and to record time for billing. If a law firm provides the freelancer access to its server to review client files, the freelancer will be able to make use of the firm's document management software. However, other freelancers will have to purchase their own technology. Given how much technology needs can vary, paying attention to what kind of investment in technology will be necessary to start a practice and its associated costs is critical.

Insurance

In the next chapter, insurance considerations are discussed in detail. As with any profession, a freelancer needs insurance for protection from unexpected events that can result in financial loss or legal liability. Professional liability insurance protects from claims of negligence or legal malpractice. General liability insurance and property insurance protect against claims of property damage or bodily injury. Cyber liability insurance protects against data breaches or cyberattacks. Health, disability, and life insurance protect against illness, incapacity, and death. Overall, insurance is an important tool that can help a freelancer manage risk and protect financial well-being. The cost of insurance depends on factors like the nature of a freelancer's practice, the location of the practice, coverage limits and deductibles, and the availability of coverage.

Professional Fees

Professional fees need to be considered in the costs of starting a freelancing practice as well. The failure to properly report taxes can result in expensive penalties and interest charges. While many freelancers will be able to handle tax filings and payments themselves, especially with the proliferation of online tax software, some will not have the expertise or the desire to do so. Depending on the complexity of a freelancer's tax situation, paying a tax professional might be necessary.

A certified public accountant (CPA) is a licensed professional who meets specific educational, experience, and licensing requirements. An accountant, on the other hand, generally has less formal education and is not licensed, but can still provide valuable services like bookkeeping and tax preparation. Ultimately, the decision of whether a freelancer will handle taxes or hire a CPA or an accountant to do that work will depend on the freelancer's particular financial situation, level of comfort with tax matters, and the desired level of expertise or guidance.

A freelancer may require the assistance of other professionals as well. A lawyer might be necessary to help set up the right type of business entity and to ensure compliance with applicable laws. Especially if trying to obtain financing, a business consultant might be a sensible cost to help develop a business plan. Many law firms pay a subscription fee to an information technology (IT) professional to manage technology needs and to deal with problems when they arise. These types of professional services, if necessary, should be factored into a start-up budget.

Licensing and bar association fees are often overlooked. Some jurisdictions have mandatory bar associations. Mandatory bar dues can be costly. Even if bar membership is not mandatory, part of a freelancer's marketing strategy might include joining a bar association for networking purposes.

In addition, all freelancers will need to maintain their professional licenses. Even if that does not come with a direct fee, all jurisdictions require some amount of continuing education to maintain a law license. Therefore, at a minimum, a freelancer should allocate funds for continuing education classes.

However, while continuing education classes can be quite costly, there are ways to minimize those costs. A membership as a solo practitioner in the American Bar Association (ABA), which, in 2023, was only $75 for newer lawyers and $150 for lawyers with more than 10 years of practice, provides members with access to hundreds of free continuing education classes. In states where continuing education classes are about $100 per credit hour and lawyers need 15 credit hours to maintain their law licenses, the ABA's $75 or $150 fee provides a real opportunity to minimize the costs of staying licensed.

Different jurisdictions have different licensing fees or business permit costs. It is essential to research the specific requirements of where a freelance law practice is registered to determine any such fees or costs. Generally, a home-based freelance business will have fewer licensing or permit requirements than other business types. Be aware that the type of business structure used to set up a freelance law practice can impact licensing and permit requirements. A corporation, for example, might have different permitting requirements than a sole proprietorship.

Bank Accounts

In addition to thinking about start-up costs, there are also other financial considerations important to starting a freelancing business that do not cost money. One such consideration is the types of bank account a freelancer will need. There are several different types of bank accounts that are generally necessary to effectively manage finances in the context of a law practice. A freelancer will need an operating account, which is the primary account used to manage day-to-day finances. The operating account is usually used to pay rent, if necessary, to purchase equipment and supplies, to pay for any necessary insurance policies, and to pay for legal software—in short, any expense necessary for the operation of a freelancer's law practice.

Most lawyers and law firms are required to have an IOLTA account. IOLTA stands for Interest on Lawyer Trust Accounts. A trust account is used to hold retainers—client funds that are paid in advance of services being rendered. For example, if a client pays a retainer, that retainer must be held in a special, interest-bearing trust account that is separate from the law firm's operating funds because the retainer has not yet been earned until a lawyer provides services. Settlement checks will also go into an IOLTA trust account prior to being disbursed.

However, because a freelancer does not deal directly with the end client but is hired by a law firm or lawyer, a freelancer should not be handling any client money. Therefore, many states will not require a freelancer to have an IOLTA trust account. A freelancer should check the state rules applicable to IOLTA accounts because violating the trust account rules can result in disciplinary proceedings against a lawyer. Mismanaging trust accounts is one of the surest ways for a lawyer to get suspended or disbarred.

If a freelancer wants to process credit or debit card payments for invoiced legal services, a merchant services account might be necessary. This type of account is typically linked to an operating account and is used to deposit funds received from credit or debit card transactions. To process credit or debit card payments, a freelancer would choose a payment gateway, which is software that securely processes online transactions. Many times, billing software includes a payment gateway. Along with a payment gateway, a freelancer will need a payment processor that will provide instructions about how to pay for services. Again, billing software may provide a payment processing system as well.

Once a freelancer has a merchant services account and a payment gateway and processor set up, it is possible to start accepting credit or debit card payments. The law firm who hired the freelancer can enter its credit card information on the freelancer's website and the payment gateway will securely transmit that information to the payment processor. The payment processor will settle the transaction by transferring funds from the client law firm's account to the freelancer's merchant services account, which the freelancer can then transfer to the operating account. While this process may seem overly complicated, practice management software has made it easy. Tabs3 software, for example, has a billing function in Tabs3Pay that allows lawyers to accept credit card and ACH payments. FreshBooks accounting software functions the same way.

Retirement Accounts

In addition to the different kinds of bank accounts necessary to optimize a freelance law practice, a freelancer should also consider whether to set up a retirement account. There are various retirement plan options available to a freelancer who is solo practitioner, only a few of which are touched on here. A traditional Individual Retirement Account (IRA) is probably the simplest and allows a freelancer to contribute pre-tax income. Contributing pre-tax income reduces taxable income. For example, if a freelancer earns $80,000 and contributes $5,000 to an IRA, instead of being taxed on $80,000, income tax would only be calculated on $75,000.

An IRA grows tax-deferred. This means that the $5,000 contributed can increase in value without the growth being taxed. However, at retirement, the amounts withdrawn are subject to income tax. In 2023, a freelancer could contribute up to $6,500 annually to an IRA, with the limit increased to $7,500 for those aged 50 and older.

A Roth IRA, which is a variation of the traditional IRA, has the same contribution limits as a traditional IRA but the amount contributed is after-tax dollars, and, therefore, subject to income tax. Accordingly, a freelancer earning $80,000 and contributing $5,000 to a Roth IRA would be taxed on the entire $80,000. The contribution of $5,000 would be in after-tax dollars but would still grow tax free. However, unlike a traditional IRA where withdrawals at retirement are taxed, withdrawals from a Roth IRA are tax free.

Another variation on the traditional IRA is a Simplified Employee Pension (SEP) IRA. A SEP IRA is a retirement plan that allows self-employed individuals to contribute a percentage of their income to a retirement account. Like a traditional IRA, SEP IRA contributions are with pre-tax dollars and earnings grow tax deferred until withdrawal. SEP IRAs allow for greater contributions than traditional IRAs. In 2023, the contributions to a SEP IRA were limited to the lesser of 25 percent of compensation or $66,000 for those under 50. For those 50 and older, there was a $73,500 limit.

A Solo 401(k) plan is also available for self-employed individuals and has the same high contribution limits as the SEP IRA. Solo 401(k) plans often get confused with Individual 401(k) plans. An Individual 401(k) is like a Solo 401(k) but offers the ability for a freelancer to make both an employee contribution and an employer contribution on behalf of the business. Total contributions to an Individual 401(k) can consist of 100 percent of a self-employed individual's income, unlike a Solo 401(k) that limits contributions to 25 percent. In addition, a freelancer can make an employer contribution of up to 25 percent of compensation with an Individual 401(k). The limit of employee contributions in 2023 for an Individual 401(k) plan was $22,500 for those under 50 and $30,000 for those 50 and older. The 2023 total limit on contributions for an Individual 401(k), both employee and employer, was $66,000 for those under 50 and $73,500 for those 50 and older.

A simplistic example of how an Individual 401(k) works can be found on the Internal Revenue Service (IRS) website: Ben, age 51, earned $50,000. He funded his Individual 401(k) with $19,500 in regular contributions plus $6,500 in catch-up contributions because he is over 50. His business also contributed 25 percent of his compensation to the retirement plan, or $12,500. Therefore, total retirement plan contributions were $38,500.

As shown by the IRS's example, Ben was able to put more than three-quarters of his earnings toward retirement—$38,500 of the $50,000 earned. While this might not be realistic for a freelancer without another source of income, for a freelancer in a dual income household, an Individual 401(k) can be a tremendous vehicle to build retirement savings quickly.

There are other types of retirement plans as well. Each has its own rules and limitations. For example, there may be income restrictions, penalties for early withdrawals, different rules for borrowing from a retirement plan, and varying administrative requirements and fees. When considering a retirement plan, it is important to bear all these factors in mind. Consulting with a financial advisor or a tax professional who can assess an individual's financial situation, retirement needs, and preferences can help a freelancer select the most suitable retirement plan.

A cornerstone of building wealth is saving for retirement. This is in part because retirement accounts like 401(k)s and IRAs often have significant tax advantages. The tax efficiencies from these types of retirement accounts allows your money to compound and grow more effectively than investments in taxable accounts will. This compounding of interest allows wealth to snowball over a career.

Enforcing a disciplined approach to wealth building through regular retirement contributions, which can be deducted automatically from your paycheck or bank account, will help a freelancer stick to retirement savings goals even when faced with the temptation to spend, ensuring the freelancer consistently sets aside a portion of income for the future.

Especially during times of high inflation like today, which erodes the purchasing power of money, saving for retirement by investing in assets that tend to outpace inflation can help protect wealth from the erosive impact of rising prices. That is why saving for retirement should be one of the foundations of wealth-building strategies. By taking advantage of retirement savings vehicles like 401(k)s and IRAs, it is possible to create a solid financial foundation that will support a freelancer's lifestyle well after the end of a career.

The power of saving for retirement in a tax-preferred account like a 401(k) or an IRA is illustrated by the following example that compares saving $10,000 per year for 20 years in a tax-preferred account versus a non-qualified account, assuming an annual growth rate of 7 percent.

In a tax-preferred account like a 401(k) or an IRA, assuming an annual growth rate of 7 percent and contributing $10,000 per year for 20 years, the future value would be $572,752. In a non-qualified account on the other hand, which does not have the advantage of tax-deferred growth, a freelancer would have to pay taxes on each year's investment gains. Assuming a 20 percent tax rate on the gains, the future value would only be $387,442.

In the preceding scenario, the tax-deferred growth results in a significantly higher future value compared to the non-qualified account. The difference in future value only increases the more a freelancer puts in a tax-preferred account. For example, if a freelancer saves $15,000 annually instead of $10,000, all other assumptions remaining the same, the future value in a tax-preferred account will be $1,403,293, but only $871,745 in the non-qualified account. This is because the tax-deferred growth allows money to compound on the initial investment as well as on the gains, leading to a substantially larger value over time. It becomes easy to see why using a tax-preferred account to save for retirement is a remarkable way to build wealth.

Health Savings Account

A health savings account (HSA) is another tax-advantaged savings account that allows individuals to save and pay for qualified medical expenses. It works in conjunction with a high-deductible health plan. Contribution limits for an HSA were $3,650 for individuals and $7,300 for families in 2023. Those 55 and older could make an additional catch-up contribution of $1,000.

HSAs, like traditional IRAs and 401(k) plans, reduce taxable income. In addition, like those types of retirement plans, contributions to HSAs grow tax free. Qualified withdrawals for certain medical expenses are also tax-free, and contributed amounts can be carried over from year to year so they are not lost if not used. Therefore, a freelancer can continue to accumulate HSA funds and use them for qualified medical expenses in future years. Many times, individuals use HSAs to pay for medical expenses that traditional health insurance plans do not cover, such as dental and vision care.

In sum, thinking about start-up costs, as well as other financial considerations, is critical when starting a freelancing practice. It allows the freelancer to plan and to budget effectively. By estimating and planning for start-up costs, a freelancer can avoid the risk of running out of money before a practice becomes profitable.

Start-up costs and other financial considerations can also help a freelancer determine how much funding is necessary to start a practice, which is imperative if seeking financing. Proper planning will allow a freelancer to make informed decisions about how to prioritize expenses and to determine how long it is possible to operate without generating a profit.

Ultimately, considering start-up costs and financial needs is essential for setting realistic goals, establishing a sound financial plan, and increasing the chances of success for a freelance practice. By carefully considering start-up costs and financial needs, a freelancer will increase the chances of building a sustainable and successful law practice and maximizing wealth.

A key consideration when talking about maximizing wealth is protecting it. Other than the personal liability protections achieved through different corporate structures, insurance is an essential tool when it comes to safeguarding capital.

——————————————————————

CHAPTER 9

Safeguarding Success

The Essential Insurance Arsenal for Starting a Freelance Practice

"My motto has always been that you can't say, 'Oh, it won't happen to me.' You have to say 'That can happen to me.' So always be aware that things can happen."

—Venus Williams

Life is unpredictable. Mistakes, accidents, and illness can happen any time. These kinds of unexpected events can have devastating financial consequences. Stories persist about people who were bankrupt by unforeseen medical expenses. Lawyers are as prone as any professional to malpractice claims, which are costly even if resolved favorably. A house fire can wipe out a lifetime of savings that home equity represents. Insurance provides a way to manage the financial risk of unforeseen events like these by placing the financial burden for them on an insurance company.

Without insurance, a freelancer would have to bear the full cost of an unforeseen event, like a legal malpractice claim or damage to business property, which can be prohibitively expensive. Even in personal matters, the absence of insurance can be financially devastating. The need for costly medical treatment without health insurance, for example, can cause financial distress that is hard to recover from. A fire that destroys computer equipment can result in a hefty replacement cost for someone without property insurance. Just the legal costs alone of defending a legal malpractice lawsuit can be extremely expensive without insurance, even if the lawsuit is ultimately dismissed.

Insurance can provide peace of mind by reducing uncertainty, which will help a freelancer focus on building a law practice with confidence. The need for insurance is an essential risk management tool, regardless of the size of a freelancer's law practice. Whether the risk is property damage, theft, a cyberattack, accidents, lawsuits, or professional negligence, insurance can help minimize the financial impact when unexpected events occur, allowing a freelancer to focus on providing quality legal services and maximizing wealth.

There are many different types of insurance a freelancer should consider when starting a law practice. Deciding which types of insurance to purchase depends on an assessment of the risks involved absent coverage that will mitigate against unforeseen and financially impactful events.

For example, not having a health insurance policy carries the risk of having to pay out of pocket for expensive medical care, or foregoing the care altogether. A freelancer practicing law without an errors and omissions policy is gambling that there is never a negligence claim and if there is, there are sufficient financial resources available to defend or resolve it. Not having property insurance coverage means that a freelancer is willing to shoulder the burden of replacing office equipment and furniture if there is a fire or a flood. Although most freelancers will not carry all the types of coverage discussed in this chapter, consideration should be given to them before deciding what kind of insurance is necessary versus what risks a freelancer is willing to shoulder.

Professional Liability Insurance

Professional liability insurance, also called errors and omissions or legal malpractice insurance, provides protection from claims resulting from negligence in providing legal services. For example, if a freelancer who is responsible for the due diligence involved in a purchase and sale transaction fails to uncover material information that could lead to a financial loss or legal consequences for a client, like an unmitigated environmental contaminant or a land encumbrance, that failure could give rise to a legal malpractice claim. Similarly, a freelancer who provides incorrect legal advice or fails to provide information about relevant legal implications could be liable for legal malpractice. A freelancer who fails to thoroughly research a legal issue, leading to a missed argument at trial, could also face a professional negligence claim.

Even failing to adhere to professional or ethical responsibilities can give rise to legal malpractice. Many jurisdictions consider the applicable professional code of ethics or code of conduct as a standard of care for practicing law. Therefore, for example, if a freelancer has a conflict of interest and fails to properly disclose it or obtain client consent, violating the rules of professional responsibility, the violation could give rise to a legal malpractice claim.

There is some measure of professional liability protection for a freelancer providing services to a lawyer or law firm as an independent contractor, rather than as an employee of the law firm. The law firm is ultimately responsible to its client for the legal services provided, even if a freelancer performed those legal services.

For example, if a freelancer drafts a docketing statement for an appeal and forgets to include an issue to be argued on appeal, resulting in the appellate court declining to consider that issue, the client may have a malpractice claim against the law firm who filed the docketing statement without adequately reviewing the freelancer's draft. The client would typically sue the law firm for legal malpractice directly, not the freelancer.

Even if the client sues the freelancer as well as the hiring law firm, a law firm's errors and omissions policies often provide coverage not just for lawyer employees of the law firm but also for independent contractors performing legal services. In other words, it is possible that a freelancer will be covered under a law firm's legal malpractice policy for any legal services performed.

A freelancer can always check with the client law firm to determine whether the legal malpractice coverage encompasses a freelancer's legal services. If a freelancer only has a few clients, it is more feasible to check whether there is coverage than if a freelancer is working for a lot of different law firms. However, even if there is coverage for a freelancer, unless freelancers want to continually check to see whether malpractice coverage is in place and whether the policy covers independent contractors, they should plan on obtaining their own malpractice policies.

This is particularly true because even if the ultimate client does not sue the freelancer for legal malpractice, and even if the client law firm's policy covers the work of the freelancer as an independent contractor, the law firm could still turn around and seek indemnification from a freelancer for the freelancer's professional negligence. Even though freelancers are independent contractors, they are still responsible for their own actions and can still be held liable for negligently performing legal services. Therefore, it is advisable for freelancers to consider obtaining their own professional liability policies.

States vary as to the cost of professional liability policies, which will often depend on the availability of professional liability insurers in the state. States that have more competition among carriers will likely have more competitive prices. Some states, however, only have one or two carriers that will provide legal malpractice coverage, which will make obtaining coverage more expensive.

The area of practice will also determine the cost of a policy. Certain practice areas, like personal injury or medical malpractice, are considered higher risk. Lawyers practicing in the high-risk fields may face higher premiums for professional liability coverage.

Firm size or revenue can also impact the cost of legal malpractice insurance. A small firm with lower revenue will typically pay lower premiums because there is less exposure to potential malpractice claims than a large firm would have with its many lawyers, greater number of clients, and higher revenue. Some professional liability carriers will even offer a lower cost policy for freelancers who only work part-time.

As with all other types of insurance, the amount of a deductible can affect professional liability insurance premiums. Policies with lower deductibles will typically have higher premiums. Whether to accept a higher deductible to reduce premium costs will depend on a freelancer's risk tolerance and willingness to assume a greater financial consequence in terms of out-of-pocket costs in the event of a legal malpractice claim.

For example, a freelancer who provides legal research and brief writing services that is reviewed by the law firm prior to filing, who never signs any court filings, and who does not interact directly with the ultimate client has a much lower risk of being subject to a legal malpractice claim than a freelancer drafting a contract, presenting it to the end client on behalf of the law firm, and discussing revisions with that client. The freelancer doing legal research and writing might be more willing, therefore, to have a cheaper professional liability policy but with a much high deductible.

General Liability Insurance

In addition to professional liability coverage, a freelancer should also consider obtaining general liability insurance, especially if working outside of the home. Most businesses have general liability coverage, which provides insurance for claims of bodily injury or property damage that occur on a law firm's premises or because of its operations, such as slip and fall accidents or damage to a client's property.

A homeowner's policy may provide coverage for these risks for freelancers working remotely from home. However, homeowners' policies might contain an exclusion if business is conducted on the residential property that is insured, so it is important to review the policy to see what is covered.

If working from somebody else's office or if renting space, that office should have its own general liability policy. However, it is important to determine whether general liability insurance is in place and what it covers so that a freelancer does not inadvertently assume the risk of accidents or property damage.

Property Insurance

Property insurance provides coverage for damage to a freelancer's physical assets, such as damage to or the destruction of a building, equipment, or furniture resulting from events like a fire, flood, or vandalism. Again, if working remotely from home, a homeowner's policy might provide property insurance coverage for a home office if there is no exclusion for space being used for business purposes.

If renting space, a freelancer will likely need to purchase property insurance coverage. Even though most landlords will have a general liability policy, that type of policy will not provide coverage for a freelancing tenant's personal property or liability within the office space itself. For example, if renting space in an office building, while the landlord's general liability policy will likely cover liability from accidents or property damage occurring in the common spaces, such as vandalism to a vehicle in the parking lot or injuries to a visitor who slipped and fell in the lobby, that coverage does not usually extend to the space a freelancer rents or to the freelancer's personal property.

Take the case of a fire in an office building that destroyed a freelancer's property within the rented office itself. The landlord's general liability policy would likely not provide coverage. Likewise, if the freelancer accidently caused damage to property within the office space or injured somebody else within the office space, it is likewise doubtful that the landlord's general liability policy will provide coverage. Therefore, for example, if a freelancer accidently started a fire in the microwave in rented office space, causing smoke damage to the furniture and equipment and injuring those who were present during the fire due to smoke inhalation, the freelancer's insurance policy, not the landlord's general liability policy, would likely be the source of coverage for any claims arising from the property damage caused by smoke from the fire and the resulting injuries.

Cyber Liability Insurance

In addition to professional liability insurance, general liability insurance, and property coverage, there are also many other kinds of liability insurance. With the advent of technology has come an insurance product called cyber liability insurance. If a freelancer is collecting and storing sensitive client information, or even if a freelancer has remote access to a law firm's server and databases containing client information, there is a risk of data breaches or cyberattacks.

Cyber liability insurance provides coverage for the costs of data breaches or cyberattacks, such as response and recovery costs. For example, data breach response costs can encompass the expenses associated with investigating a data breach and notifying affected individuals, as well as the expenses for providing credit-monitoring services. Many people have received notices in the mail from financial institutions or other organizations offering free credit-monitoring services for a year due to a data breach. The investigation to determine that there was a data breach, the cost of notifying consumers of that data breach, and the cost of the free credit-monitoring services are all costs that were likely covered by a cyber insurance policy.

In addition, if a data breach or a cyberattack causes a freelancer to lose income because of a disruption in business operations, cyber insurance may also cover the resulting financial losses. For example, a freelancer who cannot work for a month while trying to restore client databases could take advantage of cyber insurance to protect against the lost income. Cyber insurance may also cover costs related to ransomware attacks, including coverage for the ransom payment.

Cyber insurance policies vary tremendously depending on the insurance company, the jurisdiction, and the policy itself. Therefore, a freelancer who is considering a cyber liability policy should review the policy terms and conditions carefully to understand what is covered and what is excluded to make sure the policy fits the freelancer's needs.

In addition, just like insurers providing legal malpractice coverage will want to make sure a freelancer has the appropriate safeguards in place to protect against malpractice claims, like a redundant calendaring system or a process to prevent conflicts of interest, insurers providing cyber insurance policies will want assurances that there are proper security measures in place to protect against cyberattacks and data breaches prior to issuing a policy.

Workers' Compensation Insurance

While a lawyer or a law firm with employees should consider other types of insurance, such as workers' compensation or employment-related practices liability insurance (EPLI) coverage, a freelancer working alone will not need to. However, if a freelancer has employees, other insurance, like workers' compensation insurance, could be mandatory, depending on the rules of the state where the freelancer is based.

Workers' compensation insurance provides coverage for medical expenses and lost wages for employees who are hurt or injured on the job. A legal assistant who trips at work and is injured, for example, would have a workers' compensation claim. A paralegal who is diagnosed with carpel tunnel syndrome could also have a workers' compensation claim.

EPLI Coverage

EPLI coverage, which is not mandatory, provides coverage for claims of discrimination, harassment, wrongful termination, or other employment-related issues. Because employment-related lawsuits generally include legal fees for a prevailing employee, they can become very expensive.

For example, an employee filing a discrimination lawsuit who prevails would generally be entitled to not just compensatory damages but also to the legal fees incurred in bringing a claim. That means freelancers defending an employment-related lawsuit could be on the hook not just for their own defense costs but also for the employee's attorney's fees as well. Employment-related claims are some of the most expensive kinds of disputes litigated. EPLI coverage helps mitigate the risk associated with this kind of legal dispute.

Directors and Officers (D&O) Liability Insurance

For freelancers who form corporations, D&O liability insurance provides coverage for directors and officers who may be held personally liable for the decisions made on behalf of the law firm. An example of a claim that D&O coverage would typically insure are allegations of innocent but nonetheless illegal errors like improper tax accounting. In that case, D&O insurance could help cover the legal costs associated with defending against those allegations, as well as any damages or penalties awarded or agreed to in the settlement of the claim.

Life Insurance

Another type of coverage a freelancer should consider is life insurance. While a law firm might provide life insurance coverage to its employees, a freelancer will not have the advantage of that kind of employment benefit.

There are different types of life insurance policies available. Each has its own pros and cons. Term life insurance is the simplest and cheapest. Term life insurance provides coverage for a specific and limited period, such as 10, 20, or 30 years. If the policyholder dies within the policy term, a set death benefit is paid to the beneficiary.

A freelancer pays premiums during the policy term and when the term expires, premium payments stop and the death benefit is no longer available. If, for example, a freelancer with young kids wanted to protect against the absence of income in the case of death to ensure there would be sufficient money for the family's living expenses and college tuition for the kids, that freelancer could take out a 20-year or a 30-year term life insurance policy that would end after college when the children were in their twenties or thirties and able to earn a living for themselves.

Whole life insurance, on the other hand, provides a permanent death benefit for a policyholder's entire life if the policyholder pays premiums. Whole life policies can be used as a savings or investment method as well because one of the components of a whole life policy, aside from the death benefit, is the cash value of the policy, which can grow tax-deferred over time. In addition, the cash value can be used to pay premiums or can be withdrawn or borrowed against, subject to certain limitations. Whole life policies are usually much more expensive than term life policies. Moreover, if a policyholder surrenders the policy while alive or withdraws some of the cash value, taxes and possibly a fee on the cash value of the policy or on the amount withdrawn would be owed.

Universal life insurance is like whole life insurance in that it provides a permanent death benefit for the entire life of the policyholder subject to the payment of premiums. However, universal life policies are generally more flexible than whole life policies in terms of premium payments and death benefit amounts. For example, with a universal life insurance policy, the policyholder generally has the flexibility to adjust premium payments over time, subject to certain limitations. This allows the policyholder to increase or decrease premium payments based on varying financial circumstances or needs. A universal life policyholder can also adjust the death benefit amount over time, again, subject to certain limitations.

Variable life insurance is like whole life and universal life insurance in that it provides a permanent death benefit and includes a cash value component that can be invested in a variety of options, including stocks, bonds, and mutual funds. However, a policyholder generally has more control with a variable life insurance policy than with other types of life insurance policies over how to invest the cash value component of the policy.

Variable life insurance premiums are usually fixed and higher than whole or universal life insurance premiums. In addition, the death benefit of a variable life insurance policy is tied to the performance of the investment component of the policy so that as the value of the investment component fluctuates, so does the death benefit.

Whole life, universal life, and variable life insurance policies have fees and charges that a term life policy will not have. While many consider these types of insurance policies to be investments, the significant fees associated with these insurance products will eat into any return. Therefore, prior to purchasing any life insurance policy, it is important to carefully consider the need, the investment options, and the fees and charges associated with the policy. In addition, there are many overlapping features of whole, universal, and variable life insurance policies, including characteristics not discussed here. An insurance professional or an investment advisor can detail policy benefits, drawbacks, and differences.

In most cases, the insurance company will pay the agent or broker who sells a life insurance policy a commission. Commissions are usually a percentage of the premiums paid by a policyholder so a freelancer should be aware that the higher the premiums, the larger a commission an agent or broker is likely to receive. In other words, an agent or broker might have a financial incentive to try and sell a higher priced policy. However, because the commission cost is already factored into the premium amount, it does not add additional cost to the policy. Therefore, a freelancer can usually engage an insurance or investment professional to help with life insurance needs without directly paying the professional, understanding the potential conflict due to the nature of how such a professional is paid.

Disability Insurance

In addition to life insurance protection, disability insurance coverage is also an option. Again, disability insurance might be an employment benefit provided to law firm employees that a freelancer, as an independent contractor, will not be able to take advantage of.

Disability insurance is a type of coverage that provides income replacement to a freelancer who becomes physically or mentally disabled and is unable to work. While the amount of the disability benefit typically depends on a freelancer's income (the higher the income, the higher the disability benefit), disability insurance never covers 100 percent of lost earnings due to a disability.

Disability benefits may be for a limited time or long term, such as for a period of two years or until the freelancer reaches retirement age. Sometimes, there is a waiting period after a disability to trigger coverage.

Health Insurance

Health insurance is arguably the most important non-liability insurance product that a freelancer will need. If not covered by somebody else's health insurance policy, such as a spouse's, purchasing health insurance will probably be the biggest insurance expense for a freelancer.

Finding and purchasing health insurance can be a formidable process. The first step is simply to determine health-care needs. This includes understanding the type of medical care that may be necessary, including the need for doctor visits and prescription drugs. A freelancer without significant medical needs might be able to consider an entirely different health-care policy than a freelancer who has diabetes and needs a $1,500 monthly prescription for semaglutide.

In the former case, the freelancer without significant medical needs might be able to choose a high deductible plan with much lower premiums, anticipating that there will not be much of a need to access medical care so the higher deductible would not present a big concern. In the latter case, a plan with higher premiums but a lower deductible might be more beneficial to a freelancer with $18,000 in annual prescription drug costs.

Once a freelancer understands health-care needs, it is possible to research the different health insurance plans that are available to meet those needs. Different states have different health-care plans available and even within the same state, the availability of plans may differ depending on the locality. Rural areas, for example, might have different coverage options than cities. A freelancer can look at private plans through health insurance companies offering coverage in a particular state like United Health or Blue Cross Blue Shield or can start by looking at the Health Insurance Marketplace, which is operated by the federal government.

After researching options, a freelancer can then compare available plans based on cost, deductibles, copays, the types of coverage available, and the network of health-care providers. Choosing a plan will depend on a variety of circumstances like health-care needs and budget, in addition to whether a plan includes access to preferred health-care providers. Cost will be affected by different factors. For example, as already noted, a higher deductible might lower monthly premiums. A health maintenance organization (HMO) plan with access limited to providers within a defined network might be less expensive than a preferred provider organization (PPO) plan with access to out-of-network providers.

In addition, insurers often offer different levels of health-care plans, commonly referred to as tiers. For example, the same insurer can offer bronze, silver, gold, and platinum plans. There are different levels of coverage and cost-sharing depending on the tier. A bronze plan might have the lowest premiums but higher out-of-pocket costs, a good option for freelancers who are generally healthy and do not have a need for frequent medical services. A silver plan usually strikes a balance between premium costs and out-of-pocket costs, so would typically have higher premiums than a bronze plan but not as many out-of-pocket costs. A gold plan generally has the highest premiums, but provides more comprehensive coverage. This makes a gold plan a better option for freelancers who anticipate needing regular medical care due to ongoing health-care needs. Platinum plans are not as common, but would provide the highest level of coverage, meaning the lowest level of out-of-pocket expenses. However, that comprehensive coverage would come at the price of higher premiums. For a freelancer requiring frequent medical care or who has significant health-care expenses, a platinum plan, if available, might be the best option.

After choosing a health insurance plan, a freelancer must apply for coverage. This is generally a simple, online process. Once an insurer approves the insurance application, a freelancer will start paying premiums to trigger coverage. There are many options for paying premiums, including monthly or quarterly payments, payments through automatic deductions from an operating account, or credit card payments. Once coverage is active, the freelancer can start using the health insurance to access medical care.

It is important to understand a health insurance plan's benefits, deductibles, copayments, and network of providers to avoid unexpected costs. For example, a freelancer who goes outside of an HMO network might have to cover the cost of the out-of-network provider. A more expensive PPO plan, however, would allow a freelancer to choose any provider and still have some coverage, although out-of-pocket expenses might be higher for an out-of-network provider than one who is in network. A freelancer who lives in a city with a large network of providers might be fine with an HMO plan. On the other hand, a freelancer from a rural area who needs access to specialists who are not available locally might require a more expensive PPO plan so that out-of-network medical care is at least partially covered.

If researching and choosing a health insurance plan that fits medical and budgetary needs and applying for coverage seems like too daunting or overwhelming of a task, there are insurance agents or brokers who can provide guidance through the process. Typically, as with life insurance plans, the health insurance company pays the agent or broker a commission and the freelancer trying to navigate the process of obtaining health-care coverage will not have to pay the agent or broker a fee. There are also online tools available to help compare the different plans available that will help a freelancer make an informed decision.

In sum, although liability and other types of insurance are significant expenses, and perhaps the biggest expense a freelancer will have in starting a practice, ensuring the necessary insurance coverage is important because it provides financial protection against unexpected events, such as accidents, illness, property damage, or inadvertent negligence. Insurance can help a freelancer manage risk by transferring the financial burden of these kinds of unexpected events to an insurance company. It will help protect a freelancer against financial loss that might be too costly to bear and provides peace of mind by helping to mitigate potential financial risk. Therefore, insurance is a cost a freelancer cannot ignore when starting a practice.

Another cost a freelancer should not ignore is the cost associated with technology. Because it is technology that has leveled the playing field between solo practitioners and large law firms, a freelancer should carefully assess technological needs and the cost of technology when starting a practice.

CHAPTER 10

Tech-savvy Transformation

Boosting Productivity and Revenue through Technological Empowerment

"Information technology and business are becoming inextricably interwoven. I don't think anybody can talk meaningfully about one without talking about the other."

—Bill Gates

Over the past few decades, technology has revolutionized almost every aspect of our lives. It is impossible to imagine anymore a time without smart phones. The legal profession is no exception. From research to communication to practice management, technology has significantly changed the way lawyers work and interact with clients and with each other.

With the advent of legal research software, for example, new lawyers coming out of law school do not remember spending days in a law library pouring through law books trying to find the most up-to-date holdings on an assigned topic, and law firms no longer have massive law libraries filled with books. The days of law firms employing runners to take documents to court to file them are over because filings are now electronic. The job of a filing clerk has disappeared from law firms because documents are now digitized.

Generative artificial intelligence (AI) has already dramatically reshaped the legal profession even more. The following example is illustrative:

Query: What is the burden of proof for establishing legal malpractice in New Mexico?

ChatGPT response: In New Mexico, the burden of proof for establishing legal malpractice is generally governed by the preponderance of the evidence standard. This means that the plaintiff must prove that it is more likely than not that the attorney committed malpractice.

To meet this burden of proof, the plaintiff must present evidence and arguments that demonstrate the following elements:

1. Duty: The plaintiff must establish that an attorney-client relationship existed, creating a duty of care owed by the attorney to the client.

This is typically proven through a written agreement, engagement letter, or other documentation.

2. Breach: The plaintiff must show that the attorney breached the duty of care owed to the client. This requires demonstrating that the attorney's actions or omissions fell below the standard of care expected of a reasonably competent attorney in similar circumstances. Expert testimony is often crucial in establishing the standard of care and proving the attorney's breach.

3. Causation: The plaintiff must establish a causal connection between the attorney's breach of duty and the harm suffered. It is necessary to demonstrate that if the attorney had not been negligent, the client would have had a better outcome in the underlying legal matter. This can be challenging and often requires expert testimony or other forms of evidence to establish the link between the attorney's actions and the client's damages.

4. Damages: The plaintiff must prove that they suffered actual damages as a direct result of the attorney's negligence. This can include financial losses, such as lost opportunities, increased legal costs, or a negative judgment. Non-economic damages, such as emotional distress, may also be considered, although quantifying them can be more difficult.

To support their claim, plaintiffs must gather relevant evidence, such as correspondence, legal documents, and records, that demonstrate the attorney's negligence and the resulting harm. It is important to consult with a qualified attorney experienced in legal malpractice cases in New Mexico to ensure that all the necessary elements are met and the burden of proof is properly addressed.

It is worth noting that legal malpractice claims in New Mexico are subject to a three-year statute of limitations. Generally, the clock starts ticking from the date the client discovered or should have discovered the attorney's negligence. However, there is a maximum limit of six years from the date of the alleged malpractice, regardless of when it was discovered.

Overall, while the burden of proof for legal malpractice in New Mexico is based on the preponderance of the evidence standard, successfully establishing a claim requires careful documentation, legal expertise, and often the involvement of expert witnesses.

In less than 15 seconds, ChatGPT generated this response, which is a generally accurate synopsis of New Mexico law on legal malpractice. Following is another example in a transactional context:

Query: Draft a short contract for the rental of office space between a freelance lawyer and a management company. The parties negotiated that

the management company will provide access to a shared conference room, a shared receptionist, and standard office equipment like a copier, scanner, office furniture, and high-speed internet. The lawyer will supply all computer equipment.
ChatGPT response:

[Your Name]
[Your Address]
[City, State, ZIP]
[Email Address]
[Phone Number]

[Date]

[Management Company Name]
[Management Company Address]
[City, State, ZIP]
Subject: Office Space Rental Agreement

Dear [Management Company Name],

This Office Space Rental Agreement (the "Agreement") is entered into between [Your Name] ("Tenant") and [Management Company Name] ("Management Company") on this [Date].

1. Office Space:
   a. Tenant agrees to rent office space located at [Address of Office Space] (the "Premises") from Management Company.
   b. The rented premises shall include access to a shared conference room, a shared receptionist, and standard office equipment, including a copier, scanner, office furniture, and high-speed internet. Tenant acknowledges that they shall be responsible for supplying their own computer equipment.
2. Term:
   a. The term of this Agreement shall commence on [Start Date] and continue for a period of [Number of Months/Years]. The Agreement may be extended by mutual written agreement of both parties.
3. Rent:
   a. Tenant agrees to pay a monthly rent of [Rent Amount] for the use of the office space and facilities provided by Management Company.
   b. Rent shall be due on the [Due Date] of each month, payable in advance.
   c. Tenant shall make all rental payments by [Payment Method] to the account specified by Management Company.

4. Security Deposit:

   a. Tenant shall provide a security deposit in the amount of [Security Deposit Amount]. The security deposit shall be refunded to Tenant within [Number of Days] days of the termination of this Agreement, less any deductions for damages or unpaid rent.

5. Termination:

   a. Either party may terminate this Agreement by providing [Notice Period] written notice to the other party.
   b. In the event of early termination by Tenant, Tenant shall remain responsible for payment of rent until the end of the notice period or until a new tenant is found, whichever occurs first.

6. Use and Maintenance:

   a. Tenant shall use the office space and facilities in a lawful manner and in accordance with all applicable laws and regulations.
   b. Tenant shall maintain the office space and equipment in good condition, and any damages caused by Tenant's negligence or intentional acts shall be repaired at Tenant's expense.

7. Governing Law:

   a. This Agreement shall be governed by and construed in accordance with the laws of the state of [State], without regard to its conflict of laws principles.

8. Entire Agreement:

   a. This Agreement constitutes the entire agreement between the parties and supersedes any prior understandings or agreements, whether written or oral, relating to the subject matter hereof.

Please indicate your acceptance of the terms and conditions of this Agreement by signing below. Return one signed copy to the address mentioned above.

Thank you for your attention, and we look forward to a mutually beneficial business relationship.

Sincerely,
[Your Name]

_____

[Your Name] Date Tenant

Accepted and Agreed:

_____

[Management Company Name] Date Management Company

Again, the agreement generated in seconds by ChatGPT contains all the basic elements of a rental contract.

Technology has changed the legal industry forever, allowing lawyers to work more efficiently and effectively than ever before. Understanding and knowing how to use it allows freelancers to improve the quality of legal services they can provide to clients by doing so more efficiently and effectively, which will ultimately increase the bottom line.

PC versus Mac

There are many ways technology can help freelancers become more productive, leading to an increase in revenue. But first, the basics. Personal computer (PC) or Apple Macintosh (Mac)? Choosing between a PC and a Mac depends on various factors, including personal preferences, software requirements, budget considerations, and compatibility needs. The pros of using a PC are that PCs tend to have a wider range of price options, making them more budget friendly for lawyers, especially freelancers just starting out. PCs are also more compatible generally with a broader range of software applications, including software specific to the legal profession like case management software, legal research software, and document management software.

However, PCs are more susceptible to malware and viruses compared to Macs. The increased security risk is a particular concern for freelancers who may be dealing with attorney-client privileged or confidential information. In addition, some users find PCs to be less intuitive when compared to Macs. PCs may also require more frequent updates and maintenance, which could be time-consuming for busy freelancers.

Macs are known for their robust security features, making them less vulnerable to malware and viruses. The intuitive user interface of Macs is a plus, creating a better user experience, depending on preference. For freelancers using iPhones or iPads, Macs offer seamless integration, facilitating workflow efficiency.

On the other hand, Macs tend to be more expensive upfront compared to PCs, which may be a significant factor for a freelancer on a tight budget. While Macs have improved their compatibility with many software applications over the years, there are still instances where specific legal software is not available or fully compatible with a Mac. Hardware customization options are also more limited on Macs than PCs, which may be a drawback for users with specific hardware requirements.

A freelancer should evaluate individual preferences, software requirements, budget constraints, security considerations, and compatibility with other devices and software before deciding whether to go the route of a PC or Mac.

Desktop versus Laptop

Again, there are pros and cons of working on a desktop versus a laptop. A choice will depend on specific work requirements, mobility needs, and personal preferences. Many lawyers do not choose. They maintain flexibility by using both. However, a freelancer with budget constraints might have to choose one option or the other.

Desktop computers typically offer better performance than laptops, especially in terms of processing power, storage capacity, and graphics capability. For a freelancer dealing with resource-intensive tasks, such as video editing or complex document processing, this is an important consideration. Desktop setups can also be optimized for comfort and flexibility, with multiple and adjustable monitors and ergonomic keyboards. Many lawyers who become used to working with two or more large monitors find it very difficult to work on a laptop. In addition, desktop computers often provide better value in terms of the performance-to-cost ratio compared to laptops with similar specifications. Desktops are also more easily upgradable than laptops. Being able to upgrade the central processing unit (CPU), graphics processing unit (GPU), random access memory (RAM), and storage allows a freelancer to better keep up with evolving technology requirements.

However, desktops are not portable, limiting the ability to work from different locations outside of where the desktop is situated. Desktop setups also require more space than a laptop, which may pose a constraint for those with smaller offices or in a home office environment. In addition, desktops require additional hardware, like monitors, keyboards, and a mouse, which will increase overall costs.

Laptops provide freelancers with the flexibility to work from anywhere, whether it is the office, courtroom, conference room during client meetings, or while traveling. Laptops are also compact so do not require a lot of dedicated desk space, making them ideal for freelancers with limited workspace. Laptops come with built-in peripherals like a keyboard, trackpad, and webcam, reducing the need to purchase accessories. In addition, many laptop models now offer a longer battery life, meaning that a freelancer can work for hours without being tethered to a power outlet.

On the downside, laptops have performance limitations compared to desktops due to space and power constraints, which may negatively affect computing speed. Laptops are also less upgradable than desktops, with limited options for upgrading components like CPU and GPU, potentially leading to a shorter usable lifespan. In addition, laptops are more susceptible to damage or theft, which can pose a risk to confidential legal data if it is not adequately protected.

There is a third option. An "all-in-one" (AIO) computer combines some features of a desktop and some of a laptop. Some of the hardware is integrated so it takes up less space. An AIO computer looks like a simple monitor, although it is slightly thicker, because it has the hardware components built into the back of the same structure as the monitor. Therefore, an AIO computer will integrate into one unit all the key components like the monitor, the CPU, memory, storage, and often a speaker and webcam as well. Unlike a traditional desktop setup where the monitor, CPU tower, and peripherals are separate, an AIO computer combines these components into a streamlined design. It combines the functionality of a traditional desktop setup with the space-saving benefits of a laptop.

However, an AIO computer has the same limitations as a laptop regarding its upgradability because its components, like the CPU, GPU, RAM, and storage, are integrated into the monitor. In addition, if a component fails in an AIO computer, repairing or replacing it can be more expensive compared to a traditional desktop because components are often proprietary and specialized, requiring professional service or manufacturer support for repairs. Unlike traditional desktops where the components are separate, an issue with any part of an AIO computer can affect the entire system. For example, a problem with the monitor can render the entire AIO computer unusable. Therefore, while an AIO computer offers convenience and space-saving benefits, it may not be suitable for a user who prioritizes upgradeability, repairability, or customization options.

Ultimately, the decision between a desktop and a laptop, or a hybrid-like option such as an AIO computer, will depend on work requirements, mobility needs, workspace limitations, and personal preferences. There is no perfect choice, each having its pros and cons. While some freelancers may benefit from a combination of two, using a desktop or AIO computer for primary office work and a laptop for on-the-go productivity, for those who need to make a choice, it is essential to prioritize needs and choose the option that best satisfies the highest-ranking priorities.

Monitors

If using a desktop, monitor setup should be considered. Desktop monitor setups can vary significantly, depending on a user's needs, preferences, and available space. Some of the more common setups are described next.

The most basic is a single monitor setup. It consists of a single monitor connected to the computer. Providing a straightforward and clutter-free workspace, this type of setup is ideal for users with limited desk space or for those who prefer simplicity.

However, a dual monitor setup has become more common. With a dual monitor setup, two monitors are connected to the computer, side by side or stacked vertically. This kind of setup offers increased screen real estate, allowing users to multitask by spreading out applications across both monitors. For example, a user can have legal research software up on one monitor while typing a brief on the other. Dual monitors can improve workflow by making certain tasks easier, like referencing multiple documents while writing, comparing data or documents on two screens, or working on multiple applications simultaneously.

It is also possible to have a triple monitor setup, which would appeal to a freelancer where extensive multitasking and visual information processing is required.

In addition to deciding how many monitors to use, the type of monitor is also important. Ultrawide monitors have an aspect ratio wider than the standard 16:9. Typically, they have a 21:9 or 32:9 aspect ratio, which offers a panoramic view and eliminates the bezel gap present in multi-monitor setups, providing a seamless viewing experience.

For a vertical monitor setup, just rotate a regular monitor 90 degrees to a portrait orientation instead of the traditional landscape orientation. This setup may be ideal for tasks that involve viewing or editing long documents. Using a vertical monitor to work on documents like a legal brief or a long contract will reduce the need for excessive scrolling.

Curved monitors have a slight curvature in the display. This curvature is designed to provide a more immersive viewing experience by reducing distortion at the screen edges and enhancing perception and depth. Although curved monitors are often used by gamers, they are said to reduce eye strain, so are good for users who spend extended periods in front of the screen.

Importantly, flat screen televisions can be used as monitors and are sometimes cheaper. Therefore, those with budget constraints should consider buying a small television and using it as a monitor.

Freelancers can mix and match different configurations based on their specific needs, preferences, and budget constraints. For example, for those with a small office and not a lot of desk space, hanging a television on the wall in front of a desk to use as a monitor will free up desk space. Monitor configurations are limited only by the imagination.

Printers, Scanners, and Copiers

Printers, scanners, and copiers are other types of hardware to consider when setting up an office. Whether there is a need for a printer, scanner, or copier depends on many factors. For example, for a freelancer who frequently needs to print documents, like contracts, briefs, correspondence, or research, having a printer provides convenience and flexibility, allowing the freelancer to produce hard copies of documents whenever needed. By the same token, a freelancer who often deals with physical documents that need to be converted into digital format would find a scanner useful.

However, printers, scanners, and copiers cost money and take up space. A freelancer who only needs to print documents occasionally or who does not often need to convert physical documents into digital format can take advantage of different venues for using printers, scanners, or copiers to avoid the need to purchase them. Often, local or state bar associations or law school libraries will have printers, scanners, or copiers that lawyers can use free of charge.

There is also a middle ground to consider. Like AIO computers, there are also AIO printers that include scanning and copying capabilities as well. There are cost-efficient models available for a couple of hundred dollars that are small and space-efficient.

If choosing to purchase a printer, scanner, copier, or an AIO model, consider factors like print quality, print speed, scanning resolution, connectivity options, and the total cost, which would include ink and toner costs.

Other Hardware Considerations

To be able to work efficiently and to collaborate with lawyer or law firm clients, a freelancer will need networking equipment, like routers, switches, and access points, to ensure reliable internet connectivity and network access for all devices in the office. In choosing networking equipment, factors to consider are wireless range, network speed, security features, and scalability.

If phone communication is necessary with something other than a personal cell phone, consider using Voice over Internet Protocol (VoIP) phones instead of a traditional landline. VoIP phones use the internet to make calls, offering cost savings. VoIP phones also offer advanced features like voicemail to email and call forwarding.

Install uninterruptible power supply (UPS) units to provide backup power in case of a power failure. UPS units help prevent data loss and equipment damage by providing temporary power during outages and stabilizing voltage fluctuations. UPS units may be particularly important in areas where internet outages are frequent. Consider capacity, run time, number of outlets, and surge protection features when looking at UPS units.

In addition to cloud storage services to securely store and back up data, there are also network-attached storage (NAS) devices or external hard drives as another option. Consider storage capacity, data transfer speeds, redundancy, and data security features when choosing a storage or backup solution.

There are many peripherals that are necessary for or that complement a computing setup. These peripherals include keyboards, mice, webcams, and speakers. There are ergonomic peripherals that promote productivity during prolonged use that may cost more at the outset. However, the cost may be outweighed by the comfort the ergonomics provide.

Word Processing Options

There are many different word processing options available, each with its own features, pricing, and target audience. Perhaps the most common is Microsoft Word. Word is arguably the most widely used word processing application for professionals, offering a comprehensive set of features for creating, editing, formatting, and sharing documents. Word is part of the Microsoft Office suite and is available or both Windows and Mac platforms. It offers various subscription plans as part of Microsoft 365 (formerly Office 365) or can be purchased as a standalone product.

Google Docs is a cloud-based word processing tool offered by Google as part of Google Drive. It allows users to create, edit, collaborate on, and share documents online in real time. Google Docs is accessible from any device with an internet connection and web browser. It offers seamless integration with other Google services like Gmail and Google Calendar.

Other less well-known word processing applications include Apple Pages, LibreOffice Writer, Apache OpenOffice Writer, and Zoho Writer. Pages is an application developed by Apple for Apple devices. It offers a range of templates, formatting tools, and collaboration features for Apple devices that are free to use. Pages can also be accessed via iCloud on the web. LibreOffice Writer is also free. It is an open-source word processing application that offers a comprehensive set of features comparable to Word, including support for multiple file formats, templates, and extensions. LibreOffice is available for Windows, macOS, and Linux platforms. Zoho Writer is a cloud-based word processing tool that provides features for creating, editing, collaborating on, and sharing documents online. Like Word and LibreOffice, it is part of a "suite" of productivity tools like spreadsheets and presentations.

These are just a few examples of word processing options available to users and there are many more. The choice of which software to use depends on many of the same factors already discussed, like the range of features, compatibility, collaboration capabilities, pricing, and personal preference.

Legal Research Platforms

Legal research used to be a time-consuming and labor-intensive process. Lawyers spent hours sifting through books and treatises to find relevant case law. Today, legal research has become much easier and faster thanks to paid online databases like LexisNexis and Westlaw or free legal research platforms like Findlaw or Justia. These legal databases allow lawyers to search for relevant cases, statutes, and other legal resources.

Some legal research platforms today allow lawyers to search for all potentially relevant cases, then filter results by legal issue, fact pattern, motion type, or other parameters. Briefs can be input and automatically cite checked. With legal research tools, lawyers can identify points of law in cases that have been overruled or invalidated, identify related cases that have a pattern of being cited together, examine case histories, search for key terms within cases, and use litigation analytics to evaluate judges, jurisdictions, and lawyers to help strategize and create realistic expectations for litigation outcomes. A lawyer today, especially a litigator, cannot be competitive without using online legal research tools.

Communications Technology

Similarly, communications technology is now essential to any law practice because it allows lawyers to correspond and talk easily and instantaneously regardless of location. This has, in large part, facilitated the ability to do freelance work. Email, videoconferencing, and instant messaging are all tools a freelancer must understand how to make good use of.

It is hard to imagine doing anything today, including practicing law, without using email. Even lawyers practicing before the advent of email cannot imagine practicing today without it. Freelancers can use email to send and receive documents, to communicate with clients, and to collaborate with colleagues. Email can be a tool for a freelancer to provide added value to clients by keeping a hiring lawyer regularly informed about the progress of a project. Routine updates about work builds stronger relationships and provides a higher level of customer service.

Email encryption technology helps maintain the confidentiality of client information by protecting the contents of an email message or an attachment from unauthorized access. Encryption works by converting an email or an attached document into a code that can only be deciphered by a person with the correct key. The sender and recipient can either have the same key or there can be two different keys, one to encrypt and the other to decrypt the email or attachment. If using a single key, the sender and recipient can both read the message or open an attached document with the same code. With different keys, the sender will encrypt a message with one code and the recipient will use a second code to decrypt the message.

To use email encryption, both the sender and recipient need to have compatible email programs and encryption software. The sender would typically compose a message and encrypt it before sending. The recipient receiving the encrypted email would use the key to decrypt the message and access its contents. Email encryption is important for sending confidential or sensitive information like financial documents or medical records. By encrypting these types of emails or attachments, freelancers can ensure that only the intended recipient can read the information, reducing the risk of data breaches or unauthorized users accessing the information. As with email, there are also messaging apps that provide the means to encrypt messages and documents.

Videoconferencing technology, like email, also allows for communication regardless of location, reducing the need for travel. It has revolutionized the practice of law. A freelancer can use videoconferencing to attend meetings, to conduct depositions, or even to appear in court for hearings. Being able to participate in a meeting via videoconferencing instead of driving to the office to attend it in person or attending a deposition via videoconferencing rather than flying to the state where the witness lives saves time and costs by eliminating travel expenses like airfare, hotel accommodations, and meals. Gone are the days when a client will pay for a lawyer to fly to another city to attend a two-hour deposition.

Eliminating time-consuming travel to attend in-person meetings also increases productivity, leaving more time for paid work. This is especially important for a freelancer who will likely not be able to charge for the 30-minute drive to a law firm to accept or discuss an assignment or who cannot charge for the 20 minutes it takes for all the meeting attendees to arrive. Facilitating billable work as opposed to non-billable time spent commuting or waiting helps a freelancer increase net profits.

Videoconferencing is particularly important for freelancers working in a different place than where the law firm that hired them is located. For example, a freelancer who lives in rural Idaho can remotely participate in meetings at a Coeur d'Alene law firm. For the same reasons, videoconferencing has also increased accessibility for lawyers with disabilities.

In addition to email and videoconferencing, instant messaging tools are another type of digital communication platform that allows freelancers to communicate with colleagues in real time. Most instant messaging tools are free to use so users can communicate with anybody who has the same application installed on their device. While there are multiple personal instant messaging platforms like Skype, WhatsApp, and Facebook Messenger, there are also professional instant messaging tools like Microsoft Teams.

One of the biggest advantages of communications technology is its speed. Email and instant messaging allow for real-time communication. Users can receive and respond to messages immediately, which is especially important for time-sensitive matters. Another advantage of communications technology is its convenience. With nearly all lawyers today using mobile devices, users can communicate with each other anywhere and anytime, providing increased flexibility. For example, a freelancer who takes a three-week vacation might not bring a laptop to the beach but will undoubtedly have a smart phone handy. That freelancer would, therefore, still be able to communicate with a client through instant messaging or email who is paying for a subscription-based service with unlimited access to legal advice.

Communications technology tools offer a variety of helpful features to enhance interactions. Instant messaging users can create group chats so multiple lawyers can weigh in on a matter. Email users can do something similar by creating different groups for different legal matters. These tools allow for collaborative discussions and decision making.

Case Management Software

Case management software also has built-in communication tools. For example, most case management software has secure client portals and messaging features. However, case management software offers so much more. It also helps organize work by streamlining case management. Case management software features include document organization, task and deadline scheduling, and case progress tracking. Some case management software also handles billing and accounting tasks, such as generating invoices, tracking time, and generating financial reports. Some popular case management software options include Clio, MyCase, and Zola Suite. Each of these platforms has many features in common, like document management, time tracking, billing, and invoicing, and communication tools. However, each platform also has its own unique characteristics, pricing structures, and user interfaces.

One of the most significant advantages of case management software is its time-saving features. Automating tasks like billing and invoicing, generating reports, and scheduling can free up time for freelancers to focus on their billable work. For example, a freelancer can simply record time spent working, and case management software will generate a professional looking invoice. The freelancer will not have to spend any time formatting the invoice and can deliver the invoice electronically to a client with the click of a button.

A freelancer can also set reminders for upcoming deadlines with case management software, which will then send alerts to the freelancer as the deadlines approach. This tool will allow a freelancer to optimize workflow. In addition, a freelancer can easily track different metrics with case management software like expenses, accounts payable or receivable, billable hours, and revenue. Generating reports on key metrics will provide insight into all areas of operations and their impact on net revenue.

Although case management software does not come without a cost, it helps alleviate the need for a freelancer to hire staff to do administrative tasks, reducing overhead. Any time software provides a greater opportunity for a freelancer to spend time working and generating revenue as opposed to focusing on administrative tasks, it will have a positive impact on the bottom line.

Document Management Software

Different from case management software is document management software. Document management systems are solutions designed to help lawyers organize, store, and manage their documents and files electronically. Today, most law firms use electronic document management tools. These tools keep all relevant case information in one place, including notes, client documents, and communications, eliminating the need for physical files and paperwork. All the information stored is searchable, allowing a freelancer to access information quickly and efficiently.

Document management systems also have features for scanning, indexing, storing, and retrieving electronic documents. Lawyers can access documents from any computer with the necessary log in credentials because they are stored and managed in the cloud. Some popular document management platforms for lawyers include Worldox, Clio, SharePoint, and Google Drive. Again, like case management software, document management systems all share common features, but have their own unique features as well, in addition to their own pricing models and user interfaces.

One of the biggest advantages of document management systems is that they eliminate the need for the physical storage of paper files. By digitizing documents, a freelancer can reduce paper and the need for space to store the paper, like room for filing cabinets. The need for less space will reduce overhead or, at a minimum, give a freelancer more options for workspace, given the absence of expansive storage requirements. In addition, document management systems allow multiple users to access and work on the same document or file simultaneously from two different locations. This is important for freelancers who work remotely or for a freelancer who is part of a legal team all working on the same file together. Document management systems also have security features that include user authentication, access control, and audit trails, which helps protect against unauthorized access.

AI

As illustrated by the examples at the beginning of this chapter, AI has been a transformational tool for the legal profession. Lawyers can already use generative AI to help write articles or legal memoranda, to assist with drafting legal briefs and contracts, or even to help prepare deposition questions. Consider the following example:

Query: Prepare questions for a deposition regarding the qualifications of a structural engineer who will be serving as an expert witness in a case involving roof damage from high winds.
ChatGPT response:

1. Could you please state your full name, professional title, and current occupation for the record?
2. How long have you been working as a structural engineer, and could you provide a brief overview of your professional experience in this field?
3. Have you ever served as an expert witness in a court case related to roof damage from high winds? If so, could you please provide details of those cases, including the outcome and your role in assisting the court?

4. What qualifications and certifications do you hold as a structural engineer that are relevant to assessing roof damage caused by high winds?

5. Can you describe any specific training or educational programs you have completed that have enhanced your expertise in evaluating wind-related roof damage?

6. Are you a member of any professional associations or organizations related to structural engineering? If so, could you please name them and provide any leadership roles or notable contributions you have made within these organizations?

7. How frequently do you encounter cases involving roof damage caused by high winds in your professional practice?

8. Can you explain the methodology or approach you typically use when evaluating the extent and cause of roof damage resulting from high winds?

9. Do you have experience in conducting thorough investigations of roof structures to determine if they were constructed or designed to withstand high winds? If so, could you please describe the techniques and tools you employ during these investigations?

10. Are there any specific industry guidelines or standards that you typically refer to when assessing the structural integrity of roofs in relation to high wind events?

11. Have you authored or co-authored any publications, research papers, or reports related to wind-induced roof damage or the structural integrity of roofs in high wind conditions?

12. Can you provide a list of previous cases or projects in which you have been involved that specifically dealt with roof damage caused by high winds, including the outcomes or conclusions drawn from those cases?

13. Have you ever been subject to disciplinary action or faced any complaints related to your professional conduct or the quality of your work as a structural engineer? If yes, please provide details.

14. Are there any conflicts of interest or affiliations that you have that may impact your impartiality or objectivity in providing expert testimony in this case?

15. Is there anything else you believe is relevant to your qualifications as an expert witness in this case involving roof damage from high winds?

The more specific the query, the more specific the response:

Query: Prepare questions for the cross-examination of a plaintiff in a slip and fall case. The plaintiff lied in her deposition and stated she did not have a preexisting back injury. However, medical records showed that prior to the slip and fall, she had suffered from two herniated discs that required orthopedic treatment, including epidural injections for pain and physical therapy.

ChatGPT's response:

1. Good morning/afternoon, Ms. [Plaintiff's Name]. During your deposition, you stated that you did not have a preexisting back injury. Is that correct?

2. Are you aware that medical records obtained from your health-care provider indicate that you had been diagnosed with two herniated discs prior to the date of the slip and fall incident in question?

3. According to the medical records, did you receive orthopedic treatment for your herniated discs, including epidural injections for pain management and physical therapy?

4. How would you explain the discrepancy between your deposition statement and the documented medical records regarding your preexisting back injury?

5. Can you clarify whether you intentionally withheld information about your preexisting back condition during your deposition?

6. Did you discuss your medical history, including the herniated discs, with your attorney prior to the deposition?

7. Did your attorney advise you on the importance of providing complete and truthful information during the deposition?

8. Have you filed any previous personal injury claims or lawsuits related to your back injury or the herniated discs?

9. Were you taking any medication or undergoing any treatment specifically for your back condition at the time of the slip and fall incident?

10. How would you characterize the level of pain or discomfort you experienced in your back before the slip and fall incident?

11. Did your preexisting back condition impact your ability to perform certain activities or engage in physical exertion?

12. Did you seek medical attention or treatment for your back injury following the slip and fall incident?

13. Have you made any claims or filed any lawsuits related to your back injury or herniated discs subsequent to the slip and fall incident?

14. Were you aware that the information you provided during the deposition is legally binding and could impact the outcome of this case?

15. In light of the documented medical records, why should the court or the jury believe your statement that you did not have a preexisting back injury when it appears to contradict the medical evidence?

These cross-examination questions show that ChatGPT is not perfect. Questions 6 and 7, for example, probably invade the attorney-client privilege. Nonetheless, all lawyers can take advantage of generative AI to streamline their work. As incredible as this technology already is, generative AI technology is still in its infancy. Its capabilities will continue to increase at dizzying speeds. A freelancer who can effectively leverage this technology will have a powerful tool to dramatically increase productivity.

Accounting Software

Although technology can be very expensive, there are many cost-effective solutions. FreshBooks, for example, provides very inexpensive billing and accounting software that is intuitive and extremely easy to use. Depending on a freelancer's needs, as of 2023, pricing started at under 10 dollars a month, with a premium plan costing under 30 dollars a month. For between 120 and 360 dollars annually, FreshBooks provides billing and invoicing features, including time tracking, different invoicing templates that a freelancer can personalize, and payment software that has many different automated payment options.

FreshBooks software also has accounting and tax functions so it acts like a bookkeeper by, for example, tracking invoices, spending, payments, mileage, and expenses. Freelancers can generate many different types of reports with FreshBooks, including cash flow and expense reports, as well as client account statements. FreshBooks also automates client communications, such as sending payment reminders. If there is a problem, FreshBooks provides award-winning customer support with the ability to reach an actual human familiar with the software who will answer the phone to help if the need arises, a rapidly vanishing perk in today's world.

Every freelancer will have different technology needs and should understand those needs before purchasing a lot of expensive technology. A freelancer who helps with litigation, for example, will have a different need for legal research software than a lawyer who has a transactional practice. Similarly, a freelancer with a single or just a few clients may not necessarily have the need for complicated billing software. Assessing technology needs will help a freelancer make cost-effective choices and help guard against spending a lot of money on technology that will not be useful.

Deian McBryde, Esq., is a lawyer from Albuquerque, New Mexico, and has this advice about technology:

> Be mindful that a lot of the software companies are going to sell you 200 bells and whistles that sound amazing, but you will never have time to use. The most important things in managing my law practice are people and dates. So, I need technology that will help me keep my calendar straight and keep up with relationships. Family law is not legal research intensive—I can use the free legal research software from our state bar or use the research databases at our local law school—so I do not need expensive legal research software. But I do need great calendar software and I am always trying to find better ways to know what is going on with my cases and my relationships. One of the best "investments" we have made is signing up for a

website to send birthday cards to clients and referral sources. It is not high tech at all but it meets an important value for my firm and for me. So, know your technology needs and do not overbuy.[1]

Kerline Jean-Louis, Esq., a lawyer from Sommerville, Massachusetts, explains one of the ways she uses technology to automate routine tasks to free up time to build her client base:

Calendly is one example of how I use technology to automate routine tasks. Once a potential client books a consultation through my website, the software sends a welcome email and a consultation guide that I created to give potential clients an idea about what to expect, which is very helpful for people who have never dealt with a lawyer or the legal process before. The software also sends automatic text reminders, which minimizes no-shows and allows me to better manage my calendar. Rather than me having to expend the effort to manually align schedules, send reminders, and reach out to potential clients, the software does it for me and thereby enhances the client experience. By streamlining scheduling and acclimating new clients, the software frees up my time to serve more clients and to build my practice.[2]

Technology has transformed and modernized the practice of law. From research to communication to document and case management software to generative AI, technology has made it easier for lawyers to do their jobs. It has facilitated the practice of law particularly for freelancers by providing remote access, increasing efficiencies, and reducing overhead, which allows freelancers to focus more on work and generating revenue. As technology continues to evolve, it is likely that freelancers will see even greater changes in the upcoming years and continue to find new ways to leverage technology to improve their work, to better serve their clients, and to maximize profits.

Understanding the nuts and bolts of starting a freelance law practice is just the beginning, whether that is knowing how to create a business plan, choosing the right work environment, determining an effective billing model, picking the best corporate structure, appreciating financial start-up costs, understanding how to protect assets, or using technology to level the playing field. But starting a freelance practice is only the beginning. Building and sustaining a practice requires clients. Therefore, a successful freelancer must also be a rainmaker. Although many lawyers have an inherent aversion to rainmaking, there are different approaches to suit everybody, even those who are not comfortable with the idea of business development.

---

1 D. McBryde, Esq., personal communication, Aug. 30, 2023.
2 K. Jean-Louis, Esq., personal communication, Sept. 21, 2023.

PART III

Mastering the Art
of Rainmaking

CHAPTER 11

Achieving Rainmaking Success by Finding a Niche

"I think the greatest of people in society carved niches that represented the unique expression of their combinations of talents, and if everyone had the luxury of expressing the unique combinations of talents in this world, our society would be transformed overnight."

—Neil DeGrasse Tyson

One of the most natural ways to develop clients is by finding a niche in the law. A February 24, 2023, online article in *Forbes* by Henry DeVries talked about "finding riches in the niches." The article, "Discover the Rainmaker Secrets of Riches in the Niches," emphasized that "[w]hen you become an authority in a niche, you don't chase business, it chases you." The legal field is vast with many niche areas of focus. Finding a niche can be a way for freelancers to differentiate themselves, attract clients, and build successful practices.

After graduating law school and trying to find a job, Elijah quickly realized that the field of law was fiercely competitive. Achieving success would require something more than just hard work and dedication. Frustrated by the inability to find a job that he was even remotely passionate about, Elijah embarked on a quest to find his own niche.

A niche is a specialized area of focus in the law that sets a freelancer apart from the competition. It could mean practicing in a specific area of the law, such as intellectual property or employment law. It could also mean representing a particular industry, like health care or the hospitality industry. Or, a niche could be a unique approach to providing legal services, such as offering high-quality legal services at an affordable rate or offering legal services according to a novel billing model.

Elijah started looking for a way to find his own niche. One day, while waiting for friends at a local bar for happy hour, Elijah overheard a conversation between two entrepreneurs discussing opening a retail marijuana store after the state legislature legalized recreational marijuana. They were discussing all kinds of issues surrounding the growth, distribution, and sale of marijuana. Because marijuana is still illegal under federal law, the discussion turned to whether they could deduct certain business expenses on a federal tax return. They also wondered about zoning issues and what kind of training was necessary for employees to sell marijuana to the public.

Intrigued, Elijah started researching this area of the law. Because there were plenty of states where marijuana had been legal for years, he started looking for legal seminars in those states that he could attend remotely. He delved into the world of marijuana law, learning about the business aspects of it, in addition to zoning, tax, environmental, and intellectual property issues particular to the field. Elijah discovered that this area of law offered a lot of potential for a practitioner in his state because it was a relatively untapped field compared to other areas of the law, marijuana only recently having become legal in his state.

Elijah started networking with lawyers and experts from other states in the field. He became an expert himself, building a solid foundation of knowledge in the area of marijuana law. During a conference that Elijah decided to attend in person because of the speakers and the sizable audience, he met a practitioner who had built a practice in another state focusing solely on marijuana law. Elijah proposed that if that lawyer wanted to open a practice in his state, Elijah would freelance for him. As a new lawyer just out of law school, Elijah explained that he did not want to open his own practice and he wanted to retain the flexibility that freelancing would allow him, as opposed to becoming an associate at a law firm. So started Elijah's journey as a freelance marijuana lawyer.

Finding a niche is a natural way to generate clients. By focusing on a particular area of practice, freelancers can position themselves as experts in that area, which can help attract law firms as clients that are seeking a lawyer with a specialty. Having a niche can also help a freelancer develop a more focused marketing strategy. Instead of trying to market services to a broad range of lawyers or law firms, a freelancer who has identified a niche can target marketing efforts to those most likely to need the specific services offered. Elijah, for example, would only target law firms as clients that had an established marijuana law practice.

Identifying a niche is not always easy, but there are different strategies that can be helpful. One of the simplest is to identify interests or passions. For example, a law student interested in commercial transactions at Boston College Law School who annotated case law for the Uniform Commercial Code Reporter-Digest might already be a long way toward developing a niche in the area of law involving secured transactions. An outdoors enthusiast could specialize in environmental law. A lawyer for whom philanthropy is important could provide legal services relevant to the nonprofit world.

A legal issue that has had a personal impact can also serve as the basis for identifying a niche. For example, a lawyer whose parents went through a nasty divorce that ended up in court might develop a niche in collaborative separations and focus on alternative dispute resolution as an alternative to litigation for resolving marriage dissolution and custody issues. Perhaps that lawyer could provide arbitration and mediation services on a freelance basis. A lawyer with learning differences might specialize in educational law to provide advocacy services to a law firm with students with learning differences as clients. On the flip side of that coin, the lawyer could advise law firms who represent schools on compliance issues regarding special education and the Individuals with Disabilities Education Act (IDEA).

A niche can also arise from specialized experience. A seasoned lawyer who has spent years practicing in a particular area of law might already have a niche. For example, a prosecutor or public defender switching from public practice to the private sector would have a lot of experience handling DUI cases and would be able to create a niche providing freelance services to criminal defense law firms specializing in DUI defense. If practicing law is a second career, the first career might translate into a niche. A medical professional who decided to become a lawyer would have an obvious niche in the medical malpractice arena. A journalist might provide civil rights representation on First Amendment issues. An obvious path for a human resources specialist to develop a niche in the law would be to practice in the area of employment law.

Another way to find a niche is to assess relevant skills and experience. In other words, evaluate whether there are certain skills that are particularly applicable to a particular area of the law. Strong communication skills, a knack for persuasion, and the ability to relate to others are invaluable skills in litigation. Negotiation skills are a huge selling point for transactional work that involves deal making. A proficiency in writing is vital for appellate work. A technical background in science, engineering, or technology is important for an intellectual property lawyer. Fluency in a second language is invaluable for immigration work. Family lawyers need strong interpersonal skills. Attention to detail is critical for a lawyer providing due diligence services.

A freelancer can also look for gaps in the market to find a niche. Elijah discovered that there was a scarcity of lawyers practicing marijuana law in his state because marijuana had only recently become legal there. Therefore, the area of marijuana law in his state was underserved by lawyers. Looking for areas with a high demand for legal services but a limited supply of lawyers specializing in that area can help a freelancer discover a niche.

Another way to develop a niche is by thinking about the types of clients a freelancer wants to attract and the legal issues they are most likely to need help with. For example, a freelancer might choose to focus on an older population and on legal issues affecting the elderly. That type of legal work could take many forms. Freelancers interested in transactional work could create a niche working for law firms that provide estate planning or long-term care planning services. With a different focus on guardianship proceedings for the elderly, a freelancer would target law firms as clients that provided guardianship services. Older clients often need legal advice on social security and retirement planning to navigate the complexities of social security eligibility requirements, strategies for maximizing benefits, and tax implications. A freelancer interested in the financial aspects impacting an older population could provide legal services to a law firm that works with older clients on those types of issues. Elder abuse and neglect are serious problems that can occur in a variety of settings, including nursing homes, assisted living facilities, or even in the home. A freelancer interested in appearance work could work with a law firm specializing in nursing home litigation. By focusing on a specific client population, a freelancer can develop a niche by helping law firms who have those population segments as clients with the legal issues that are most likely to affect them.

A freelancer can also develop a niche by exploring new and emerging areas of the law like Elijah did. Lawyers who understand marijuana cultivation and distribution law are in high demand because it is still a relatively new field of law. Growers and distributers must comply with new and changing laws and regulations relating to the production, distribution, and sale of marijuana. Because the federal government still considers marijuana to be illegal, although many states have legalized it for medical or recreational purposes, there is a complex legal landscape that a lawyer can help navigate involving the conflicts between federal and state law. Industry professionals may need legal advice about the best business entity to form to have the most protection from legal liability. New kinds of contractual provisions will be tested, like leases to acquire property to grow marijuana or marijuana distribution agreements.

A similar emerging area of the law comes with states starting to decriminalize psilocybin and other psychedelics. The healing centers in Colorado that will be established to facilitate the use of psilocybin will need lawyers to advise them about policies and procedures, including educational or professional requirements for the practitioners in the healing centers who accompany patients on their journeys. Like the growing and distribution of marijuana, healing centers providing psilocybin-assisted therapy may need to obtain special licenses or comply with state and local regulations governing the provision of those services. Healing centers will also need legal help to implement risk management tools and safety measures to minimize the potential for harm to patients, which might include protocols for client screening, appropriate dosing procedures, adequate supervision by trained professionals, and the maintenance of a safe environment. There will likely also be privacy law implications for healing centers, such as compliance with the Health Insurance Portability and Accountability Act (HIPAA). It is easy to see how a freelancer could develop a niche advising law firms with clients in the psilocybin- or psychedelic-assisted therapy industries.

With the increasing popularity of cryptocurrency and blockchain technology, there is a growing need for lawyers with expertise in those areas as well. Because cryptocurrency and blockchain technology is relatively new, it presents a unique set of legal challenges. As with any emerging technology, legal advice regarding new technologies is not only essential to ensure compliance with existing laws and regulations but also to navigate the rapidly evolving legal landscape. For example, because cryptocurrency and blockchain technology operate outside traditional financial systems, regulators are still developing rules to govern their use, including securities, anti-money laundering, and tax regulations. In addition, because this new technology presents untested opportunities for fraud and cybercrime, legal advice is necessary to implement robust security measures to protect against threats. Because the legal issues facing cryptocurrency and blockchain professionals are so new and unique and because they are rapidly evolving, a freelancer who specializes in this emerging area of the law will quickly establish a niche.

One of the most recent and rapidly evolving industries is artificial intelligence (AI). The legal issues surrounding the use of AI are complex and untested. For example, AI technology can create, invent, and improve upon products, services, and processes, raising questions about who owns the intellectual property rights to these innovations. "Heart on My Sleeve," an AI-generated song that went viral in 2023, used generative AI technology to imitate Drake's singing style. As a result, lawyers are now advising about patentability of a music style, as opposed to simply copyrighting lyrics.

Because AI relies heavily on data, lawyers are needed to assist in ensuring compliance with data privacy laws and regulations, as well as to advise on data ownership, licensing, and sharing agreements. Looking toward the future, as AI becomes even more autonomous, the question of who will be liable for harm caused by AI is sure to come up. With AI already being used in the medical field, for example, will a medical practice using AI become liable if AI fails to detect cancer? A freelancer with a niche in the law involving AI can provide legal advice about liability issues unique to that field and risk management strategies. The ethical issues surrounding AI could create a legal field of its own, with concerns about bias, discrimination, and invasion of privacy already arising. A lawyer who practices in this emerging legal field can easily create a distinctive niche.

Dr. Alberto León, PhD, a lawyer from Albuquerque, New Mexico, practices in the intellectual property arena providing specialized services to institutional clients, small businesses, and individuals focusing on the protection of and disputes involving intellectual property rights. He developed a niche representing clients in the boxing world. After his tenure as commissioner and chair of the New Mexico Athletic Commission, Alberto joined the World Boxing Council (WBC), the largest professional boxing governing body in the world. He served as a bout supervisor and special executive counsel to the WBC, after which the WBC board of governors elected Alberto as the organization's chief legal counsel.

Now, Alberto oversees the WBC's legal matters all around the world, which includes managing the WBC's intellectual property licensing projects; the enforcement and protection of the WBC's intellectual property rights; chairing the WBC José Sulaimán Boxers Fund Committee; handling contract drafting, interpretation, and disputes; providing legal advice for the WBC president and board of governors; and coordinating the activities of the Results Management

Unit of the WBC's anti-doping program. Alberto's niche in boxing law was inspired by his childhood experiences:

> My first exposure to boxing came as a child growing up in Panama and being an avid boxing fan. At that time, Panama had several world champions and was one of the meccas of the sport.[1]

His passion for boxing as a child led him to his first boxing law client when his love of boxing came through during a conversation:

> My legal career in boxing law had a serendipitous beginning. I was practicing law in Miami, Florida, and was traveling from Madrid, Spain, to Miami. On the plane, I met a boxing promoter who was traveling to Miami to finalize the negotiation of a contract for a European boxer. Over the long trip, we spent several hours talking about boxing. My love of the sport was obvious. The next day, the promoter called me at my law office and requested my help with the contract negotiations. I helped him and continued to work with him on several projects after that.[2]

After he moved from Florida to New Mexico, Alberto continued pursuing his interest in boxing, which helped position him for a lucrative career in boxing law.

> When I moved to New Mexico, one of the members of the New Mexico Athletic Commission, which regulates all unarmed combat sports in the state, who was a long-time friend and client of mine, asked me to do some pro bono work for the Commission, which I agreed to do. While doing that pro bono work, the Commission was holding its boxing judge certification program. I participated in that program and became a licensed boxing judge. I started working bouts as a boxing judge and after a short time, Governor Bill Richardson, the governor of New Mexico at the time, appointed me as a commissioner. I served as a commissioner for over seven years and as chair of the Commission for most of that time.[3]

Alberto's work with the New Mexico Athletic Commission is what ultimately led to his legal work for the WBC.

> In my role as chair of the New Mexico Athletic Commission, I became acquainted with the leaders of the professional boxing sanctioning

---

1 A. León, JD, PhD, personal communication, Sept. 11, 2023.
2 *Id.*
3 *Id.*

organizations, including the WBC. Soon after I left the Commission, the WBC asked me to join its organization, which I did.[4]

Alberto's work with the WBC provided him with invaluable insight and experience in many important areas of sports law, which has led to attracting national and international clients outside of the boxing industry for whom he acts as a legal consultant, technical advisor, and expert witness.

The WBC is the most respected and largest professional boxing sanctioning organization in the world. As such, the WBC has created and manages numerous programs in which I am involved both as legal counsel and as a strategic advisor. Those roles provide me with daily exposure to promoters, suppliers of boxing products and services, government officials, boxing managers, and many others involved in the sport. My association with the WBC at the highest levels also lends a lot of credibility to my knowledge and experience about many aspects of the sport. I have been able to combine my boxing law and intellectual property practice to do work for United States-based and international clients I met only due to my position with the WBC. That work includes license negotiation and documentation, patent and trademark protection and maintenance, proceedings before United States federal agencies, and much more.[5]

As shown by Alberto's experience, creating a niche and becoming an expert in a specific area of the law led to a rewarding and very profitable career.

Kerline Jean-Louis, Esq., from Somerville, Massachusetts, also developed a niche in the intellectual property law arena. Her niche is very different than Alberto's, showing that even within the same area of law, there can be vastly different focuses. Kerline realized, as she was creating and building her own brand, how important brand protection was.

Your brand is one of your most valuable assets. Protecting your brand ensures a positive image and reputation in the eyes of your clients and the public. Clients are more likely to trust and hire a lawyer they perceive as competent and reliable. Brand protection helps promote and maintain that trust. Protecting your brand through trademark legal services allows you to grow your brand with peace of mind. It puts others on notice that you are the owner of your brand, prevents others from making money off your brand, gives you the power to stop others from improperly using your brand, and allows you to pass on your legal rights as part of your legacy.[6]

---

4 *Id.*
5 *Id.*
6 K. Jean-Louis, Esq., personal communication, Sept. 21, 2023.

Kerline turned what she learned from the development of her own brand into a thriving law practice.

Understanding how important it was for the success of her own law practice to create and protect her brand, Kerline transitioned from representing clients in criminal defense, immigration, and civil litigation matters to assisting entrepreneurs, creatives, and business owners protect their brands just like she did for herself when she started her own law practice. As a first-generation Haitian-American, Kerline was particularly passionate about closing the racial wealth gap and helping traditionally underserved clients with the trademarking process. The niche she created, based off her own experience in starting a law firm and her passion for helping those without access to legal services, was to create affordable, client-centered, value-driven trademark services, particularly for traditionally underserved communities, including trademark clearance searches, trademark application preparation, responses to trademark office actions, trademark monitoring, trademark maintenance, and trademark enforcement. In just a few years, with two of them being during the COVID-19 pandemic, Kerline built a successful law practice by creating a niche in the area of trademark law and brand protection.

By specializing in a high-demand, niche area of the law and by developing a reputation as an expert in that field, a freelancer can attract more clients, command higher fees, and ultimately build a more profitable freelance practice. For freelancers who are uncomfortable with the traditional idea of rainmaking that involves long and expensive lunches, golf games, and wooing clients, developing a niche is a different way to accomplish the same thing. For lawyers who find it difficult to directly solicit clients for work, there are also other ways of developing clients besides finding or creating a niche. One of those ways is through web-based marketing and advertising.

CHAPTER 12

Igniting Your Freelance Success through Strategic Marketing and Advertising

"Launching products is easy—it's . . . all of the marketing that is hard."
—Jessica Alba

In today's highly competitive legal market, effective advertising and marketing strategies are critical to the success of a law practice, especially for freelancers. Freelancers face unique challenges in attracting and retaining clients. Without a solid advertising and marketing plan, it can be difficult to stand out from other lawyers and to generate a steady stream of work.

Advertising and marketing a freelance business involve the promotion of legal services to potential clients and building a strong brand identity that resonates with a target client market. It encompasses a wide range of activities, including the creation of a website, the development of a social media presence, networking, creating content, and even something as simple as providing excellent legal services and engaging in reliable communications with clients.

Although advertising and marketing are related, they refer to different things. Marketing is the overall strategy that a freelancer uses to promote the legal services being offered. Marketing activities can include market research, such as how many lawyers in a community are offering a particular type of legal services or whether there is an underserved client market. Marketing can involve developing a special type of legal services being offered, like a collaborative family law practice that uses a non-confrontational approach toward separation, divorce, or custody issues. Branding is also a type of marketing. For example, a freelancer can focus on establishing a brand that portrays professionalism or that can provide market differentiation by focusing on a commitment to understanding potential clients' unique needs. Pricing is a type of marketing as well. Nontraditional pricing models can set a freelancer apart from other lawyers.

While marketing is the umbrella, advertising is just one component of marketing. Advertising is simply a way of communicating with the ultimate users of the freelancing legal services—the lawyers and law firms that will be hiring a freelancer. For a freelance law practice, that means creating and distributing promotional messages through various channels to reach a target group of clients. Advertising can take the form of print ads, such as ads in a state or local bar association's newsletter, which many lawyers read. Online ads have started replacing print ads. More and more commonly, advertising occurs through social media posts and websites.

In short, marketing is broader than advertising. Marketing is about creating a strategic plan to reach target lawyers and law firms, whereas advertising is about conveying promotional messages to that audience. There are many benefits to marketing and advertising any business. It brings increased visibility, which can generate clients. Whether marketing promotes the services offered, highlights the experience of those providing services, showcases successful outcomes, or provides client testimonials, marketing efforts that communicate the value offered to clients and that differentiate a freelancer's services from competitors is invaluable to increasing clients and driving revenue.

Marc Enger, from St. Louis, Missouri, is the owner of Propel Marketing Services. He offers this insight:

> Often, when talking to small business owners, we hear a reluctance related to marketing budgets. The sense is that marketing is a hard cost with at best a soft, if not unknown, return on investment (ROI). Like putting money into a brokerage account that is managed with a growth or income strategy, when you decide on a marketing strategy, you are investing in a set of objectives. As with a stock portfolio, you monitor your marketing objectives to see what is working well and what is not. And then you adjust to improve performance over time. Your marketing plan can set a baseline to see what marketing activities yield what results. You should be able to see how each of the tactics you are investing in contributes to your business goals. You monitor their effectiveness and you modify and adapt marketing strategies depending on what is working and what is not. Over time, as your target audience becomes more aware of your brand, becomes familiar with what you do and how they would benefit, engages with you via social media and content marketing, and as you learn more about them, the impact of your marketing efforts will continue to grow at an even higher rate of return. But it all starts with a sound strategic marketing plan designed around your business objectives.[1]

Marketing allows a freelancer to build credibility and trust with a target audience. In a more and more crowded freelance marketplace, lawyers and law firms need to be able to trust that a freelancer has the expertise necessary to deliver quality work for them. Effective advertising and marketing can help establish that trust by delivering valuable content or demonstrating leadership in a particular practice area as a trusted legal authority.

---

1 M. Enger, personal communication, Aug. 27, 2023.

For example, a professional looking website can showcase a freelancer's legal experience and provide testimonials from satisfied lawyers. Creating content such as authoring an article about a current legal issue can help establish a freelancer as an authority in that area of law. Social media platforms are also an effective way to establish credibility by allowing freelancers to engage with potential lawyers or law firms who might be clients.

Freelancers can showcase their expertise by commenting on social media regarding a legal issue in the news. For example, there was a lot of First Amendment discussion surrounding Colin Kaepernick's decision to kneel for the national anthem. Providing a comment on social media based on the law rather than a legally unsupported opinion could have helped establish a lawyer as an authority in the area of civil rights law. With advertising and marketing, freelancers can reach a wider audience and generate paying clients. This can be especially important for freelancers just starting out who do not yet have an established client base.

There is a lot of pre-planning that goes into developing a marketing strategy. Before creating a marketing strategy and engaging in marketing efforts, a freelancer needs to have a clear understanding of the necessary direction marketing efforts will take. There is no set way to do this, but a good place to start is with something called a SWOT analysis. SWOT stands for Strengths, Weaknesses, Opportunities, and Threats. Strengths and weaknesses are internal to the freelancer. Strengths are the factors that give a freelancer a competitive advantage, like a freelancer's experience. Weaknesses are factors that might hinder a freelancer's success. For example, for a lawyer who just graduated law school, the lack of experience could be a weakness.

Opportunities and threats are external. An opportunity is an outside influence that can provide a chance to generate clients or to grow a freelancer's business. Threats are something outside a freelancer's control that could jeopardize a freelancer's business. For example, while many lawyers experienced a negative business impact from the COVID-19 pandemic, it created the opportunity for remote workers to thrive. Depending on a lawyer's position in the marketplace, the pandemic could have created an opportunity or could have been a threat.

While strengths, weaknesses, opportunities, and threats can all be different, sometimes one freelancer's strength (experience) is a weakness for another (inexperience) or sometimes an external event (the pandemic) can create an opportunity for some (remote work) while posing a threat for others (business disruption). Understanding the internal and external factors that can impact a legal freelance business will go a long way toward helping create an effective marketing plan.

For a freelance law practice, internal strengths may be low overhead costs and a niche area of specialty in the law. On the other hand, a freelance business operating remotely from home might lack the resources to compete with larger law firms, which would be a weakness. Capitalizing on a growing demand for legal services in a specific niche area when there are not a lot of lawyers servicing clients in that field of law might present an external opportunity. However, competition from larger law firms that have lawyers experienced in most fields of law could present an external threat to the success of a freelance practice.

By conducting a SWOT analysis, a freelancer can identify key areas on which to focus marketing efforts and develop strategies. For example, if there is an opportunity in a particular niche market that is underserved, a freelancer can develop a targeted marketing campaign to reach law firms that cater to that audience. If, on the other hand, a freelancer identifies a lack of the same resources as a larger law firm as a weakness, marketing can focus on how the freelancer has leveraged technology to provide the same high-level services that a big law firm can provide despite lesser resources. A SWOT analysis can reveal how to turn weaknesses into strengths or threats into opportunities.

After performing a SWOT analysis, another critical step in developing a marketing strategy is to identify a target market by determining the specific group of lawyers or law firms that the freelancer wants as a client base. This is the group a freelancer will target with marketing efforts. For example, a freelancer who only wants to work for solo practitioners or small law firms could target marketing efforts on providing that group with a cushion by absorbing work if they become too busy. A freelancer who specializes in family law might want to target law firms working with people going through a divorce. A freelancer with a science background who passed the patent bar might target large law firms that represent technology start-ups or entrepreneurs. The more clearly defined the target market, the easier it will be to create a marketing strategy.

After conducting a SWOT analysis and defining a target market, a freelancer should establish marketing objectives. An acronym commonly used for defining marketing objectives is SMART, which stands for Specific, Measurable, Achievable, Relevant, and Time-bound. These objectives will help a freelancer track progress, measure success, and ensure that objectives are both well-defined and attainable. Examples of marketing objectives might include increasing website traffic with a specific demographic within a certain time period. The objective is very specific so satisfies the "S" aspect in the SMART analysis. It could be even more specific if the objective were to increase website traffic by a certain amount, like 10 percent. Progress can be measured by looking at website analytics, which addresses the "M" in the SMART analysis. Increasing website traffic is feasible or achievable by employing search engine optimization (SEO) techniques or by boosting website content, fulfilling the "A" in the SMART analysis. Increasing website traffic is clearly relevant to a marketing strategy in that it increases visibility, thereby attracting potential clients, checking the box for "R." Finally, the objective can be time-bound by setting milestones for achieving it. For example, the objective can be stated as increasing website traffic by 10 percent per quarter, fulfilling the last portion of the SMART analysis, "T."

A social media objective for a new freelance law practice could be to expand social media presence by increasing the number of followers by 20 percent in the first year. The objective is very specific in terms of time, amount, and plan. It is measurable by using analytics and tracking the growth in followers, likes, comments, and shares. Increasing social media presence is achievable by posting relevant content and engaging with followers. Social media advertising is also relevant because it provides a cost- and time-effective way to reach a broad audience and to connect with potential clients.

Using an in-person approach as opposed to an online approach, an objective might be to increase referrals by cultivating relationships with existing clients. A different objective along those lines might be to increase referrals from other lawyers through networking. While the overall objective is the same—increasing referrals—the objective is much more specific in terms of the source of those referrals—clients versus other lawyers.

Using either example, the objective is measurable by tracking the number of referrals received from the referral source. Either objective is also achievable. For the former example, a freelancer can achieve the objective of increasing client referrals by building strong relationships with existing clients through excellent service and reliable communication. For the latter, a freelancer can achieve the objective of increasing referrals from other lawyers or colleagues by attending local bar association events, engaging in pro-bono legal service opportunities to increase exposure among colleagues, or engaging in community organizations that attract lawyers, like chambers of commerce or organizations involved in economic development initiatives. Either goal is obviously relevant because increased referrals lead to more clients, which results in the growth of a freelance law practice. Finally, by adding milestones onto the objective, it becomes time-bound.

A final step in developing a marketing strategy is to conduct market research. This involves gathering relevant data and insights about the target client base, competition, industry trends, and client expectations. Using a freelancer specializing in estate planning as an example, market research could involve considering demographic data such as age. While estate planning efforts often suggest preparing for death, which might point to an older demographic, many people with young children have estate planning needs as well. Although an older person's estate planning needs might involve a health-care directive, power of attorney, or who to leave money to upon passing, a younger person's estate planning needs might revolve around guardianship issues and who will care for young children in the event of an untimely death.

Because of the perception that estate planning involves people who have a lot of money, market research might show that estate planning for young families who have not yet built wealth is an underserved market and need. Marketing efforts targeted toward helping law firms provide legal services to a younger demographic without a lot of assets would look much different than marketing efforts focusing on helping a law firm with a wealthier, older client demographic.

Market research for an estate planning freelancer could also look at trends in estate planning law in terms of how to charge. For example, market research may reveal the typical legal fees to probate a simple and uncontested estate. Understanding that those fees are in the $3,000 to $5,000 range in a particular jurisdiction will prevent a freelancer from establishing a flat-fee rate that exceeds that amount and driving away potential law firms as clients. Knowing that under federal law, any facility receiving Medicare or Medicaid reimbursements is required to use advance directives could help with messaging to a law firm serving a demographic that receives federal entitlements.

Conducting market research will also allow a freelancer to better understand the competitive landscape. Doing so is helpful for differentiating a freelancer from other lawyers. For example, if traditional law firms charge by the hour, even simple and uncontested probate costs are uncertain. There is a big difference in a probate that costs $3,000 versus one that costs $5,000 for somebody with limited means. A freelancer can take advantage of the typical, hourly billing model and offer a fixed fee for probating a simple, uncontested estate.

If the targeted demographic is elderly with mobility challenges, understanding that demographic's preferences to not travel downtown and navigate parking and a high-rise office building might lead a freelancer to rent an office in a one-story building with easy parking or even to visit with potential clients at their place of residence as part of the legal services the freelancer provides to a larger law firm. Offering a different pricing strategy or a novel way of providing legal services will allow a freelancer to create a unique value proposition and to provide differentiation in a competitive field that hiring lawyers or law firms will find attractive.

By thoroughly researching the estate planning market, a freelancer will better understand the target market, which can lead to identifying opportunities. A freelancer can gain valuable insights to inform service offerings, which can create competitive differentiation. Discovering the best approaches for client engagement through market research will lead to an understanding of how to attract and serve a target client market effectively, which will impact a freelancer's marketing strategies directed to the lawyers and law firms that serve that market.

By conducting a situational analysis and identifying internal strengths and weaknesses, as well as external opportunities and threats, pinpointing a target client base, setting marketing objectives, and researching the target market, a freelancer will be able to determine a unique value proposition and positioning within the target market. After doing that work, the freelancer can develop a comprehensive marketing strategy, defining key marketing messages that will best resonate with the target client base.

Once the message is identified, a freelancer can tailor marketing strategies to effectively communicate that message and choose the most appropriate marketing channels to reach and engage the target client base. The channels can be online, offline, or a combination of both. They can include advertising, content marketing, social media engagement, or in-person marketing through networking. For example, freelancers specializing in business law can develop informative content to post on a website or LinkedIn. They can provide links to articles establishing the freelancer's expertise in the realm of business transactions.

Business law freelancers can also create blogs and periodically address common issues that arise for business lawyers. Speaking engagements are a great way to conduct in-person marketing. Local, state, and national bar associations provide many such opportunities through continuing legal education seminars (CLEs). Speaking at CLEs not only helps establish a freelancer as an authority in a particular area of law but also creates networking opportunities and referral prospects because those attending the CLE are lawyers.

Marketing efforts can be expensive. Social media advertising and joining bar associations for in-person networking opportunities are not free. A freelancer needs to develop a budget with a realistic allocation of financial resources to support the marketing strategies. A budget should include costs for such activities as developing and maintaining a website, SEO, social media marketing, email marketing, online directories and listings, printing costs for business cards or brochures, registration fees for networking events or conferences, the expense of joining a bar association, and analytic tools to measure online marketing performance. A budget should allow for a balanced approach, allocating financial resources to both online and offline marketing channels.

There is no single marketing approach that is right for everybody. The following example shows how diverse marketing efforts can be. Kerline Jean-Louis, Esq., works just outside Boston, Massachusetts. Her marketing efforts are wholly different than another lawyer from Boston. Kerline actively engages in social media marketing to build her practice. One of the ways she does that is by creating and sharing content through social media platforms like Instagram, TikTok, and YouTube. For example, she produces long form content like educational webinars for YouTube and uses snippets from those webinars to post short-form content on Instagram or TikTok.

One example of her content marketing involved a discussion of why common names used to describe brands, like using "Queen" in a name for Black beauty products, might not be entitled to protection. The audience viewing that content would understand by engaging with that content what kinds of names are protectable before spending a lot of time and effort to come up with and promote a brand.

Creating content allows you to reach a broader audience and increase your brand's visibility. Consistently producing and sharing valuable content makes people more aware of your brand and positions your brand as authoritative in your niche area of practice. Providing insights, answering questions, and offering solutions to common problems builds trust and credibility, encourages engagement, helps potential clients understand how your legal services can meet their needs, and helps differentiate your brand from competitors by showcasing your unique values and approach. You can have great branding and provide exceptional services but if people are not aware of them, you will not be able to generate clients.[2]

Compare Kerline's approach with the tactic used by the other lawyer from Boston who does not advertise, does not use social media, does not have a website, and does not create content to promote herself. As a freelancer, she took her passion for writing, a skill she developed while working on a law review and clerking for a judge, and used it to develop long-term relationships with law firms by providing value through exceptional brief writing in complex litigation matters. She generates clients purely through word-of-mouth and referrals from professional colleagues.

Outlines of two very different sample marketing plans can be found in Appendix D. One focuses on a transactional, real estate lawyer marketing primarily through online methods. The other involves a litigator engaging mostly with in-person marketing efforts.

Once a freelancer puts a marketing plan into action, monitoring the results is imperative. A freelancer should constantly assess and adjust marketing strategies based on performance and market feedback. For example, website analytics provide metrics on traffic, and social media analytics provide metrics on clicks, including demographic information about who is viewing the online channels. Use the data and insights gained by these analytics to measure the effectiveness of the marketing strategies and to identify areas for improvement.

If a freelancer who is targeting large law firms is mostly reaching solo practitioners online, the marketing strategies should be refined and resources reallocated to reach the target client base. That might mean advertising through different social media channels or re-messaging to try and attract a different audience. If a freelancer who is tracking the results of social media marketing discovers a lack of engagement with target clients through social media but has generated numerous client referrals through speaking engagements, that freelancer can decrease social media presence and concentrate on securing more speaking engagements.

Kerline offered an example of the importance of continually evaluating marketing strategies. On her website, Kerline regularly posts blogs. One blog she posted was titled, "Taco Tuesday Trademark Beef." The blog focused on Taco Bell's 2023 campaign using Lebron James to support its petition to cancel the trademark "Taco Tuesday." Lebron James had unsuccessfully tried to trademark the phrase "Taco Tuesday" in 2019. Taco Bell's position was that the

---

2 K. Jean-Louis, personal communication, Sept. 21, 2023.

phrase "Taco Tuesday" had become so generic in its use that it was no longer entitled to trademark protection, a principle called genericide, which Kerline explained in her blog. However, after posting her article, Kerline learned from using social media analytics that her blog did not generate interest from her target audience; rather, because Lebron James was featured in the blog, it generated interest from sports enthusiasts. Kerline learned a valuable lesson that enabled her to better focus her content to reach her target audience.

Creating a marketing plan is an iterative process. Flexibility is key. Regularly review, adapt, and refine a marketing plan to optimize results and to maximize ROI. In the words of Marc Enger, owner of Propel Marketing Services, a marketing plan, when properly structured, should function like an investment portfolio—invest to achieve certain objectives, monitor performance, and adjust over time to increase your ROI.

While many freelancers have built their practice entirely through marketing and advertising efforts, others have found different ways. There are many ways to attract clients for freelancers who prefer not to engage in formal marketing or advertising.

CHAPTER 13

From the Theoretical to the Practical

Attracting Clients

"That we are responsible for our own fate, we reap what we sow, we get what we give, we pull in what we pull out. I know these things for sure."

—Madonna

Many lawyers have an aversion even to the word "rainmaking." Lawyers go to law school to learn how to practice law, not to learn how to market themselves or to study the skills of business development. As a result, many lawyers feel ill-equipped to be rainmakers. In addition, the fear of rejection drives a distaste for rainmaking. The idea of asking for work but not getting it feels uncomfortable. Practically, the constant pressure to work and generate revenue creates a time constraint that hinders business development activities.

However, like it or not, rainmaking in some form is critical to the growth and sustainability of a freelance law practice. While generating clients is often perceived as a challenging task, it need not be as difficult as it seems. There are practical, stress-free ways to generate clients so that rainmaking becomes a natural part of any freelance law practice.

Building relationships is at the core of rainmaking. Establishing a strong, personal relationship with a client will lead to business opportunities. Satisfied clients will relay to referral sources how pleased they are with a freelancer's services, which will in turn lead to increased referrals. Similarly, a client with ongoing legal needs who is pleased with a freelancer's services will keep coming back. One of the most effective ways to build client relationships is through excellent work. No amount of schmoozing will make a client happy or keep a client coming back if the work is not satisfactory.

The importance of doing good work cannot be overemphasized when it comes to maintaining existing client loyalty and generating new clients. It is impossible to build trust or credibility with a client if the services provided are inadequate. Clients pay a lot of money for legal services and expect competent and effective representation in return. Consistently delivering high-quality legal work not only demonstrates a freelancer's expertise, competence, and

114

commitment to achieving the best outcomes possible, but it also inspires confidence and fosters a freelancer's reputation in the community.

There is a strong likelihood that a satisfied client will come back and provide repeat business. A satisfied client will also speak highly of the legal services provided, which could result in referrals or other clients seeking a freelancer's legal services. An unsatisfied client will not exhibit that sort of loyalty. Satisfied and loyal clients not only drive revenue through repeat business but also become valuable brand ambassadors through word-of-mouth.

Providing high-quality legal services to other lawyers and law firms is the single most important way to attract and maintain clients. Satisfied lawyers and law firms often refer other lawyers who need litigation support to a freelancer who provides excellent work product. Many freelancers do not engage in any marketing efforts. Word-of-mouth referrals is what sustains their freelance law practices. Delivering exceptional legal work keeps clients coming back. One freelance lawyer in Boston, Massachusetts, has been doing legal work for the same law firm for three decades. All of her current business is repeat business from the satisfied lawyers and referrals from those lawyers. Prioritizing the quality of the legal work provided to lawyer and law firm clients is an investment in long-term success. Building a reputation for excellence can lead to a steady stream of clients without engaging in formal rainmaking efforts, which can create stability and growth of a freelance law practice.

Importantly, client satisfaction is not necessarily outcome dependent. A civil litigator, for example, is not likely to take many cases to trial and win because the overwhelming majority of civil cases—more than 98 percent of them—settle before trial. Settling means compromising. Compromising means that neither side gets entirely what they want. On the plaintiff's side, that means that a client who receives a $500,000 settlement might not be pleased if the settlement was substantially less than a seven-figure expectation. Conversely, an insurer in a state where there have been nuclear wrongful death verdicts in trucking cases might view a multimillion-dollar settlement favorably because it came in under policy limits. Even if a freelancer is working on one of the rare cases that goes to trial, a client who pays a lawyer hundreds of thousands of dollars to win at trial might not feel good about the outcome if a $75,000 settlement had been possible without an admission of liability and a confidentiality clause.

Managing expectations is crucial to client satisfaction. Even what seems to be a relatively small legal matter for a lawyer can involve high stakes or be emotionally charged for the ultimate client. By setting realistic expectations from the outset, a freelancer can prevent unrealistic hopes or unreasonable expectations about outcomes. When clients have realistic understandings of potential outcomes, risks, challenges, timing, and costs associated with their cases, the prospect of an unpleasant surprise that will jeopardize client satisfaction is drastically reduced. Advising a client about what to expect will make that client more likely to trust the freelancer's judgment, fostering a collaborative relationship. Being transparent about how decisions are made and involving clients in the decision making ensures that clients will feel informed and involved in their legal representation.

A key to creating realistic expectations is to be clear, open, and consistent with communications. One of the leading reasons for client dissatisfaction regarding any type of professional service is a lack of communication. A hiring lawyer who cannot get a response from a freelancer to a question or who never hears status updates from the freelancer about an assigned project is not going to be a satisfied client, regardless of outcome.

In addition to taking the steps to ensure client satisfaction as a natural way to become a rainmaker, professional networking is another stress-free way to engage in rainmaking. Local, state, and national bar associations provide ideal opportunities for networking that give freelancers a way to build relationships with colleagues, which can result in referrals and can ultimately generate clients. Bar associations frequently organize networking events, conferences, and continuing legal education seminars (CLEs). Attending these kinds of events allows a freelancer to meet other lawyers who can become referral sources.

> Deian, McBryde, Albuquerque, New Mexico. I spent a lot of time and energy during law school making friends, and not just my law school classmates. The three things I would say about law school is to learn rules not cases, make friends, and find mentors. By the time I opened my law office, I had referrals coming in relatively quickly. My tip for starting—you are going to get so many ideas, millions of ideas—is to make friends, get to know people, and create authentic connections. When I opened my firm, my first year's budget for marketing was mostly buying coffee, buying lunch, and buying drinks to create relationships in the legal community and develop cheerleaders as referral sources. And it was really useful. We opened in June. By September, we had our first profitable month, thanks to clients referred through personal or professional relationships, not online marketing or SEO.[1]

Attending bar association events in a particular practice area is a great way to meet potential referral sources. For example, going to a CLE put on by the business law section of a bar association and attending the networking event after the seminar will help a freelancer connect with other lawyers practicing in the same field of law. During breaks or at a post-event networking reception, the freelancer can try to connect with attendees. This type of networking will make it quickly known that a freelancer is available to provide legal services. Establishing a personal connection with a colleague does not take a lot of effort and can lead to referrals or even collaborative work together.

---

1 D. McBryde, Esq., personal communication, Aug. 29, 2023.

Bar associations and other law-related practice entities have practice groups that focus on demographics, general areas of law, or specific practice settings. For example, state bar associations will generally have a young lawyers division and a senior lawyers division. There are national, state, and local chapters of minority bar associations like those for Hispanic, Asian, Black, women, and LGBTQ+ lawyers. There are also many bar-related groups organized around general areas of the law like a defense lawyers association or a trial lawyers association. In addition, there are many bar groups organized around specific practice settings like estate planning, employment, criminal, or tax law. Joining these groups allows a freelancer to connect with lawyers who share similar practice interests. Active participation in groups or committees by attending meetings, contributing to discussions, or volunteering for leadership positions will help establish a freelancer as an engaged member of the legal community and will facilitate networking within a freelancer's niche practice area.

Lisa Dickinson, Esq., a lawyer from Spokane, Washington, has been very involved in local, state, and national bar groups. Nationally, among many other positions, she has served on the American Bar Association's (ABA) House of Delegates, the ABA's Standing Committee on Membership, Standing Committee on Professionalism, and Standing Committee on Technology and Information Systems, in addition to the ABA Cybersecurity Task Force and the governing bodies for the ABA Solo, Small Firm and General Practice Division and the Tort, Trial & Insurance Practice Section.

Because of the many alliances Lisa has formed in the legal community from her bar association activities, she is able to easily associate with lawyers across the country when those resources are needed in litigation matters to better serve her clients. She has also associated with lawyers outside her jurisdiction as local counsel and has acted as outside general counsel for businesses with needs in her region. Networking and building relationships with other lawyers on a national scale through her bar association work significantly bolstered the growth and success of Lisa's law practice. By establishing connections nationally, Lisa was able to tap into a vast pool of knowledge, experience, and potential referrals. Collaborating with colleagues from different jurisdictions not only led to cross-referrals and co-counseling opportunities but also increased Lisa's visibility and fostered her reputation as a well-connected and highly respected legal professional.

Networking does not need to be limited to the legal community. Freelancers can network within the non-legal community the same way they can network within bar associations. For example, a freelancer whose niche involves environmental issues can volunteer for a nonprofit organization that encourages environmentally conscious behaviors through community partnerships. Doing so not only provides exposure for the freelancer through the environmental nonprofit but also through the community businesses and organizations the nonprofit partners with.

Showcasing expertise is another way that significantly contributes to rain-making success. Freelancers can position themselves as trusted authorities in their practice areas by providing valuable content, whether through writing or speaking. Volunteering to speak at a CLE or to give a presentation to a trade group is a great way to gain exposure to an audience that can serve as a good client referral source. Blogging, contributing articles to a newsletter, or posting long- or short-form content on social media is another way to gain exposure to a target client base by sharing insights and providing practical legal information.

Networking and showcasing expertise to build a reputation and generate referrals is a cost-effective way of rainmaking because a freelancer does not have to spend thousands of dollars for these kinds of professional network-ing opportunities. For example, as of 2023, solo practitioners like freelancers could join the ABA's Solo, Small Firm & General Practice Division (GPSolo) for $150 annually. For a new lawyer practicing 10 years or less, the cost was only $75. The benefits accessible to GPSolo members more than outweigh the cost of membership. GPSolo members have access to a wide variety of free practice resources like webinars and CLEs, mentoring groups, podcasts, and publications. One of the most significant benefits, however, is the opportunities GPSolo provides to network and to build a reputation by writing and speaking.

Members of GPSolo can contribute to the GPSolo Magazine. Each issue explores a topic of interest, whether a substantive area of the law, ways to leverage technology, law practice management, or wellness in the legal prac-tice. Members can also contribute to the GPSolo eReport, which is a monthly e-newsletter. Writing an article for the GPSolo Magazine or eReport is a great way to get published.

There are also hundreds of CLEs a GPSolo member can volunteer to speak at that are viewed by a national audience. In addition, GPSolo hosts four con-ferences annually in different locations that provide incredible, in-person net-working opportunities. The registration for the winter meeting has always been free and there are scholarships available for the other meetings. GPSolo also organizes roundtable events members can participate in; has many opportuni-ties to serve on committees to advance a particular practice area of expertise; and has an internet discussion forum, SoloSez, for solo practitioners and small firm lawyers.

In short, joining the ABA and becoming a member of GPSolo can pro-vide a freelancer with numerous ways to network. The ABA has many groups besides GPSolo that provide similar opportunities in targeted areas of the law, like the Business Law Section, the Litigation Section, and many others. With the ABA's focus on diversity in the legal profession, minority lawyers, young lawyers, retired lawyers, military lawyers, and lawyers from any practice set-ting or group can find a home. Whether a freelancer has a regulatory law focus, found a niche in air and space law, provides freelancing services in alter-native dispute resolution, practices entertainment or sports law, specializes in international law, needs tips on law practice management, or is a minority or underrepresented lawyer, the ABA has a multitude of groups, committees, publications, seminars, and events that provide networking opportunities.

There are also many legal services platforms where freelancers can advertise their services. LAWCLERK, Avvo, Lawyer Exchange, UpCounsel, LegalMatch, and Rocket Lawyer are some such platforms. Legal services platforms provide a newer model for connecting freelancers with lawyers that have specific legal needs. The legal services platforms serve as the intermediaries, connecting the lawyer clients with freelancers who help support them. Many solo practitioners or small firms use the support of freelancers through legal services platforms instead of hiring associates, and some freelancers make a living on only work generated through those platforms.

The lawyers or clients who need assistance create a profile on the legal services platform. They provide information about their specific legal needs. For example, they can describe a specific legal project they need help with, such as drafting a contract, legal analysis, document review, research and writing, or motion practice. Or, they can post that they need ongoing help in a particular practice area of law or with a specific case. Once the lawyer posts a project or a particular need, the platform's algorithm matches the project or need with freelance lawyers who have created a profile on the platform who have the relevant expertise and availability to provide the needed services. The freelancer then applies for the project or job described and the lawyer reviews the profiles of the freelancer applicants and selects the one or ones best suited for the project. Once a selection is made, the lawyer and freelancer can communicate directly about project details, deadlines, and any other project requirements.

Rainmaking is not a one-time effort. Persistence and consistency are key. Freelancers should build rainmaking efforts into their regular business activities. Success may not come immediately. However, making rainmaking activities routine and dedicating time to rainmaking efforts will eventually lead to success. Rainmaking does not have to be difficult. It can even be fun. Building professional and client relationships, showcasing expertise, and developing a professional reputation will lead to an increased client base, sustained business growth, and professional success. Rather than becoming something to dislike, rainmaking can become a natural and rewarding part of a freelance practice. Having an idea now of the many different rainmaking strategies to build a practice, it is time to turn to the operational aspects of a freelance law practice to make sure it is sustainable on a day-to-day and on a long-term basis.

PART IV

The Art of Operating a Successful Freelance Practice

CHAPTER 14

Appreciating the Flow of Freelance Finances

"Never take your eyes off the cash flow because it's the lifeblood of business."
—Sir Richard Branson

After months of planning, Emma finally got her freelance law practice off the ground. She has a law firm client providing her with 20 to 30 hours of work a week and the word is out that she is available for work. Now that Emma is generating revenue, she needs to start thinking about cash flow. Managing cash flow is critical to the success of any business. Cash flow refers to the amount of money coming in and going out of Emma's freelance law practice. Managing cash flow is essential to ensure that there is enough cash available for her to cover expenses. Emma must effectively manage cash flow to make sure her freelance practice does not run out of money.

Managing cash flow starts with figuring out the amount of money coming in. Once Emma has been in business for a while as a freelancer, there will be historical data to analyze, which will help her project revenue based on past performance. She will understand from a historical perspective how much she can charge clients and how much they are willing to pay for her services. However, forecasting revenue without that historical context is much trickier.

One strategy Emma can use to forecast cash flow is to conduct market research to estimate potential revenue. For example, rather than guessing how much a freelancer typically charges for the type of work Emma will provide in her locale, she can do some research. That might involve asking other freelancers in her area how much they typically charge, finding out from law firms how much they typically pay, or trying to learn that information from another source, like a legal services freelancing platform that will have information about market-driven rates.

Having a good understanding of cash flow, however, is not as simple as just knowing how much a law firm will pay Emma for the legal services she provides. Emma must also understand when she will be paid. For example, law firms that do insurance defense work sometimes only bill insurance companies on a quarterly basis. Therefore, if Emma is freelancing for a law firm that only receives quarterly payments, she should understand whether the law firm will pay her quarterly when it can collect from its insurer client or whether the law firm will pay Emma monthly if she invoices the law firm every 30 days. If the law firm pays Emma monthly even though the insurance client has not yet paid the law firm, then the law firm might run into cash flow problems itself.

It is easy to see how the timing of payments can impact cash flow. If a law firm pays Emma quarterly rather than monthly, then Emma will need more cash reserves to pay her monthly bills. The necessity of building cash reserves is not necessarily a bad thing, especially if Emma can generate good will with her client by agreeing to quarterly payments. It is simply something Emma needs to plan for. If Emma has monthly bills but is not paid on a monthly basis, she will have to either build cash reserves sufficient to satisfy her monthly obligations or find another way to pay her bills, such as accessing a line of credit.

The other side of cash flow is expenses. Understanding expenses will allow a freelancer to keep sufficient cash on hand to pay the bills necessary to sustain a law practice. Emma can estimate her expenses and cash outflows by understanding her needs as a freelancer. If she works remotely from home, for example, she will avoid rental costs. However, she will have to purchase her own office equipment. Emma can easily estimate the cost of any office equipment she needs by looking online or going into a store that sells office equipment. If Emma needs to purchase a higher speed internet package, she can readily determine that cost by calling an internet provider. The cost of necessary technology is easy to determine. An insurance agent or broker can estimate insurance-related costs. Therefore, by doing some research, Emma can accurately forecast expenses.

When forecasting either revenue or expenses, especially without the benefit of historical data, it is important to start with conservative estimates. In other words, Emma should assume lower revenue and higher expenses than she expects to have. By starting conservatively, Emma will avoid overestimating her cash inflows or underestimating her cash outflows, which can lead to financial problems down the line. As Emma starts freelancing, she can adjust her cash flow projections based on actual results. This involves comparing her projections to her actual revenue and expenses and adjusting her cash flow projections based on any variances. By adjusting cash flow projections regularly, Emma can ensure that her forecasts remain accurate and up-to-date.

Assume Emma started her freelance law practice with $25,000, which she self-financed. She forecasts earning $5,000 every month from Law Firm ABC. Her first payment will be in February after she invoices for January's work. She also forecasts quarterly payments of $15,000 for her work for Law Firm XYZ. Her subscription work brings her $25,000 annually, payable twice a year in January and June. Emma pays bar dues every January of $800. She pays quarterly health insurance premiums of $5,000. Her joint office space costs $500 per month to rent. Emma pays $2,500 each month for a legal research license. Her professional liability insurance premium of $1,500 is paid once a year in

April. She forecasts $200 per month in marketing expenses. Given this forecast, Emma's cash flow statement would look like this:

	Jan.	*Feb.*	*Mar.*	*Apr.*	*May*	*June*
Starting Cash Balance	25,000	28,500	30,300	47,100	42,400	44,200
Revenue						
Law Firm ABC		5,000	5,000	5,000	5,000	5,000
Law Firm XYZ			15,000			15,000
Subscription work	12,500					12,500
Total	**12,500**	**5,000**	**20,000**	**5,000**	**5,000**	**32,500**
Expenses						
Bar Dues	800					
Health Insurance Premiums	5,000			5,000		
Joint Office Space rent	500	500	500	500	500	500
Legal Research License	2,500	2,500	2,500	2,500	2,500	2,500
Malpractice Insurance				1,500		
Marketing Expenses	200	200	200	200	200	200
Total	**9,000**	**3,200**	**3,200**	**9,700**	**3,200**	**3,200**
Net Cash Flow	**3,500**	**1,800**	**16,800**	**(4,700)**	**1,800**	**29,300**
Ending Cash Balance	**28,500**	**30,300**	**47,100**	**42,400**	**44,200**	**73,500**

There is a lot of useful information that this cash flow statement can tell Emma. For example, Emma can see that in the month of April, she will have a negative cash flow, meaning that she will spend more than she brings in. However, because she has accumulated a positive cash balance from previous months, Emma can absorb the negative cash flow without having to borrow money. Emma can also see from the cash flow statement that June is a big month for her because all her clients pay her that month, the only time that will happen in the year. Therefore, if Emma were contemplating a big expense, such as buying new office equipment, June would be a good month for her to make that purchase. If Emma had borrowed the $25,000 to start her law practice instead of self-financing it, interest and principal payments on the loan until she paid it back would also be included in the cash flow statement.

Extrapolating the cash flow statement through December shows the following:

	July	*Aug.*	*Sept.*	*Oct.*	*Nov.*	*Dec.*
Starting Cash Balance	73,500	70,300	72,100	88,900	85,700	87,500
Revenue						
Law Firm ABC	5,000	5,000	5,000	5,000	5,000	5,000
Law Firm XYZ			15,000			15,000
Subscription work						
Total	**5,000**	**5,000**	**20,000**	**5,000**	**5,000**	**20,000**

(Continued)

	July	Aug.	Sept.	Oct.	Nov.	Dec.
Expenses						
Bar Dues						
Health Insurance Premiums	5,000			5,000		
Joint Office Space rent	500	500	500	500	500	500
Legal Research License	2,500	2,500	2,500	2,500	2,500	2,500
Malpractice Insurance						
Marketing Expenses	200	200	200	200	200	200
Total	**8,200**	**3,200**	**3,200**	**8,200**	**3,200**	**3,200**
Net Cash Flow	**(3,200)**	**1,800**	**16,800**	**(3,200)**	**1,800**	**16,800**
Ending Cash Balance	**70,300**	**72,100**	**88,900**	**85,700**	**87,500**	**104,300**

By understanding that she will end the year with a cash balance forecasted at $104,300, Emma can decide how much she wants to contribute to her 401(k). She can also look at her cash flow statement and determine when she wants to make those contributions. For example, she can make retirement contributions quarterly in March, June, September, and December, all positive cash flow months for her. Emma will also understand at the beginning of the year how much she might earn by subtracting her ending cash balance of $104,300 from her beginning cash balance of $25,000.

By estimating income of $79,300 and deciding how much to contribute to her retirement account, Emma can go through another iteration of her cash flow statement to make it more accurate by estimating taxes. Without considering deductions for expenses, if Emma decided to contribute $20,000 to a 401(k), she would be taxed on $59,300, which would put her in the 22 percent tax rate in 2023 if she were a single filer. Assuming a state tax rate of 5 percent, Emma would be paying 27 percent in taxes, or $16,011, which she could include in her cash flow statement. On the other hand, if Emma wanted to put the $20,000 into a Roth IRA instead, she would be taxed on her total income of $79,300, which, although she would remain in the same federal tax bracket, would amount to $21,411 in income tax liability.

Although Emma's forecast shows that there will never be a month where her ending cash balance is negative despite some months of negative cash flow, if her forecast were to show a month with a negative cash balance, Emma would know ahead of time she would have to find the cash to meet her expenses that month. She could do that by increasing revenue. Perhaps she could seek an additional project from one of her clients and bill enough to make up the difference. Or, she could access a line of credit and pay it back once her cash flow and ending cash balance were positive again in subsequent months.

Forecasting revenue and expenses is not the only part of the cash flow equation. Managing revenue and expenses is also important. Managing the revenue side of cash flow requires active monitoring. Monitoring revenue means tracking the actual cash coming in against forecasts. This will allow Emma to understand, for example, whether her client pays on time or late, and if so, how late. Monitoring revenue will allow Emma to identify potential problems early and take corrective action in a timely manner. For example, if Law Firm ABC is always late paying invoices, she can offer it terms to encourage prompt payment by proposing discounts for early payment or imposing late fees for overdue payments. If the law firm continues to be untimely with payments, Emma can consider not doing further work until the firm brings its account current.

On the other hand, if Emma is confident the firm will pay her eventually and she does not want to give up the firm as a client, she can access a line of credit from the bank to provide liquidity until the firm brings its account current. If she does not want to access a line of credit, Emma can build up cash reserves so that she does not need to use a line of credit. Alternatively, she can look for ways to increase revenue to manage cash flow. For example, Emma can increase revenue through productivity and efficiency. Or, she can increase revenue by diversifying revenue streams. Maybe Emma can expand her practice areas to serve new clients or invest in marketing and business development to attract new clients.

In addition to managing revenue, controlling expenses is the other side of the cash flow calculation. To have positive cash flow, the money coming in must exceed the money flowing out. Therefore, the less money flowing out, the better the cash flow. As a freelancer, there are many creative ways to reduce costs.

For example, rather than purchasing a legal research license for $2,500 monthly, it might be cheaper for Emma to pay Law Firm ABC to add her as an additional user to its existing license. Using free research software would be another way, especially if there is free access to the legal research software Emma likes using at her local bar office, law school, or courthouse library. If Emma has the flexibility, spending a couple of hours a day at the courthouse would be a way to avoid the cost of paying $2,500 for access to a legal research platform.

Emma has already saved money on renting an office by choosing to lease a joint office space for only $500 per month. However, if she were willing to work from home and had the space, that would avoid office rental costs altogether.

Emma does not have the cost of expensive case management software because she uses Microsoft Office 365's built-in administration tools. Likewise, Emma does not pay for expensive, complicated, bookkeeping software because she only spends $15 monthly for three clients for intuitive, easy-to-use, accounting software like FreshBooks, which also includes invoicing and payment features designed especially for freelancers. At only $180 annually, the amount was negligible enough that Emma did not include it in her cash flow projections.

There are so many ways to reduce expenses as a freelancer. Joining the American Bar Association (ABA) is one way. As of 2023, it costs a solo practitioner like a freelancer either $75 or $150 annually to join the ABA, depending on years in practice. One of the advantages to joining is the ABA's content in the form of e-publications and podcasts, much of which involves law practice management tips for streamlining expenses. In addition, the ABA has hundreds of hours of free continuing legal education (CLE) programs available to members that make the cost of joining well worth it. A freelancer can avoid the substantial cost of having to pay for CLE courses to obtain the credits necessary to maintain licensure by taking advantage of the ABA's free CLE database.

Discovering how to minimize expenses is just as important to cash flow as maximizing revenue because there are only two ways to improve cash flow—increase revenue or decrease expenses. A freelancer who has minimal expenses can work less and still net the same amount of revenue as one who has considerable expenses.

One of the biggest expenses that impacts cash flow is taxes. Because a freelancer is an independent contractor, making estimated federal and state income tax payments will be necessary. Some freelancers set up a separate tax account that is used to manage estimated quarterly taxes. In other words, they build up cash reserves in a separate account that is only used for paying taxes.

A handful of states also impose gross receipts tax (GRT) on legal services. It is a tax on the total amount of revenue generated from legal services provided without deduction for expenses. GRT is typically calculated as a percentage of revenue generated from legal services, and the rate varies among states and even among localities within the same state. However, freelancers who work in states where legal services are subject to GRT can obtain a non-taxable transaction certificate, also known as an exemption certificate. It is a document that the law firm paying the freelancer must provide to the freelancer to indicate that the legal services being provided are exempt from GRT. A law firm paying a freelancer in a GRT state charges the client GRT, including on the legal services the freelancer is providing. Because the law firm is charging GRT on the freelancer's legal services, it provides an exemption certificate to the freelancer so GRT is not charged twice on the same services. That way, the freelancer does not have to pay GRT.

A freelancer, as an independent contractor, will also be responsible for paying self-employment taxes. Self-employment tax is a tax paid by individuals working for themselves on the net earnings from self-employment, which is calculated by subtracting business expenses from income. The self-employment tax includes Social Security tax and Medicare tax. As of 2023, the Social Security tax rate was 12.4 percent and the Medicare tax rate was 2.9 percent. Therefore, for self-employed freelancers, the total self-employment tax would be 15.3 percent. Self-employment tax is generally paid quarterly, along with the estimated income tax payments.

In addition to forecasting and monitoring revenue and expenses, managing cash flow will require a freelancer to prepare for contingencies. If, for example, Emma experiences a negative cash flow month that falls at the same time her tax payments are due, Emma must still be able to pay the taxes due to avoid penalties and interest. There are different ways to prepare for emergencies or unexpected expenses that can affect cash flow. Emma can build an emergency, cash reserve fund to cover unforeseen expenses or can secure a line of credit from her bank to provide liquidity in times of financial need.

Regardless of how big the numbers may be on a balance sheet, no business can succeed without managing cash flow. Effective cash flow management means a law practice has enough liquidity to cover day-to-day operating expenses, as well as any unexpected costs that may arise. This will provide financial stability.

Having adequate cash flow means a freelance law practice has sufficient working capital, which is essential for not only ongoing operations, but also for investing in opportunities for growth like marketing, new technology, or professional development. Working capital will also help freelancers weather financial downturns, a slowdown in work, or financial emergencies.

Freelancers often have periodic financial obligations, like estimated tax payments, insurance premiums, and professional association dues. Managing cash flow ensures they have the funds available to meet these obligations in a timely manner to avoid penalties or late fees or legal issues due to nonpayment. If a freelancer has taken on debt to start a law practice, effective cash flow management ensures that the freelancer has the financial resources to service that debt.

Managing cash flow is the first step. Monitoring cash flow is also essential. Monitoring cash flow will provide valuable insights into a law practice's financial health, which will help freelancers make informed decisions about pricing legal services, resource allocation, and strategic planning based on real-time financial data. Sound cash flow management and monitoring will contribute to the long-term sustainability of a freelance law practice by helping to ensure the practice can withstand fluctuations in the economy or workload fluctuations. It will also impact well-being. Unpredictable cash flow can lead to financial stress. Effective cash flow management will reduce stress and enhance the overall satisfaction practicing law.

Successful cash flow management is its own form of marketing. The timely payment of bills and timely invoicing clients will enhance a freelancer's professional reputation. Creditors, vendors, and clients are more likely to view a freelance law practice favorably if financial commitments are consistently met. Maintaining a good reputation is critical for a freelancer to succeed in a competitive legal landscape.

Managing cash flow is a critical component of running a successful freelancing practice. A freelancer manages cash flow effectively by accurate forecasting, regular monitoring, managing accounts receivable and payable, and controlling expenses. While forecasting cash flow for a new freelancing practice can be challenging, especially when historical data is limited, conducting market research, creating realistic assumptions, using projections, starting conservatively, and adjusting projections regularly will help provide accurate cash flow projections that will allow a freelancer to manage finances effectively. However, managing cash flow is not enough. Managing workflow is also critical to building and sustaining a successful freelance law practice.

CHAPTER 15

Effective Workflow Management for Freelance Success

"The shorter way to do many things is to only do one thing at a time."

—Mozart

Effective time management is essential for a freelancer to enhance productivity. Enhancing productivity helps maximize revenue. By completing tasks in less time, a freelancer can take on additional, revenue-generating work. Alternatively, a freelancer can guard the additional time created by working more efficiently for personal pursuits.

Mastering skills to enhance productivity can contribute significantly to the success of a freelance law practice and to achieving a work-life balance. Time management is multifaceted and involves prioritizing tasks to manage workflow. Doing this requires goal setting, planning, and scheduling. By managing time well, freelancers can reduce stress, maximize the time spent doing paid work, and create ample personal time outside the practice of law.

The importance of time management cannot be overstated. That there are professionals who specialize in time management and offer services to individuals seeking to improve their time management skills underscores how important time management is. Time management is what will enable a freelancer to build a sustainable practice.

There are many time management myths. In today's fast-paced and interconnected world, multitasking has become a common way to manage the demands of work. Multitasking is the simultaneous handling of more than one task or activity. There are many examples of multitasking in the practice of law. Having a Zoom meeting up on one computer monitor while working on a legal brief or drafting a document at the same time is one common example. Emailing during a deposition is another. Talking on the phone while drafting a document is also a common example of multitasking. Who has not participated in a Zoom meeting with the camera off and muted, while taking a phone call, at the same time as typing something on a computer? While multitasking may seem like a productive way to accomplish numerous different responsibilities at the same time, multitasking actually leads to decreased productivity and can have a negative impact on the quality of work.

When attempting to multitask, focus and attention is necessarily divided among different tasks. It is impossible to give the same focus to drafting a letter when also trying to concentrate on what is happening during a Zoom meeting. As a result, the ability to pay attention to each task diminishes, which can lead to a work product that does not have the same quality as it would have had if the lawyer had been focused on one project at a time. Constantly switching between tasks can lead to errors and slower task completion times. The quality of work can also suffer when attention to detail is compromised because of divided attention. This is particularly a risk in the legal field, which requires accuracy and precision. Therefore, contrary to popular belief, multitasking does not enhance productivity.

To mitigate the dangers of multitasking and to improve overall performance, it is important to adopt effective time management strategies, such as prioritizing tasks, time blocking, and managing workflow. By focusing on one task at a time, the most important tasks first, and by looking ahead and allocating dedicated periods of time for specific activities, a freelancer will increase productivity and be able to generate a higher quality work product.

Prioritizing activities is critical for making the most out of limited time. Ranking activities necessary to sustain a freelance law practice based on their importance, urgency, and impact on a law practice enables a freelancer to focus on high-value tasks, to meet deadlines, and to leave time for the business aspects of running the practice. For example, if it is the beginning of the month and a freelancer has not invoiced law firms for work performed in the previous month, even though billing is an administrative task rather than a revenue producing one, billing might have a higher importance than drafting documents that the client law firm is not expecting until the middle of the month. If there is a continuing legal education (CLE) deadline to obtain credits by the end of the calendar year and the Christmas holiday is fast approaching, it might be more urgent to make time to attend a CLE than to finish a legal project when the client law firm will be closed during the holidays anyway. While legal work is what generates revenue and, therefore, might always seem like the highest priority, sometimes administrative tasks or professional development will be more important in the short term than billable work.

Most freelancers are responsible not only for generating revenue through billable work, but must also handle the administrative aspects of maintaining a thriving practice. Prioritizing tasks becomes crucial for a freelancer to ensure that both the client work is being performed effectively and that the law practice is being managed efficiently. Start by creating a comprehensive list of all the tasks that need to be accomplished, including client work, administrative tasks like billing, marketing and business development, and professional development. The list for a Monday might look like this:

- Draft estate planning documents due to Law Firm ABC
- Draft status letter due to Law Firm XYZ
- Content development for website
- Time tracking

Now assess the importance of each task. Consider deadlines, client needs, and the impact on revenue. For example, prioritize tasks that directly contribute to revenue generation and client satisfaction, like addressing client inquiries and delivering legal services to a client. In the preceding example, drafting the documents and status letter would take priority over the marketing activity of developing content for a website. However, time tracking is also a priority to make sure the freelancer captures the time spent every day working on paid legal projects.

After identifying the different tasks that need to be accomplished and assessing the importance of each, block time for the different activities. Dedicating a focused block of time for client work will allow for uninterrupted concentration. The best time to record time is as a freelancer has completed a particular legal task. By doing that, there is no need to block time for billing. It is the most efficient way to capture time, which will result in maximizing revenue. However, most lawyers do not record their time as they are working. In that case, recording time at the end of a workday will go a long way to making sure all billable time is invoiced. Therefore, block time at the end of each workday to record time.

In the preceding example, a freelancer could block time in the morning to draft the estate planning documents, take a lunch break, spend until mid-afternoon drafting a comprehensive status report, and then record the time spent that day working. With the client work complete for the day and the time spent working recorded, the freelancer can turn to marketing efforts during the last part of the day.

What the freelancer should not do is start the day writing an article for a blog that is part of marketing efforts even though that is more enjoyable than drafting legal documents or a status report. It is too easy to get caught up in that project and then not have enough time during the workday to complete the legal work that is going to generate revenue. That means either the work is not completed, getting pushed off to another day, or the freelancer works later than intended to finish the work, negatively impacting work-life balance.

Whether considering work on a daily, weekly, or monthly basis, be sure to allocate specific time blocks for revenue-generating work, administrative tasks, marketing efforts, and professional development. Prioritize them in terms of the relative importance of each task, any deadlines, and the impact on revenue. By having dedicated times for different tasks, a freelancer can ensure that all areas necessary to sustain a law practice receive attention in a timely manner.

Managing workflow is critical for time management. It is impossible to prioritize if there are five projects each requiring hours of attention that are all due on the same day. Planning ahead, therefore, is critical to managing workflow. Looking at the tasks that need to be completed every week or every month will help with prioritization. It is rare that a freelancer will have multiple clients assigning projects that all have the same, immediate deadlines. Set realistic deadlines to complete each task. Make sure to build in time buffers to accommodate unexpected events or emergencies.

For example, a freelancer who does not manage workload well and who is coming up on a client deadline to complete a project the next day will not be able to take the time necessary to respond to an emergency inquiry from a potential new client that requires a few hours of research. However, had the freelancer built in a buffer to complete the project, there would be no problem spending a few hours to meet the needs of a potential new client. If a freelancer has good workflow management and can expeditiously respond to a potential new client inquiry, there is a much greater potential to secure that new client than if the freelancer had to put the potential client off for a few days to meet a deadline for another client.

Similarly, suppose a client has an unexpected family emergency and needs a freelancer to take over a project for a few days. A freelancer who is overcommitted will not be able to do that. A freelancer who has good time management skills has a better chance of being able to step in, resulting in client satisfaction and appreciation for the freelancer, which will hopefully lead to repeat work.

Emergencies or unexpected events need not be work related. If a freelancer is required to take care of a sick child who is home from school, building in a buffer and not running right up against deadlines will avoid the need to explain to a client that the freelancer was unable to complete a project because of a sick kid. If a freelancer plans on completing a project a few days before the deadline, then spending half a day with a plumber when a frozen pipe bursts will not cause undue stress regarding work. By planning ahead, a freelancer can proactively manage workload and avoid last-minute rushes.

Regularly review and assess how tasks are prioritized and adjust if necessary. As circumstances change, adjust the prioritization. If, for example, an out of state friend decides to pay a visit, by blocking off time for that visit in advance, a freelancer can see what work-related projects need to be moved and can adjust scheduling to accommodate that work at another time. Being flexible and open to reevaluating a task list not only allows a freelancer to make changes to balance work and life, but also ensures that a freelancer can focus on the most important and high-impact activities at any given time while at work, thereby increasing productivity and maximizing revenue.

One of the challenges of managing workflow is knowing how to handle large projects. Large projects can be overwhelming and lead to procrastination.

Break them down. By breaking down a large project into smaller, more manageable tasks, it is easier to make steady progress, to maintain momentum, to complete the project in a timely manner, and to avoid feeling overwhelmed.

For example, suppose there is an assignment to provide a status report in a complex litigation case involving multiple defendants and a voluminous amount of documentary and testimonial evidence. First review the pleadings to get an overview of the allegations in the case and the defenses raised. Then go through any motions that have been filed to gain insight into any legal issues that are central to the case. Next, analyze the written discovery responses to determine the evidence that will be relied on by the parties to support the claims and defenses. Conduct any legal research necessary to evaluate the primary issues identified in the pleadings or other court filings. Evaluate the evidence and the legal arguments to assess the factual and legal strengths and weaknesses of the parties' respective positions. Finally, describe each step in a status report. By breaking down a large project into these smaller tasks, a freelancer can structure an approach to completing the assignment.

Or, take the example of a freelance lawyer working on drafting a contract for a client who is starting a new business venture. First, identify the business objectives. Next, research industry standards, regulations, and compliance requirements. Then analyze contracts for similar businesses and identify commonly used provisions and relevant legal issues. Create an outline of the contract structure, including key provisions like definitions, obligations, payment terms, intellectual property considerations, and dispute resolution.

After creating the outline, collaborate with the client law firm to make sure the outline aligns with the client's goals before turning to drafting the contract itself. Begin drafting the contract by focusing on the essential contractual provisions—the parties' identities, the purpose of the agreement, and the key contractual obligations. Then customize the contract. Identify additional provisions that should be included based on client-specific requirements or industry and legal standards. Review the contract once a draft is complete to ensure clarity, consistency, and accuracy.

Breaking down a project to its smaller components will make projects seem less overwhelming and will allow a freelancer to approach the project systematically. Managing workload is one of the biggest challenges most lawyers face. The variability of work in terms of complexity, type of work, and deadlines makes it difficult to establish a consistent workflow. Unexpected family interruptions, client emergencies, or court appearances often disrupt planned workflows. While flexibility is key, there are two things that are invaluable in managing workload.

The first is to manage expectations. Most lawyers usually know well beforehand if they are going to be out of the office for an extended period, whether it is for a trial, to attend a conference, or to go on vacation. Inform clients well in advance. Set up an out-of-office message for any client who emails or calls during that time, stating the period of absence with a way of contact in the case of emergencies only. Effective communication with clients and professional colleagues is a critical aspect of managing workload.

The second way to help manage workload is to automate routine, administrative tasks as much as possible to enable a freelancer to focus on billable work instead. Automation eliminates the need to manually perform repetitive jobs, which frees up time for higher-value activities. Automated processes are also consistent and reliable, reducing the risk of errors that can occur when a lawyer does the same tasks over and over again manually. Automatization helps freelancers work smarter, not harder, so it is a valuable tool for managing workflow.

By implementing these strategies, freelance lawyers can effectively prioritize tasks, balance workflow, and optimize time management, striking a balance between revenue-generating work, administrative responsibilities, professional development, and personal time. Time management allows for a more structured and organized approach to freelancing, which will result in increased productivity, client satisfaction, work-life balance, and overall success. As illustrated earlier, one of the components of managing workflow is to make sure to budget time to operate a practice. While seemingly a no-brainer, making the time for law firm administration is easier said than done.

CHAPTER 16

Budgeting Time to Administer a Freelance Practice

"It takes as much energy to wish as it does to plan."

—Eleanor Roosevelt

No freelance law practice is going to run itself. Running a successful free-lance law practice requires more than just legal expertise. One of the biggest pitfalls to becoming a freelancer is not calculating for the time necessary to administer a practice. Freelancers must not only provide legal services, but need to also effectively manage the administrative aspects of their law practice to make sure it functions smoothly and effectively. Billing, financial recordkeeping, scheduling, document management, IT management, and other administrative tasks all take time. Allocating the time to complete administrative tasks rather than leaving them as an afterthought is critical.

Effective administration helps sustain and build a freelancer's professional reputation. Timely responses to inquiries, prompt billing, and well-maintained records demonstrate professionalism and instill confidence in the hiring law firms and lawyers. A well-managed practice creates a positive impression and enhances a freelancer's reputation. A poorly managed practice, on the other hand, does just the opposite. Little things go a long way. For example, a freelancer who timely invoices law firms every month creates an air of professionalism that will not be there for a freelancer who always must be reminded by a hiring law firm to send out invoices.

Running any law practice involves various administrative aspects that are essential for its smooth operation. Sound financial management is critical for any freelance law practice to thrive. This includes budgeting, recording time, billing clients, tracking expenses, handling accounts receivable and payable, financial reporting, and tax compliance. Allocating time for these types of financially related administrative tasks will help freelancers avoid unnecessary financial complications.

Tax Reporting

Timely tax reporting will avoid the need to pay penalties and interest for late payments. Spending time on accounts receivable and payable will ensure the timely collection and payment of invoices, which will result in an accurate financial picture. Having an accurate financial picture is critical for maintaining a healthy cash flow. In short, in the absence of effective financial management, a freelancer cannot make informed decisions about a practice's growth and profitability.

Time Tracking and Invoicing

For those freelancers who bill hourly, one of the most important tips for effective time management is to bill contemporaneously with the legal services being provided. An easy way to do that is to leave time management or billing software open on the computer while working. That way, each time a task is completed, the freelancer can immediately record the time it took to complete the task. At a minimum, a freelancer who bills hourly should record all time for the day by the end of each day. It is much easier to capture time when recording it contemporaneously with working than to try and recreate the time at the end of the month when it is time to invoice a client.

In the busy and demanding nature of a freelance law practice, it is easy for lawyers to inadvertently forget to bill for certain tasks. Imagine how hard it would be on the thirtieth day of the month to try and remember the numerous phone calls, emails, and other interactions with clients, the exact nature of legal research performed during the first few days of the month, or how much time was spent drafting a contract. This work, when totaled, can take hours of time but may be overlooked when trying to remember it nearly a month later. To minimize the chances of forgetting to bill for certain tasks, it is critical for freelancers to diligently record their time.

Whether billing hourly or according to a different billing model, timely invoicing is also critical for reasons already discussed. Sending out bills every month or regularly is not only important for accurate financial projections and cash flow but also reveals a sense of professionalism that untimely invoicing will negate.

Document Management

In addition to financial administrative tasks, document management takes time as well. Document management involves the tasks related to organizing and storing legal documents so they can be retrieved efficiently. For example, a freelancer who works on multiple cases for different law firms should develop processes to store documents in a hierarchy of folders, first by the name of hiring law firm and then by the ultimate client being served by the hiring law firm. Within the client file, documents can be stored based on the type of document. Different types of documents can include correspondence, pleadings, motions, or other court filings, legal memoranda, contracts, discovery, and client-produced documentation. This method would look something like the following:

- ABC Law Firm
  - Client X
    - Client Documents
    - Correspondence
    - Discovery
    - Expert Witnesses
    - Lay Witnesses
    - Motions
    - Pleadings
  - Client Y
    - Contracts and Leases
    - Corporate Organization Documents
    - Financial Documents
    - Minutes of Board Meetings
    - Negotiation of CEO's Employment Contract
    - Solar Lease
- XYZ Law Firm
  - Client A
    - Administrative Agency Records
    - District Court Litigation
    - Appellate Litigation
  - Client B
    - Residential Purchase Agreement and Addenda
    - Inspections
    - Repair Work
    - Title Documents

In this example, the freelancer's two clients are ABC Law Firm and XYZ Law Firm. ABC Law Firm engaged the freelancer to work on matters for Client X and Client Y. Client X is involved in a lawsuit. Therefore, the folders under Client X are organized pursuant to the type of litigation documents such as pleadings, discovery, and lay and expert witnesses. Client Y is a corporate client needing different types of business advice. Client Y's documents are organized according to the types of corporate documents pursuant to which it operates, such as organizational documents and meeting minutes, as well as according to the specific matters the freelancer is helping ABC Law Firm with, like the negotiation of the CEO's employment contract and a solar lease.

XYZ Law Firm engaged the freelancer to help with matters involving Client A and Client B. The freelancer is drafting an appellate brief for Client A stemming from a charge of discrimination that was litigated at the administrative level before the Equal Employment Opportunity Commission (EEOC). After the EEOC issued a right to sue letter, the employee filed a district court lawsuit and won at trial. The employer then appealed the district court verdict. The freelancer organized the documents by the three different stages of litigation, the administrative, trial, and appellate stages. The freelancer is also helping XYZ Law Firm with a real estate purchase involving Client B and has organized the documents by type as they relate to the purchase transaction.

Creating a consistent file structure for organizing legal documents like folders and subfolders based on practice areas, clients, cases, or specific document types will ensure their easy identification and retrieval. Freelancers should assign unique identifiers to each document to facilitate easy retrieval. Unique identifiers can include case numbers, client names, document types, dates, or any other relevant categorization system. However, the categorization system should be the same for all documents. For example, in a litigation matter, pleadings and motions can be saved starting with the number that appears on the court docket followed by the identity of the party filing it and then the name of the court filing. This would look like:

001 Plaintiff's Complaint
002 Defendant's Answer to Complaint
003 Plaintiff's Motion to Amend Complaint
004 Defendant's Response in Opposition to Amend Complaint
005 Plaintiff's Reply in Support of Motion to Amend Complaint

Correspondence can be named by its date, the type of correspondence, and the identities of the party sending and receiving it. This would look like:

031223 letter from freelancer to Law Firm XYZ
031523 email from Law Firm XYZ to freelancer
031723 letter from freelancer to Client A (draft)
032023 status report from freelancer to Law Firm XYZ

There are many different naming and organizational conventions. The important thing is to keep them consistent to be able to search for and locate documents quickly and efficiently.

Document management also involves capturing and storing documents. For example, documents a freelancer receives that are attached to emails need to be downloaded and stored. If a freelancer has physical copies of documents, they need to be scanned into digital copies and stored.

Document retention and disposal is also a consideration. Different states have different requirements regarding document retention. For example, some states require lawyers to maintain documents for at least seven years after representation ceases. However, hiring law firms might have different requirements, especially for freelancers who might not be bound as independent contractors to the same rules for lawyers providing direct client representation.

Efficient document management ensures that freelancers can easily locate, access, and work with the necessary documents while maintaining data security and while complying with legal and client requirements. Efficient document management will enhance a freelancer's productivity. In addition to effective document management, adhering to legal and ethical standards is also fundamental to any law practice. For example, budgeting time for conflict checks is critical so a freelancer does not run afoul of the ethical prohibitions against conflicts of interest with concurrent or former clients. Allocating time to conduct conflict checks plays a crucial role in maintaining ethical standards.

Continuing Legal Education

Because the legal profession is dynamic, especially for freelancers working in an emerging area of the law, like cryptocurrency, marijuana law, or artificial intelligence, freelancers must continually make sure they stay up-to-date on relevant areas of law to not just meet their ethical obligations of competence and to maintain licensure, but also to stay relevant and to become a leader in a particular area of practice. Budgeting time for administration allows freelance lawyers to allocate the necessary hours for professional development and continuing education, which can involve attending seminars, reading legal publications, or participating in webinars. By staying updated, freelancers can continue to deliver high-quality services to their clients to maintain or improve their professional reputations in a competitive legal market.

Rainmaking

Freelancers should also budget time for client development or rainmaking. This might be time spent marketing or advertising or time to create content to publish on a website. It could also include time spent networking or at speaking engagements. Freelancers need to develop marketing and advertising strategies, effectively promote themselves, manage an online presence, network, and participate in business development activities. This all takes time.

Allocating Administrative Time

Allocating specific time blocks dedicated solely to working on administrative tasks is a way to make sure the necessary administration happens. Blocking time helps create a clear separation between legal work and administrative responsibilities. For example, a freelancer could dedicate 30 minutes at the beginning of each week to make sure a website is updated. Or, a freelancer could dedicate the last hour of a work week on a Friday to creating content to use for marketing and advertising. Building a regular bar association luncheon into a freelancer's schedule will ensure that networking activities take place.

Begin by assessing what administrative tasks need to be accomplished on a regular basis. Some might be daily, like recording time. Some might be monthly, like invoicing clients. Some might be quarterly, like tax reporting. Some tasks might not occur on a regular basis, like attending continuing education seminars. Set forth specific time slots each day, week, or month solely for administrative tasks. The last half an hour of each day could be focused on billing. The first half of the first day of each month could be focused on sending out client invoices for the services provided from the previous month. Each quarter, time can be set aside for tax reporting. By designating these blocks of time, freelancers can create a routine practice to ensure that administrative tasks receive the attention they deserve.

During the time blocked for administering a law practice, minimize distractions that can hinder productivity. This is especially important if there is an aversion for law firm administration. Turn off email and app notifications. Put cell phones on silent mode. Create a work environment conducive to completing administrative tasks by reducing possible interruptions. By blocking time for administrative tasks, freelancers can ensure that essential administrative tasks are given the attention they require.

> To run a business, lawyers must understand their own skills and what they can do themselves and where they need help. For example, should I do my own bookkeeping? During my first year in solo practice, I sat with a pile of receipts for about four and a half months because I knew how to do bookkeeping. I had done a lot of bookkeeping and thought I could take on the bookkeeping function of my firm myself. But I never got to it. Ultimately, I had to hire someone to do it and I have never done it myself since. I had the skills to do the work but not the time or bandwidth. Not to mention that every hour I spend doing a bookkeeping task was an hour less billable time. That said, I still must know what is happening in my business. I need to read accounting reports and make sure things are being reconciled properly. I cannot delegate those tasks, but I can delegate data entry. So, know your skills and understand the time commitment it takes for administration. What are you good at and what do you have the time for? If you are not great at something or do not have the time to do it well, find someone to help you.[1]

---

1 D. McBryde, Esq., personal communication, Aug. 29, 2023.

In sum, effective management of the administrative aspects of a law practice is critical to build and sustain it. It allows freelancers to focus on providing exceptional legal services to clients while also ensuring that the practice operates efficiently and maintains compliance with applicable rules and laws. However, even the best administered freelance law practice will not be successful unless freelancers are aware of certain ethical pitfalls and how to avoid them.

PART V

Avoiding Pitfalls

CHAPTER 17

The Power of
Engagement Letters

"An attorney may not be held liable for failing to act outside the scope of a retainer."

*Attallah v. Milbank, Tweed, Hadley & McCloy,
LLP*, 168 A.D.3d 1026 (N.Y. App. Div. 2019)

In 2011, the law firm of Milbank, Tweed, Hadley & McCloy agreed to represent Ahdy Attallah regarding his expulsion from the New York College of Osteopathic Medicine. As reported in the published decision, the parties executed an engagement letter that provided:

Our services will include all activities necessary and appropriate in our judgment to investigate and consider options that may be available to urge administrative reconsideration of your dismissal from the New York College of Osteopathic Medicine (the "College"). This engagement does not, however, encompass any form of litigation or, to the extent ethically prohibited in this circumstance, the threat of litigation, to resolve this matter. This engagement will end upon your re-admittance to the College or upon a determination by the attorneys working on this matter that no non-litigation mechanisms are available to assist you. The scope of the engagement may not be expanded orally or by conduct; it may only be expanded by a writing signed by our Director of Public Service.[1]

Despite the law firm's efforts to resolve the dispute on Mr. Attallah's behalf without resorting to litigation, the College refused to reconsider its dismissal of him. Mr. Attallah then sued the law firm to recover damages for legal malpractice for failing to negotiate the administrative reconsideration of his dismissal, for failing to file a lawsuit against the College, and for not providing legal advice regarding the efficacy of commencing a defamation action.

---

1 Attallah v. Milbank, Tweed, Hadley & McCloy, LLP, 168 A.D.3d 1026, 1027 (N.Y. App. Div. 2019).

The appellate court, considering the engagement letter, upheld the law firm's motion to dismiss Mr. Attallah's complaint. According to the engagement letter, the law firm never promised to negotiate an administrative resolution; rather, the law firm agreed to "investigate and consider options that may be available to urge administrative reconsideration." The appellate court found that the only promise was to investigate and consider whether there were any options available to urge the school to reconsider Mr. Attallah's expulsion. Anything else was outside the scope of engagement.

Because a lawyer cannot be held liable for failing to act outside the scope of a retainer agreement, the appellate court held that the law firm could not be held liable for its alleged failure to negotiate with the College, to commence a lawsuit against the College, or to provide advice about the viability of a defamation lawsuit. Therefore, finding that those acts fell outside the scope of the engagement letter, the appellate court upheld the dismissal of the legal malpractice complaint against the law firm.

Engagement letters are legal documents. They establish the terms and conditions of the attorney-client relationship. For freelance lawyers, they set the parameters of the relationship between the freelancer and the hiring lawyer or law firm. While engagement letters serve many purposes, one of the primary benefits of an engagement letter is the protection it can provide against legal liability for freelance lawyers.

As illustrated by the *Attallah* case, an engagement letter typically outlines the specific scope of work a freelancer agrees to undertake for a hiring lawyer or law firm. By specifically defining the scope of representation, an engagement letter not only helps to prevent misunderstandings as to the nature of the legal services to be provided, but it can also help ensure a freelancer is not held responsible for matters beyond the agreed-upon scope of representation. For example, an engagement letter that sets out a freelancer's agreement to assist a law firm only by providing legal analysis of an issue after researching it and preparing a legal memorandum will help negate any perception that the freelancer will also draft a motion based on the legal analysis.

In setting forth the scope of representation, an engagement letter can outline the exact nature of the legal services to be provided and the deadlines for doing so. For example, the engagement letter can state that a freelancer agrees to draft a motion for summary judgment within 30 days and that if the hiring law firm wants revisions, those revisions would necessitate a separate engagement. Conversely, the engagement letter can state that the freelancer will prepare a motion for summary judgment and provide a draft to the hiring law firm 10 days prior to the dispositive motions deadline so the law firm can decide whether revisions are necessary, and, if so, the freelancer will revise the draft motion and present a final version to the hiring law firm three days prior to the dispositive motion deadline.

Specifying the exact legal services a freelancer agrees to provide will also clarify compensation. Using the preceding example, if a freelancer agrees to a flat-fee rate for drafting a summary judgment motion, it is important to understand whether the flat fee includes just an initial draft or encompasses revisions as well.

Compensation provisions in an engagement letter should specify when the hiring law firm will pay a freelancer. Maybe payment will occur 30 days from the law firm's receipt of the freelancer's invoice. However, if the hiring law firm represents a governmental entity, it might only receive payment quarterly. In that event, for cash flow reasons, perhaps the hiring law firm would not want to pay the freelancer until it gets paid. Likewise, if the ultimate client is late paying the hiring law firm, the law firm might not want to pay the freelancer until it can collect its fees. Or, if the end client defaults on the obligation to pay the hiring law firm, perhaps the law firm might try not to pay the freelancer at all.

Generally, because freelancers are independent contractors, they would not bear the risk of whether the ultimate client pays late or defaults on a payment obligation to the hiring law firm. However, if a freelancer has good cash flow, provides regular legal services to a particular law firm, and has a good relationship with that law firm, then maybe the freelancer would consider waiting until the law firm collects payment from the end client before requiring payment from the law firm to provide a unique value proposition to that law firm. Regardless of the nature of the compensation arrangement, setting it forth in an engagement letter will help prevent misunderstandings.

This includes which party is responsible for paying expenses and taxes, if applicable. In states with gross receipts tax on services, for example, the engagement letter should specify which party is responsible for charging for and collecting those taxes. In addition, if the freelancer agrees to travel for a hearing or deposition, there should be an understanding as to whether the freelancer can charge for travel time or mileage.

Regarding the independent contractor relationship between a freelancer and the hiring law firm, engagement letters also often outline the duties of both parties. For example, an engagement letter can state that the hiring lawyer makes all final decisions after a review of the work product. That could mean the hiring lawyer reviews and possibly revises a brief prior to filing it, evaluates a contract prior to presenting it to the other side for consideration, or assesses a legal analysis prior to discussing it with the ultimate client. By explicitly defining the obligations of both the freelancer and the hiring lawyer or law firm, the engagement letter will help establish the standard of care, which can provide a defense against a legal malpractice claim.

This relationship between the independent contractor-freelancer and the law firm should be spelled out in the engagement letter. The engagement letter, therefore, should clearly provide that the freelancer is an independent contractor engaged by the hiring lawyer or law firm and that there is no attorney-client relationship between the freelancer and the hiring lawyer's or law firm's ultimate client. This way, the ultimate client would not have grounds to directly sue the freelancer because there is no attorney-client relationship between the two.

Engagement letters should address conflict of interest issues as well, whether to state that no conflicts exist or to address potential conflicts of interest and to confirm informed consent to the representation in situations where there is an actual or potential conflict of interest. This will help protect a freelancer against claims of breaches of professional responsibilities or ethical duties and will mitigate the risk of being held liable based on a conflict of interest situation.

Addressing legal malpractice coverage can also be useful to include in an engagement letter. For example, the engagement letter can specify whether the hiring law firm's legal malpractice policy covers the freelancer or whether the freelancer has a professional liability policy independent from the hiring law firm's policy.

Document storage and retention is another issue to cover in an engagement letter. Perhaps the hiring law firm wants a freelancer to destroy all confidential documents at the conclusion of the limited representation. Alternatively, suppose there is a state rule or law requiring the freelancer to retain documents for a certain amount of time after the representation concludes. Either way, the freelancer's obligation to retain or destroy documents should be spelled out in an engagement letter.

Engagement letters can contain a dispute resolution provision. For example, in the event of a dispute between the freelancer and a hiring lawyer or law firm, the engagement letter can specify that the parties mediate, arbitrate, or engage in some other alternative dispute resolution mechanism prior to or instead of litigating. This can help limit a freelancer's exposure, as well as litigation costs and all the uncertainties that come with litigation.

Communicating when the engagement has ended will also help prevent misunderstandings. Therefore, every time an engagement ends, a freelancer should send a letter closing the matter. For example, if a freelancer has agreed to do a due diligence document review as part of a merger and acquisition, once the due diligence is complete, the freelancer can send a letter stating that the work is complete. That way, the hiring law firm will not expect any further services from the freelancer on the matter.

While engagement letters are valuable to manage expectations, prevent misunderstandings, and limit legal liability, they are not foolproof. As illustrated by the *Attallah* case, despite an engagement letter that very specifically limited the scope of engagement, the law firm was still sued. Engagement letters will not always shield freelancers from all claims or allegations of wrongdoing. In addition, the enforceability of an engagement letter may vary depending on local laws and regulations. For example, some states may require the hiring lawyer or law firm to sign the engagement letter for it to be binding. Other states may limit the enforceability of mandatory dispute resolution provisions. Therefore, it is critical for freelancers to understand the applicable rules and laws in their state when drafting an engagement letter.

Writing engagement letters when a freelancer helps the same law firm with many projects may not be practical or necessary. For example, if a freelancer writes a motion for summary judgment, reviews a contract, prepares a legal memorandum, handles a deposition, and interviews witnesses, all in different cases but for the same law firm, sending separate engagement letters for each matter might seem like overkill. When a freelancer handles many projects for a particular lawyer or law firm, that freelancer can send a letter at the outset of the working relationship outlining general matters such as conflict of interest policies, document retention procedures, and billing arrangements, with a much simpler email for each specific matter that sets forth details about the particular project, such as scope and deadlines.

In sum, engagement letters serve as a critical framework to outline the terms, responsibilities, and expectations between a freelancer and the client lawyer or law firm. By providing a clear and written record of the scope of legal services, fees, and deadlines, engagement letters establish the foundation for a successful relationship between the parties, protecting not only the interests of both parties but also enhancing communication and minimizing the potential for misunderstandings. Engagement letters, like the sample one in Appendix E, help manage expectations and prevent scope creep, creating a proactive approach that fosters transparency, trust, and professionalism. While engagement letters are one tool in a freelance lawyer's arsenal for avoiding misunderstandings, knowing how to avoid conflicts of interest will also foster long-lasting client relationships that will lead to a successful freelance law practice.

CHAPTER 18

Avoiding Conflicts of Interest

"In the nature of law practice . . . conflicting responsibilities are encountered. Virtually all difficult ethical problems arise from conflict between a lawyer's responsibilities to clients, to the legal system and to the lawyer's own interest in remaining an ethical person . . . ."
—Preamble to the American Bar Association's Model Rules of Professional Conduct

Lawyers have a duty to avoid conflicts of interest and to ensure that their representation of clients is not compromised due to conflicting obligations. There are different guidelines regarding conflicts of interest. The American Bar Association (ABA) has promulgated Model Rules of Professional Conduct. These are only models; states have their own rules that are applicable to the lawyers licensed by those states. Most states' rules are based on the ABA's Model Rules. Therefore, consideration of the ABA's Model Rules is helpful to inform issues surrounding conflicts of interest.

Freelance lawyers, who can work independently for multiple lawyers or law firms, face particular issues when it comes to conflicts of interest that other practitioners do not have to deal with. Working with a wide range of lawyers or law firms who service diverse clients across various practice areas and locations can increase the likelihood that a conflict of interest will arise. Because working for different lawyers or law firms requires a freelancer to maintain independence and loyalty to each lawyer or law firm separately, conflicts can arise when the interests of the ultimate clients of different lawyers or law firms are opposed. For example, a freelancer helping one law firm draft standards for roadway safety for a state's department of transportation would face a conflict situation if also supporting another lawyer in a lawsuit against the department of transportation arising from the unsafe construction of a highway.

Potential conflicts can sometimes be hard for freelance lawyers to discover. Freelancers may have limited access to comprehensive information about the ultimate clients they are serving. A freelancer working on a legal analysis of a specific issue for a large law firm, for example, might not be aware of the name of the ultimate client, the identity of the client's adversaries, or even the specific legal matter the freelancer has been engaged to handle. This limited information can make it challenging to identify conflicts of interest.

Freelancers must navigate potential conflicts carefully to avoid compromising their professional integrity or violating ethical obligations. Freelancers rely heavily on their professional reputations and the trust of the lawyers and law firms hiring them. Conflicts of interest can undermine this trust and hurt a freelancer's reputation if not managed properly. Maintaining transparency, ensuring informed consent when representing potentially conflicting clients, and promptly disclosing any potential conflicts are essential to avoid violating ethical obligations, to maintain a solid professional reputation, and to build long-term relationships with hiring lawyers and law firms.

The ABA's Model Rules of Professional Conduct set forth guidance for avoiding conflicts of interest. Rules 1.7 and 1.9 are those that are most applicable in the freelancing context. Model Rule 1.7 is the conflict of interest rule for current clients:

Model Rule 1.7: Conflict of Interest: Current Clients

(a) Except as provided in paragraph (b), a lawyer shall not represent a client if the representation involves a concurrent conflict of interest. A concurrent conflict of interest exists if:

   (1) the representation of one client will be directly adverse to another client; or
   (2) there is a significant risk that the representation of one of more clients will be materially limited by the lawyer's responsibilities to another client, a former client or a third person or by a personal interest of the lawyer.

(b) Notwithstanding the existence of a concurrent conflict of interest under paragraph (a), a lawyer may represent a client if:

   (1) the lawyer reasonably believes that the lawyer will be able to provide competent and diligent representation to each affected client;
   (2) the representation is not prohibited by law;
   (3) the representation does not involve the assertion of a claim by one client against another client represented by the lawyer in the same litigation or other proceeding before a tribunal; and
   (4) each affected client gives informed consent, confirmed in writing.

A scenario that would create a conflict of interest for a freelancer under Model Rule 1.7 would be if two different lawyers hired a freelancer to provide legal services related to both sides of a contract dispute involving a residential real estate transaction. For example, assume a buyer and seller entered into a residential purchase agreement that fell through because the buyer's inspection revealed a leaky roof that the seller did not want to fix. Lawyer A is seeking to enforce the terms of the purchase agreement on behalf of the seller. Lawyer B is contesting the enforceability of the purchase agreement on behalf of the buyer due to the defective roof and the seller's refusal to remedy it.

If the freelancer were to provide legal services to both Lawyer A and to Lawyer B, there would be a concurrent conflict of interest because the interests of the two ultimate clients are materially adverse to each other. Therefore, to comply with Model Rule 1.7, a freelance lawyer should decline one of the representations or obtain informed consent from both Lawyer A and Lawyer B, who, in turn, should seek informed consent from their clients, after disclosing the conflict of interest.

Knowing that there is a concurrent conflict of interest in this scenario might be easy or might be difficult. If Lawyers A and B both gave the freelancer a copy of the residential purchase agreement and asked for a legal analysis of its enforceability, the freelancer would obviously know that Lawyers A and B were representing clients who were materially adverse to each other. However, suppose Lawyer A, without providing a copy of the contract at issue, tasked the freelancer with a generic research project to analyze a particular state's law regarding the enforceability of a contract when compliance with one of its terms is onerous and Lawyer B, who provided a copy of the contract to the freelancer, tasked the freelancer with analyzing the enforceability of the contract. The freelancer would not necessarily know in that scenario that Lawyer A's and Lawyer B's clients were on opposite sides of the same real estate transaction.

However, an initial assessment of the matters of engagement based on the information available may raise red flags and help identify the potential conflict. For example, in the preceding scenario, the nature of legal services required is the same. Lawyer A and Lawyer B both want help with an issue regarding a real estate contract's enforceability. The timing of the request for services is also the same. The information, taken as a whole, suggests that the two matters might be related, warranting additional communication to determine whether a conflict exists.

Of course, seeking sufficient information up front about the nature of representation, such as the scope of work and the parties involved would alleviate the guessing game in the first place. Requesting as much relevant information as possible before providing legal services will help a freelancer make an informed decision about whether undertaking the representation would result in a conflict of interest.

Conflicts of interest do not just arise from incompatible concurrent representation. Conflicts can also occur when a freelancer is working on a matter that conflicts with legal services the freelancer provided in the past. The ABA's Model Rule 1.9 addresses that situation:

Model Rule 1.9: Duties to Former Clients

(a) A lawyer who has formerly represented a client in a matter shall not thereafter represent another person in the same or a substantially related matter in which that person's interests are materially adverse to the interests of the former client unless the former client gives informed consent, confirmed in writing.

(b) A lawyer shall not knowingly represent a person in the same or a substantially related matter in which a firm with which the lawyer formerly was associated had previously represented a client

(1) whose interests are materially adverse to that person; and

(2) about whom the lawyer had acquired information protected by Rules 1.6 and 1.9(c) that is material to the matter; unless the former client gives informed consent, confirmed in writing.

(c) A lawyer who has formerly represented a client in a matter or whose present or former firm has formerly represented a client in a matter shall not thereafter:

(1) use information relating to the representation to the disadvantage of the former client except as these Rules would permit or require with respect to a client, or when the information has become generally known; or

(2) reveal information relating to the representation except as these Rules would permit or require with respect to a client.

A situation in which a freelancer might violate Model Rule 1.9 would arise if the freelancer, who previously assisted a law firm handing a particular matter for a client, subsequently works on a substantially related matter for another law firm that is materially adverse to the interests of the former client. Take, for example, a scenario where Law Firm A engaged a freelancer to handle a trademark registration application for one of its clients, Company X. After the freelancer finishes the work for Law Firm A, Law Firm B seeks the freelancer's assistance in a trademark infringement lawsuit on behalf of its client. However, the lawsuit is one that Law Firm B filed against Company X.

In this situation, the freelancer's work for Law Firm A on behalf of Company X in a trademark-related matter, even though in the past, is substantially related to the trademark infringement lawsuit filed against Company X by Law Firm B. By working for Law Firm B on that matter, the freelancer risks violating Model Rule 1.9. Again, the freelancer should either decline Law Firm B's assignment or obtain informed consent waiving the conflict.

Freelancers can help avoid conflicts of interest by leveraging technology to manage their practice. Conflict checking software or case management software with built-in conflict checking capabilities allow a freelancer to input information about the ultimate clients and search for potential conflicts by cross-referencing existing and former clients. This type of software will help identify any conflicts before accepting new engagements.

For freelancers who do work for only a handful of law firms or who only handle a few cases, something as simple as a searchable Excel spreadsheet could serve as a conflicts database. However, for freelancers who work for many different lawyers on many different matters, a more sophisticated conflicts database will probably be necessary. Importantly, many errors and omissions insurers will require certification that a freelancer has a process for identifying and preventing conflicts of interest prior to issuing a professional liability policy.

A question about potential conflicts of interest specific to freelancers arises when a freelancer serves in an "of counsel" capacity. Sometimes, a law firm might want to list a freelancer who provides ongoing legal services as "of counsel" on its website and letterhead. Being "of counsel" typically refers to a lawyer who has a close and ongoing relationship with a law firm but is not a partner or associate. Instead, "of counsel" refers to a lawyer who serves in a consulting or advisory capacity to the law firm. If a freelancer provides ongoing legal services to multiple law firms, some or all of them might want to identify the freelancer as "of counsel" to their firms. One reason could be that a law firm's client has a policy of only paying for legal services billed by a lawyer identified on a firm's letterhead, which is the case with some insurance companies.

There is no prohibition under the ABA's Model Rules regarding a freelancer serving as "of counsel" to multiple law firms. To the contrary, the ABA has issued ethics opinions permitting a lawyer's affiliation with multiple law firms as "of counsel." In the ABA's Formal Ethics Opinion 90–357, for example, the ABA's Standing Committee on Ethics and Professional Responsibility concluded that a lawyer could be "of counsel" to multiple law firms. The limit is determined not by the number of firms a lawyer has an "of counsel" relationship with, but by the nature of the relationship between the lawyer and law firm. If there is a "close, regular, personal" relationship between the lawyer and law firm, a lawyer can be "of counsel."

Although there is no predetermined numerical limit as to how many "of counsel" relationships a freelancer can have according to the ABA's guidance, as a practical matter, the number is limited because a freelancer cannot have a close, regular, and personal relationship with too many law firms. At some point, the number of relationships would be too great to maintain the closeness, regularity, and personal nature of them that is necessary for an "of counsel" relationship.

The prevailing view in many states is in line with the ABA's guidance; however, some states have adopted the opposite rule in state ethics opinions, allowing a lawyer to only have a single "of counsel" relationship. Therefore, prior to a freelancer establishing an "of counsel" relationship with more than one law firm, it is important to review a particular state's guidance on the issue.

A freelance lawyer's diligence in avoiding conflicts of interest is critical to upholding ethical standards, protecting client interests, and maintaining a professional reputation. Upholding professional integrity and maintaining the trust of clients and the legal community require strict adherence to the ethical rules and professional obligations. A failure to do so can result in not just reputational damage, but it can also lead to legal consequences, including professional disciplinary action or legal malpractice claims. Conflicts checks, clear communication and transparency, and informed consent are essential to ensure the smooth operation of a freelance law practice that minimizes the risk of conflicts-related complications or disputes. By avoiding conflicts of interest, a freelance lawyer can provide competent and unbiased representation, fostering trust and confidence in the freelancer, as well as in the legal profession as a whole. The same can be said for maintaining client confidentiality.

CHAPTER 19

Maintaining Attorney-Client Confidentiality

"A lawyer should keep in confidence information relating to representation of a client . . . ."

—Preamble to the American Bar Association's Model Rules of Professional Conduct

Just as lawyers have a duty to avoid conflicts of interest and to ensure that their representation of clients is not compromised due to conflicting obligations, a lawyer also has a duty to keep information relating to the representation confidential. The American Bar Association (ABA) Model Rule 1.6 provides that generally, "[a] lawyer shall not reveal information relating to the representation of a client unless the client gives informed consent . . . ."

The obligation to keep information relating to the representation confidential applies to freelance lawyers working for a law firm or another lawyer. Just because a freelancer's client is another law firm or lawyer, as opposed to the ultimate client, does not mean that a freelancer can avoid the fiduciary duty of confidentiality. Many times, a freelancer will be privy to confidential client information while providing services to a lawyer or law firm. For example, a freelancer who has remote access to a law firm's server will have access to the confidential client information of all the law firm's clients, not just information about or from the client on the matter the law firm engaged the freelancer to work on. Therefore, a freelancer must prioritize client confidentiality and take the necessary steps to protect sensitive information.

Remote work raises many confidentiality issues. In a traditional law firm, it would be unusual for somebody who does not work at the firm to have direct access to electronic and hard files. Although certainly possible, someone not associated with a law firm using its computers or rifling through paper files would raise eyebrows. For a freelancer working from home, however, a child using the freelancer's computer to do homework might not seem so strange. It is likewise easy to imagine a guest wandering into a home office to use a computer to read the news or look up flight information. However, if there is access through that computer to client information, there are client confidentiality implications. That is one reason why having a dedicated workspace and equipment when working remotely that is not used for other purposes or by anybody else is so important.

Even with a dedicated workspace, however, there are still challenges in safeguarding client information. Home computers tend not to have the same security systems on them that traditional law firm computers have. For a freelancer to fulfill the fiduciary obligations pertaining to client confidentiality, it is essential to have the appropriate measures in place to protect client information, such as secure electronic file storage, a secure Wi-Fi network, and using secure devices and software. Robust security measures, such as strong passwords, two-factor authentication, data encryption, and regular software updates, are also essential to protect against data breaches.

There are many steps a freelancer can take to protect client information online. Whether storing information on a home computer, accessing a law firm's server remotely, or file sharing in the cloud, one of the most basic steps a freelancer should take to protect client information is to use strong and unique passwords. Do not use common passwords like 123456, password, qwerty, abc123, or letmein. Also avoid using easily guessable information as passwords like birthdays, addresses, a pet's name, a phone number, or other personal details. Using common passwords or passwords that are easily guessable significantly weakens security. Strong and unique passwords will combine uppercase and lowercase letters, numbers, and special characters. In addition, do not use the same password twice. That way, if somebody figures out the password to unlock a computer, that same password will not also provide access to a file storage database.

Consider using a password manager to generate and securely store complex passwords that are different for each account to avoid having to track many different passwords. A password manager helps generate unique passwords and stores them securely in an encrypted format. In other words, a password manager acts like a vault for passwords. Instead of using common or easily guessable passwords, relying on memory to recall passwords, or writing down passwords, a password manager allows for the creation of different and complex passwords for multiple accounts while only needing to remember a single master password to access the password vault.

In addition to using appropriate passwords to protect confidential information, it is possible to encrypt confidential data by enabling full-disk encryption (FDE) on a computer. This ensures that if a computer is lost or stolen, the data remains encrypted and inaccessible without the encryption key. FDE is particularly useful for portable devices like laptops or external hard drives that are more easily susceptible to loss or theft.

The process of enabling FDE will vary depending on the operating system and software tools on the computer. With Microsoft Windows, for example, FDE can be enabled through BitLocker Drive and for macOS, FDE can be enabled through FileVault. Once FDE is enabled, the data on the disk is encrypted. To access the data, a decryption key is required. The decryption key is typically a password generated during the encryption process. Before the operating system can start or the encrypted data can be accessed, the user needs to provide the decryption key during the boot process. In this way, only authorized users with the decryption key can unlock the computer and access the encrypted data.

One of the easiest ways to keep information secure is to make sure a work computer's operating system and software stay updated. Updates often include security patches that address known vulnerabilities, which will help protect computers from potential threats. Reputable antivirus software will also help detect and remove threats like malware, viruses, and other malicious software that can compromise security. In addition, a firewall will act as a barrier between a computer and potential unauthorized access attempts.

Regarding emails, freelancers should use secure methods of communication to transmit confidential client information. Secure methods of transmitting confidential information and material include encrypted emails or client portals.

Most people forget about securing their Wi-Fi network. Setting a strong and unique password for any Wi-Fi network to prevent unauthorized access is just as important as doing so for online accounts. Enable encryption like WPA2 or WPA3 to encrypt the data transmitted over a Wi-Fi network.

A virtual private network (VPN) is also helpful when connecting to the internet to prevent the unauthorized access to data. A freelancer will most likely not be able to access a law firm's server without using a VPN. A VPN encrypts internet traffic and provides an additional layer of security. Using a VPN is particularly important if working remotely or working from a public Wi-Fi network.

Finally, be mindful not just of online security but of physical security as well. Lock or turn off a computer when it is not in use. Having an office that locks is also helpful. This is especially true if a freelancer stores paper files. Paper files should be securely stored in a locking filing cabinet in a locked office so that they remain inaccessible to unauthorized users.

Maintaining confidentiality of information relating to the representation is of utmost importance in the legal profession. Lawyers often handle highly confidential information about clients, such as financial data, medical histories, criminal records, and other sensitive and personal information. Ensuring the confidentiality of client information is one of the primary ethical obligations a lawyer has. Breaching the fiduciary duty to keep client information confidential can form the basis of a legal malpractice claim if any breach of confidentiality harms the client, and a lawyer has an ethical duty under Rule 1.6(c) to "make reasonable efforts to prevent the inadvertent or unauthorized disclosure of, or unauthorized access to" client information. Therefore, a freelancer must do what is necessary to safeguard client information from unauthorized access to protect clients from potential harm through the misuse of their personal information.

Understanding how to use safeguards to protect client information is important to avoid ethical pitfalls. However, even freelancers who meet all their ethical obligations sometimes get crosswise with their clients. Knowing how to handle non-ethical conflicts when they develop is important for preserving client relationships.

CHAPTER 20

Managing the Client Relationship

"To give real service you must add something which cannot be bought or measured with money, and that is sincerity and integrity."

—Douglas Adams

As a freelancer working for other lawyers or law firms, it will sometimes be necessary to address negative feedback and even complaints. Knowing how to manage conflicts promptly and professionally is important to sustaining and growing a freelance law practice. Positive conflict resolution will help build strong client relationships and maintain a positive reputation in the legal community.

When a hiring lawyer or law firm provides negative feedback or expresses a concern, it is imperative to actively listen and show empathy. A freelancer should demonstrate the ability and willingness to understand the hiring lawyer's perspective and acknowledge the concern being expressed. By actively listening, a freelancer can gain valuable insight into the problem and, therefore, help construct a solution.

For example, take a law firm hiring a freelancer to conduct legal research. After the freelancer turns in a legal memorandum containing the research and analysis of it, the law firm expresses dissatisfaction with the quality of the research. A freelancer receiving that complaint should listen attentively to the law firm's concern and acknowledge the disappointment with the research. The freelancer can show empathy and understanding of the nature of the concern by acknowledging the impact poor research can have on the law firm's case preparation.

Everybody appreciates prompt responses to feedback, especially if the feedback is to express a complaint or concern. Therefore, a freelancer receiving criticism should acknowledge the concern as soon as possible, even if the freelancer cannot come up with a solution immediately. A freelancer can inform the hiring law firm that its message was received and can assure the firm that the freelancer is actively working to address its concerns. This simple act of acknowledging a concern will demonstrate a freelancer's commitment to resolving the issue.

Using the example of a concern with the quality of a freelancer's research, the freelancer can acknowledge the concern and ask the hiring lawyer about the specific issue that is problematic. Perhaps the hiring lawyer wanted an analysis of federal law and the freelancer provided state law research instead. Or, maybe there was a seminal case that the freelancer failed to include in the legal memorandum. Although the freelancer will probably not be able to address the concern on the spot, the freelancer, understanding the specific nature of the criticism, will be able to address it after taking time to investigate the concern further.

Once a freelancer has acknowledged the concern or complaint, it is important to conduct a thorough investigation into the matter. Gather all relevant information, review the client's file, and consult with mentors, if necessary. It is impossible to meaningfully respond to a complaint without a comprehensive understanding of the situation.

In the example about a concern with the nature of legal research conducted, a freelancer can look back through emails with the hiring law firm to see if there was any specificity about whether the law firm asked the freelancer to analyze state or federal law. Then review the research and analysis provided to the law firm to see if it complied with any requirements set forth in writing. Perhaps there was a miscommunication or an ambiguity regarding what the hiring law firm wanted. Alternatively, maybe the matter is one in which federal courts apply state law to decide the issue so that even though the case was pending in federal court, a state law analysis was nonetheless appropriate. Maybe the seminal case the hiring lawyer was thinking of had been overturned or was subject to criticism by other decisions, which is why the freelancer chose not to include it in the legal memorandum.

After investigating the matter, it is then possible to respond to the client's concerns. When responding to a client's concerns, always maintain a professional and respectful tone. Regardless of the nature of the concern, it is important to remain composed and avoid being confrontational or engaging in personal attacks. Address the client's concerns objectively and as neutrally as possible.

Transparency is key when managing client relationships, especially in a situation where there is some sort of conflict. Be honest and open about the situation, providing clear explanations of any mistakes or misunderstandings that may have occurred. Offer realistic scenarios to resolve the problem and keep the client informed of the progress being made toward resolution. Clients appreciate transparency and are more likely to trust a freelancer's ability to resolve a problem if the freelancer approaches the matter openly and honestly.

Transparency is the key to how one lawyer (anonymous) handled a legal malpractice claim. A client who had engaged the lawyer to represent him in a workers' compensation matter asked that same lawyer for help after he was involved in a motor vehicle collision. The lawyer failed to file a personal injury suit within the applicable statute of limitations, barring any recovery of underinsured motorist coverage benefits. Being open and transparent, the lawyer told his client that he had been negligent and advised his client to engage another lawyer to file a legal malpractice lawsuit. The client, taking his lawyer's advice, sued his lawyer for legal malpractice. Appreciating his lawyer's honesty and knowing from his lawyer's workers' compensation representation that the lawyer normally performed quality work, the client forgave the mistake and allowed the lawyer to continue representing him in the workers' compensation matter.

If a client's complaint is valid and stems from an error on the freelancer's part, take responsibility and offer a sincere apology. Admitting mistakes and demonstrating a commitment to rectifying them can help rebuild trust with the client. Apologize for any inconvenience caused and assure the client that steps are being taken to prevent similar issues in the future.

For example, the freelancer investigating criticism about research being from a state rather than a federal jurisdiction who discovers that the hiring law firm did, in fact, request state law research, can respond to the hiring law firm by forwarding the request for research under state law, showing that the freelancer did in fact follow instructions. Offering to conduct additional, federal law research, however, is a way to demonstrate a willingness to find common ground.

Try to find win-win solutions that satisfy the client's concerns. By doing this, it makes it easier to preserve the client relationship, even if the dispute is not due to an error on the freelancer's part. Alternatively, if the freelancer erroneously researched state law when the assignment was to analyze federal law, the freelancer should take responsibility, apologize, and offer to complete the actual assignment without further charge.

If the client asked for a federal law analysis and the freelancer provided a state law analysis because the matter was one in which federal courts apply state law to decide the issue, perhaps the freelancer failed to specify that as the reason for analyzing state rather than federal law. Again, the freelancer should apologize for not providing that explanation before advising the client that the state law analysis set forth in the legal memorandum provided the correct evaluation of the issue.

View client feedback, even if the feedback is negative, as an opportunity to learn, grow, and improve. Reflect on the issues raised by the client to evaluate processes, procedures, and strategies for the provision of legal services. Implement necessary changes to prevent similar problems in the future, which will enhance the overall quality of the legal services provided. For example, in considering the complaint about the quality of research because it was from the wrong jurisdiction, in the future, a freelancer can make sure to start a legal memorandum with the nature of the assignment to try and avoid any misunderstandings with language like the following:

Pursuant to Garcia & Savage, LLC's January 18, 2023 email, this legal memorandum addresses whether the attorney-client privilege applies to the documents requested by the Plaintiff in the federal court lawsuit styled, *Tellez v. Department of Corrections*, Case No. 1:23-CV-00619-HHP. Because state law informs the applicability of the attorney-client privilege, this legal memorandum analyzes state law to evaluate the applicability of privilege in this case, notwithstanding the case's pendency in federal court.

Billing disputes are not uncommon. Take the example of a law firm that raises a complaint about a freelancer's invoice, alleging that the number of hours billed was not commensurate with the work product. A freelancer should communicate with the law firm and acknowledge the billing concern, assuring the law firm that billing concerns are important and that the freelancer appreciates that the law firm brought up the concern for the freelancer to try and resolve. Perhaps after investigating the concerns raised, the freelancer identified a billing discrepancy. For example, maybe the freelancer inadvertently billed for the same task twice. Or, perhaps instead of billing 0.5 hours, the freelancer made a typographical error and billed 5.0 hours.

In that case, the freelancer can apologize for the inadvertence and adjust the invoice. The freelancer should also explain the steps being taken to make sure a similar billing error does not occur again, like enhancing internal checks to maintain accurate billing records. If the billing error caused the law firm any financial burden, the freelancer can discuss payment arrangements or flexible payment options to accommodate the law firm's needs. The freelancer should end the conversation about the billing error acknowledging the misunderstanding and assuring the law firm that the freelancer is committed to providing the law firm with the highest level of legal services and to resolving any disputes to the law firm's satisfaction.

However, what if the law firm believed the amount billed was too much for the services provided? A freelancer in that situation can provide the law firm with a very detailed breakdown of the time charged, explaining the specific services provided and corresponding fees. A detailed breakdown can provide a clearer understanding of the amount of time billed. For example, if a freelancer charged 2.3 hours for drafting discovery responses, that time can be broken down as follows: legal research to determine applicable legal authority supporting objections to contention interrogatories (0.4); prepare answers to interrogatories (0.8); analysis of client documents responsive to requests for production to redact privileged and confidential information (0.7); prepare responses to requests for production (0.4).

If the law firm is still not satisfied and if the freelancer wants to maintain the relationship, there can be an offer to adjust the charges to an amount the law firm believes is appropriate. The freelancer can emphasize a willingness to make sure the law firm feels it has been billed fairly and that the fees billed reflect the value of the legal services provided.

Handling negative feedback, complaints, and client conflicts effectively is critical to maintaining a successful practice. By practicing active listening,

promptly responding, showing empathy, and engaging in transparent communication, a freelancer can manage client concerns professionally and maintain
strong client relationships. How a freelancer addresses conflicts with a hiring
lawyer or law firm can significantly impact reputation and future business
opportunities. Embrace conflict situations as opportunities for growth, learning and striving to improve to provide exceptional legal services, which always
includes customer service.

Evading pitfalls means not only avoiding ethical issues and managing the
client relationship but also protecting both the freelancer and client from unexpected events like an untimely incapacity or death. More and more lawyers are
engaging in succession planning to protect themselves and their clients. Some
jurisdictions now require lawyers to have written succession plans. Succession
planning need not be difficult or time-consuming. It just takes some planning.

CHAPTER 21

Succession Planning

"To fulfill the obligation to protect client files and property, a lawyer should prepare a future plan providing for the maintenance and protection of those client interests in the event of the lawyer's death."
—American Bar Association's Standing Committee on
Ethics and Professional Responsibility, Formal
Opinion 92–369 (December 7, 1992)

Jackson's foray into legal freelancing turned into a thriving practice that allowed him to attain financial success. A freak accident left him incapacitated, unable to practice law. He was supposed to evaluate a contract dispute for a law firm client and advise the firm whether to file suit. The firm, not hearing from Jackson, assumed he found there was no actionable claim. Because the law firm failed to sue within the applicable statute of limitations, the firm's client brought a legal malpractice claim against it. The law firm, in defending the lawsuit, filed a third-party claim against Jackson.

Jackson's bills went unpaid. Collection notices started coming in. Jackson's disability policy lapsed. Insurance money that would have been available to help support Jackson's family during his incapacity was no longer an option. His legal malpractice coverage also lapsed due to nonpayment and he no longer had coverage for the third-party lawsuit. Nobody was collecting unpaid invoices for legal services rendered. Jackson had no more money coming in but various liability contingencies.

Avoiding this kind of situation is not just a matter of common sense, but in many jurisdictions, there is an ethical obligation for lawyers to have contingency or succession plans in place for the orderly disposition of client and law firm matters in the case of the lawyer's death or incapacity. Failure to comply with these ethical obligations can result in disciplinary action. Legal malpractice insurance carriers are also increasingly requiring lawyers to engage in succession planning and to certify they have a succession plan in place to obtain professional liability coverage.

As illustrated earlier, succession planning involves not only client considerations but also personal financial planning. While different jurisdictions may have their own requirements for what succession planning looks like, and although succession planning will vary depending on individual circumstances, there are some common considerations to help ensure a smooth transition of client matters and to deal with firm and personal financial matters in the case of incapacity or an untimely death.

The first step is to become familiar with any jurisdictional rules or regulations pertaining to succession planning. If a bar association, disciplinary board, or other governing body has requirements for succession planning, any plan will need to meet the specific requirements or guidelines established by those organizations.

Next, identify a successor. A successor should be a trusted colleague who can transition any outstanding legal matters in the event of death or incapacity. Successors should be lawyers who understand the ethical obligations surrounding client confidentiality. Because the successor will be privy to attorney-client privileged information, like client files and the information contained in those files, the successor should be aware of and committed to upholding the attorney-client privilege.

Transitioning matters for a freelance attorney is much simpler than for a practitioner who directly represents clients. Because a freelancer is an independent contractor and is generally not responsible for the ultimate work product, a successor's job might only involve advising the lawyer or law firm clients of the incapacity or death. The lawyer or law firm clients would then have the responsibility for ensuring the completion of any outstanding work. This is a very different scenario than if a solo practitioner had an upcoming trial and a successor would have to petition the court to put off the trial while helping transition the client to a new lawyer to take on the client's representation at trial.

A successor cannot notify a freelancer's lawyer or law firm clients about the freelancer's incapacity or death if the successor does not know who those clients are. Therefore, a succession plan needs to specify who should be notified. Because with a freelance law practice the identity of clients can change frequently, identifying current clients can easily be accomplished by keeping a running list of them on a computer. For example, if a successor can log on to the freelancer's computer and find a subfile named "Current Client Matters" under the primary file named "Freelance Law Firm, LLC" among all the freelancer's personal computer files, it will make the successor's job a lot easier. Assuming the subfile "Current Client Matters" is organized by the names of the law firm or lawyer clients and then the actual cases the freelancer is helping with, a successor should easily be able to inform clients what cases the freelancer was involved in that need attention. Organizationally, if a freelancer's computer looks something like this, a successor's job will be much easier:

- Freelance Law Firm, LLC
  - Accounts Payable
  - Accounts Receivable
  - Conflicts Database

- Closed Client Matters
- Current Client Matters
  - Client X
    - Alpenhof Due Diligence
    - Robinson Real Estate Contract Review
    - Gonzales v. School District No. 9
  - Client Y
    - DeVries v. Bustamante
    - Safire v. Geller
  - Client Z
    - Domingo Baca Outreach Project
    - French Family Foundation
    - 505 Community Foundation
- Corporate Documents
- Financials
- Leases
- Professional Liability Insurance
- Retirement/401(k) Plan
- Taxes

Organizing computer files to make open and current legal matters easily visible and accessible to a successor necessarily means a successor must have computer access. Therefore, a successor needs passwords to be able to access law-related files. If there is a concern about a successor having access to a freelancer's non-work-related, personal computer files, there are ways to password-protect individual files or folders with third-party apps. It is also possible to share certain files with a successor but not all files.

In addition, successors should have information about any bank accounts related to the law practice. In the preceding example, that information would likely be found in the subfolder titled "Financials." Consider executing a limited power of attorney that grants the chosen successor the legal authority to manage law-related financial accounts upon incapacity or death. That way, a successor could close an operations account or pay obligations out of it. A limited power of attorney would also allow a successor to call an insurer to determine whether premiums are due, notify the tax authorities of the freelancer's incapacity or death such that estimated tax payments would be subject to modification, or terminate any leases or software subscriptions.

Further ensure that financial arrangements are in place to cover expenses related to winding down the freelance law practice, which would include paying any outstanding debts or liabilities such as equipment or office leases, software subscriptions, insurance premiums, or outstanding tax obligations. Also discuss compensation with a successor beforehand so there is a clear agreement as to whether the successor expects compensation and, if so, how much.

Once consideration is given to all these factors, create a comprehensive, written, succession plan that outlines all the key details. Share this plan with relevant individuals, including the chosen successor. Referencing succession planning in an engagement letter is a way to advise clients about the existence of a succession plan, which, again, may be a jurisdictional requirement depending on where the freelancer practices law. Creating a comprehensive, written succession plan not only complies with any jurisdictional and ethical requirements to protect client interests, but will also preserve a freelancer's legacy and provide peace of mind to loved ones in the event of an unexpected incapacity or untimely death.

A freelancer who gets to the point of needing to create a succession plan will have already explored the world of legal freelancing, including the pros and cons, the mechanics of building a freelance law practice, and the considerations for growing and sustaining it. But on a personal level, rather than a professional one, how can a freelancer make sure to enjoy the fruits of a freelance lifestyle?

PART VI

Striking a Work-Life Balance

CHAPTER 22

Balancing Act

The Importance of Nurturing Success in Both Work and Life

"I've learned that you can't have everything and do everything at the same time."

—Oprah Winfrey

The legal profession is fast-paced and demanding and is associated with stress, high-pressure, and long working hours. Lawyers often move from one task to the next, juggling work and their personal lives without ever coming up for air. Many lawyers cannot find the time to attend to physical well-being. Family obligations are often swept to the side. Lawyers come to dread thinking about facing their busy work schedules.

The demanding nature of legal work takes a toll on mental health. Lawyers who face heavy workloads, tight deadlines, demanding clients, and a constant pressure to perform at a high level find that making critical decisions under that kind of strain is emotionally draining and mentally exhausting. Especially for litigators, the adversarial nature of the legal system adds an additional layer of stress. Even transactional lawyers engaged in fiercely competitive negotiations or deal making find themselves coping with these dynamics. Judges, too, must deal with daily conflict. No matter the type of law practiced or role in the legal system, the emotional toll of navigating the adversarial dynamics of the legal system, coupled with the responsibility of representing stakeholders' interests, can lead to burnout, anxiety, depression, and other mental health issues.

The long hours commonly associated with practicing law is one of the biggest contributors to the significant mental health challenges lawyers face. Private practitioners frequently work extended hours, including at night and over weekends, to meet deadlines and manage heavy caseloads. There can be constant pressure to meet billable hour targets. Even private practitioners who do not have a billable hour requirement often work long hours to complete the work necessary to move cases along. The same is true for public sector lawyers. Prosecutors and public defenders typically have more work than they can handle during normal working hours because of a lack of resources. A lack of resources is also a challenge legal services lawyers are intimately familiar with.

Many state court and administrative law judges do not have their own law clerks and, after a day on the bench spent hearing cases, must put in additional hours to read court submittals to prepare for the next day, draft opinions, and possibly even do their own research to become versant regarding the issues that they will be deciding. Federal judges have overflowing dockets.

The constant pressure to meet work-related targets can have an adverse impact on self-care and disrupt a work-life balance.

The Honorable Henry Hamilton, III from West Des Moines, Iowa, commented on how stressful the practice of law can be:

> While being a federal, administrative law judge has been a position of honor, it also comes with its fair share of stress. From the outside, it can look like judges simply preside over cases and make decisions. The reality, however, is very different. I have managed a constant clash of perspectives between the parties appearing before me. Each case brings with it a unique set of facts and positions. As a judge, I have had to weigh these perspectives and make decisions when there is often no clear right or wrong. The realization that my decisions significantly impact the lives of the parties before me has made finding a fair resolution while keeping in mind law and precedent extremely challenging. Knowing that people's futures are in my hands has added an undeniable layer of stress to my job.
>
> But the stress of a courtroom is not limited to me as a judge. The lawyers who appear before me also experience significant pressure. Tight deadlines, demanding clients, and the emotional toll of advocating for their clients' positions can take a toll on the mental well-being of any lawyer. I have seen instances when talented lawyers have stumbled during oral arguments because of anxiety, despite having obviously prepared extensively, when court documents have been misfiled because lawyers were overburdened with work, sometimes negatively impacting cases, and when lawyers seemed to have simply given up because they were burnt out.
>
> The courtroom is a demanding place where emotions run high and the stress involved can impact the experience of everybody involved. I do not think it can be overstated that finding a work-life balance is critical to preserving mental health in the legal profession.[1]

There is now a growing recognition of the mental health crisis within the legal profession. The need for increased awareness and support has become obvious. The extent to which mental health issues and substance abuse impact lawyers is alarming. Law firms, bar associations, and even legal malpractice insurers have begun promoting lawyer assistance programs, continuing education classes on well-being, and access to mental health resources.

---

1 The Hon. H. Hamilton, III, personal communication, Aug. 29, 2023.

Although slowly changing, there is still a stigma surrounding mental health issues that can discourage lawyers from seeking support. Lawyers often feel compelled to present a façade of invincibility, fearing that seeking help or even acknowledging their struggles will be seen as a sign of incompetence or failure.

In a feature article titled "There Is No Work-Life Balance" in the American Bar Association's Litigation Journal,[2] the Honorable Bridget Mary McCormack and Len Niehoff noted that there were nearly two trillion search results for the term "work-life balance." Although these results were not unique to the legal profession, given the number of legal programs, podcasts, seminars, and classes addressing the issue, clearly the mental health crisis in the legal profession needs to be addressed.

There are now systemic and personal approaches to help deal with the mental health issues facing lawyers. Fostering a culture of well-being and resilience within law firms and legal organizations is a start. Encouraging open conversations about mental health, providing training on stress management and self-care, and implementing supportive organizational policies can create an environment that values the well-being of lawyers and promotes a healthy work-life balance rather than discouraging it.

An atmosphere where lawyers are encouraged to seek help without fear of judgment or professional repercussions is vital. Providing access to confidential counseling services, establishing support networks, and promoting other mental health resources within the legal community can make a big difference. Law schools can play a role in educating future lawyers about mental health challenges and pointing them to resources to help them navigate these challenges.

The legal profession has started responding to the mental health crisis. Click on the Iowa State Bar's website and there is an entire page devoted to "Resources to lift you up," which contains links to articles and podcasts about advancing well-being within the legal profession, along with links to substance abuse prevention services and mental health treatment. The Iowa State Bar provides every member with free, confidential, around the clock access to a mental health assistance program. Law schools are also becoming more proactive. Stanford Law School, for example, has student well-being programming, a dedicated therapist for law students, and a host of other mental health resources. Brooklyn Law School offers virtual mediation sessions and therapy services with a counselor to help students manage mental health challenges.

While the legal community has recognized the mental health crisis in the legal profession and has taken steps to start addressing it, individual lawyers need to also focus on their own mental health as well. Acknowledging the challenges and taking advantage of support systems will create a healthier, more sustainable career that allows a lawyer to focus on well-being and to create a

2 Bridget M. McCormack & Leonard M. Niehoff, *There Is No Work-Life Balance*, 46(1) Litig. J. (Oct 17, 2019).

work-life balance. The importance of working toward a healthy equilibrium between a lawyer's professional and personal life cannot be overstated.

Contrary to popular belief, working longer hours does not necessarily equate to higher productivity. In fact, excessive work without breaks or time for rejuvenation can lead to diminishing returns. A well-balanced work-life routine helps maintain focus, creativity, and motivation, resulting in higher productivity levels. By prioritizing life outside of work, lawyers become better able to approach their professional responsibilities with fresh perspectives, sharper decision-making abilities, and enhanced problem-solving skills. By allowing adequate time for relaxation, hobbies, vacation, and quality time with loved ones, lawyers can recharge and return to work with increased focus and clarity. This, in turn, leads to improved performance, higher job satisfaction, and a sense of fulfillment in both lawyers' professional and personal lives.

Leaving time outside of work also positively impacts relationships. Meaningful connections made and support networks developed outside of work play a vital role in overall happiness and well-being. When lawyers allocate sufficient time and energy to nurture personal connections, there is a fostering of stronger bonds with family, friends, and significant others. By maintaining a healthy work-life balance, lawyers can be fully present in their relationships, cultivating deeper connections. Scientific studies demonstrate that social connections improve emotional well-being and can even boost the immune system.

In Melanie Bragg's June 14, 2023, feature article[3] titled "Confessions of 11 Lifelong Bar Association Enthusiasts", she observed that "[b]y actively participating in bar associations, you'll become a member of a community whose ties remain long after your initial service." She writes: "In a post-pandemic world where we hear the news of depression, anxiety, and loneliness causing so many to leave the law, the need for in-person connection in our careers is even that much greater."

The lawyers Melanie interviewed for her article all spoke of the importance of connection. For example, Carrie F. Ricci, General Counsel, United States Army, spoke in the article about how a networking opportunity at the Hispanic National Bar Association Annual Convention one year led her to pursue initiatives in the Latino community that not only "fed [her] soul," but helped her establish relationships with colleagues "through bar work [that] have made all the difference!"[4]

David Lefton, a lawyer in Cincinnati, Ohio, also summed up the benefit of making connections in Melanie's article:

> In-person bar meetings have additionally taken me out of the office and provided opportunities to get together socially, travel, and see the state and country with colleagues, all while giving back to the profession. Bar

3 Melanie Bragg, *Confessions of 11 Lifelong Bar Association Enthusiasts*, 40(3) Solo, Small Firm, & Gen. Prac. Mag. (May/June 2023).

4 *Id.*

service has afforded me opportunities to "recharge my battery" so I am more focused and a better lawyer when I am in the office. There are many benefits to bar service, but for me, bar service has provided me with a sense of community, both at the local level, statewide, and nationally.[5]

Humans are inherently social beings. From the beginning of history, humans have relied on relationships with others for survival, support, and emotional well-being. Having a strong network of friends, family, or a supportive community helps buffer against life's stresses. When faced with challenges, whether work-related or personal, lawyers with a robust support system are more resilient and, therefore, better equipped to navigate difficulties.

Connection with others is a powerful antidote to negative feelings related to work. There is now scientific evidence that human connection triggers the release of oxytocin, a hormone that reduces stress and promotes happiness. On the other hand, evidence also reveals that a lack of social connection—isolation and loneliness—thwarts good health. The pandemic highlighted the effects of social isolation and loneliness on young children who no longer had social interactions at school, on the elderly living in long-term care facilities, and on everybody in between. Creating connections is essential to finding balance.

Establishing social connections can be difficult for some. Joining groups or participating in activities related to hobbies, interests, or passions is one way to establish them. That can include taking an art or language class, finding a meet-up group to hike or bike with, or worshiping with people of the same faith. Another way to form connections is by attending social events. Volunteering is also great way to connect with people having similar interests, whether that involves helping people through pro bono legal work or spending time to benefit a local charitable organization. In addition, online communities can provide a means to engage with others about areas of interest in a way that builds connections.

The legal profession offers many networking opportunities to help build professional connections as well on the local, state, and national levels. Freelancers can become involved with any number of specialized bar associations, attend legal conferences focusing on an area of interest, join law school alumni associations, or find mentorship opportunities. Social activities often follow bar-related events like bar conventions or continuing education seminars.

A well-rounded and balanced life encompasses more than just work. By dedicating time to life outside of work, lawyers can nurture personal growth through engaging in activities that bring joy and fulfillment. Learning, exploring new avenues, pursuing personal goals, and building relationships allows lawyers to enrich their lives and enhance their sense of fulfillment, positively influencing overall well-being.

---

5 *Id.*

Having a work-life balance directly impacts job satisfaction. When lawyers can achieve a healthy equilibrium between their professional and personal lives, they are more likely to feel fulfilled in their careers. Pursuing personal interests, spending time with loved ones, and engaging in activities outside of work contribute to a greater sense of overall satisfaction with life.

Julie Houth, Esq. from San Diego, Californa, takes work-life balance very seriously:

> You have the full-blown responsibility to take care of yourself. Remember your purpose. Be purposeful. Learn how to organize and prioritize. Watch how others do it. Live a meaningful life. Do not linger in panic—it does not help you solve the problem. Sometimes you do just need a break.[6]

Striking a harmonious equilibrium between professional commitments and personal well-being should not just be an afterthought because it directly impacts the effectiveness, longevity, and overall quality of a lawyer's career. Balancing the professional with the personal provides numerous benefits, including enhanced job satisfaction, reduced burnout, improved mental and physical health, and improved relationships, allowing lawyers to not just excel in their professional roles but also to nurture their personal lives. This creates a positive ripple effect that extends to clients, co-workers, family, and friends. As the legal landscape continues to evolve, legal organizations, law firms, and individual lawyers will continue to embrace the importance of work-life balance and recognize it as being essential for the sustainability of lawyers and the legal profession. But simply talking about a work-life balance is one thing. Achieving it is another.

6 J. Houth, Esq., personal communication, Aug. 31, 2023.

CHAPTER 23

Unleashing Harmony
Mastering Work-Life Balance Strategies

"We need to do a better job of putting ourselves higher on our own 'to-do' list."

—Michelle Obama

Achieving a work-life balance means creating harmony between a lawyer's professional and personal life. It is the ability to effectively manage the demands of work while also devoting time and attention to personal pursuits, relationships, and overall well-being. It need not involve a complete separation between work and personal life. Coming home and talking about cases with a partner, taking a child to the office for a day, or even working a little while on vacation does not mean a lawyer is sacrificing a work-life balance. Because the practice of law is rarely a nine to five job, a lawyer's work and personal life will necessarily overlap to some extent.

Striking a healthy integration between work-related responsibilities and a fulfilling personal life is what is important. Talking about work over dinner is a normal part of life. If a child has a day off from school on a day when a parent must work, taking that child to work is a way to share an experience that may be more rewarding for both the parent and child than leaving a child in the care of a babysitter. Taking a few calls for an hour each morning while on vacation does not mean a vacation cannot nevertheless be relaxing and fulfilling.

Work-life balance simply means that a lawyer recognizes there are commitments and responsibilities outside of the lawyer's professional role and that the lawyer allocates time and energy to those endeavors. Maintaining a work-life balance will lead not only to increased job satisfaction, but it will reduce stress, improve relationships, result in better physical and mental health, and enhance productivity in both the personal and professional domains. It requires being intentional and setting boundaries, prioritizing self-care, and making conscious choices to ensure that work does not result in the neglect of the other important aspects of life.

Work-life balance is a subjective concept that varies for each person. Volunteering might be important for one person and lead to a sense of fulfillment, while playing a competitive sport might be what gives somebody else joy. A person who spends a week-long vacation hiking, camping, and hunting might get bored sitting on a beach, reading a book, and relaxing. Regardless of what a lawyer likes to spend time doing outside of work, the first step in achieving a work-life balance is to understand what brings joy, pleasure, or a sense of gratification or fulfillment that is not related to work. Start with thinking about what is truly important outside of work. Reflect on values and priorities to discover what matters most in life. Is it kids? A relationship with a partner? Volunteer work? Downtime away from everybody? A hobby? What are the areas in life that hold particular significance?

Then identify, of the things that are important outside of work, which ones are nonnegotiable. A lawyer with a demanding private practice who is married with kids and who wants to be present for extracurricular school activities might not have time to devote to volunteer work. A lawyer with a passion for running marathons might not have a lot of extra time outside of training to take a vacation. Understanding values and priorities for non-work-related interests will allow a lawyer to focus on what is most important outside of work.

After assessing priorities, it is possible to set goals to regularly incorporate those non-related work activities into daily life. The goals can be short term or they can be long term. They can be a one-time goal or ongoing. For example, a short-term, one-time goal might be to make time to visit family during an upcoming holiday weekend or to help a child with a particular school project. An ongoing goal could be having a family dinner at least twice a week, picking up kids from school, or walking the dog in the morning. A long-term milestone might be to achieve a fitness goal, learn a new skill, or plan a South American vacation next year.

Setting goals provides motivation and focus, increasing the likelihood of success in incorporating the prioritized activities into life by providing a clear objective to work toward. By setting clear goals, there is not only a sense of direction about a desired outcome but also a source of motivation and inspiration. By setting a goal to work toward, there will be an increased likelihood of staying committed in trying to prioritize non-work-related activities.

After setting general goals, it is possible to break them down into smaller, more manageable tasks to develop a structured approach and to create a roadmap for achieving them. While this may seem like an overly formal process to incorporate activities that are supposed to be fun, relaxing, or rewarding into daily life, understanding the steps necessary to achieve goals is important and can be very simple.

For example, if Marina sets a goal of having a family dinner on Mondays and Thursdays, the tasks necessary to accomplish that goal can be as simple as stopping at the grocery store on those days to pick up food to cook or making sure to not work late on those days so that dinner is not put off. If Marina's goal is picking up kids from school in the afternoons, her plan to accomplish that goal might be starting work earlier in the day. Walking the dog in the mornings, on the other hand, might involve planning to start work later. A fitness goal might involve setting aside time every day for training or a physical workout. Volunteer work could require Marina to block off two hours once a week on her calendar to help a local community nonprofit organization.

Only after the steps for achieving a goal are identified is it possible to effectively manage time so that it is possible to achieve those goals. Marina cannot train for a marathon, for example, if she cannot manage her schedule to make room for three-hour training runs. If Marina's goal is to eat healthier, she cannot achieve that without spending time on food preparation. Volunteering two hours a week for a local nonprofit cannot happen if Marina does not carve out that time in her work week.

Making time outside of work to engage in the steps necessary to achieve personal, non-work-related goals is one of the hardest challenges. Treating personal commitments with the same importance as work will help. This could mean using the same time management techniques for work and personal obligations. For example, just like a lawyer schedules tasks and sets reminders for work activities, the same can be done for personal undertakings. Marina can block out her schedule starting at 4:30 p.m. on Mondays and Thursdays so she has time to run to the grocery store and to make dinner by 6 p.m. If she works with a trainer twice a week to achieve a fitness goal, she can make sure that time is scheduled on her calendar.

By scheduling the time for activities outside of work just like a lawyer schedules tasks and deadlines on a legal calendar, it is easier to establish boundaries between work and personal life. If Marina knows the limits on her time, she can communicate that to hiring lawyers or law firms. That will help prevent them from scheduling a meeting when Marina is not available or from setting a deadline when she is on vacation. Not only will the hiring lawyers or law firms appreciate understanding Marina's availability so they can account for it in scheduling and managing their own needs, but in communicating the limits on her time up front, Marina will be better able to disconnect and resist the temptation to check work emails or messages during her personal time. She will be more present when off work, which will allow her to break free more easily from stress-inducing work distractions.

Treating personal time as nonnegotiable and scheduling it just like any other important work commitment will protect personal time from work-related intrusions. Establishing boundaries and communicating them will help create a culture with hiring lawyers and law firms that respects personal time. However, to maintain those boundaries, learning how to say no is critical. This might be difficult for a freelancer looking to maximize revenue or to increase cash flow. However, being selective about work-related commitments and obligations and saying no to assignments that will overwhelm a schedule or encroach on personal time is important to achieving a work-life balance. Therefore, accounting for down time in revenue and cash flow projections is critical. If financial calculations are based on a 60-hour work week, it will be difficult to create personal time for non-work-related activities.

There are no right or wrong approaches to prioritizing personal time. While some lawyers may have the need to block out time for personal pursuits, for others, incorporating personal priorities into life is a more organic process.

Susie Schultz, from Portland, oregon, has put theory into practice regarding the work-life balance:

> Balancing a demanding career and the responsibilities of being a wife and a mother is a juggling act that makes prioritizing interests beyond work and family challenging. But I cannot imagine being happy or productive at work without incorporating my passion for outdoor adventure into my life. My approach is not so much about time management—blocking out time in my schedule to do what I love. It is more about having cultivated a mindset.
>
> I have intentionally shaped my life to revolve around the outdoors. For example, most of our shared family activities incorporate outdoor exploration. Whether during an evening after the workday is over, on a weekend, or when we are taking a longer vacation, we enjoy climbing mountains, camping, skiing, fishing, mountain biking, and other outdoor activities together, as a family. I surround myself with people who enjoy doing the same thing, which helps inspire me to prioritize the outdoors in my life and reinforces my mindset, strengthening my commitment to making sure the outdoors is always front and center in my life.
>
> When I share in the outdoors with my family and friends, it strengthens our bonds, enhances our relationships, and enriches our lives. Being outside in any capacity, whether I am running a grueling race over Imogene Pass or relaxing next to a camp fire, rejuvenates me. It would be impossible for me to be successful in a fast moving, high stress career without making the outdoors an integral part of my life.[1]

When trying to find a work-life balance, flexibility is key. Life happens. Despite the best laid plans, situations arise that interrupt schedules. Work or family emergencies can interfere with dedicated personal time. Understanding that such occurrences are a part of life and embracing the flexibility to adapt to unforeseen situations is important to maintaining balance.

Remember that allowing for personal time will ultimately enhance productivity at work. Achieving a work-life balance will reduce the likelihood of experiencing burnout. A lawyer cannot work well or efficiently when in a constant state of emotional, mental, and physical exhaustion caused by work-related stress. Prioritizing personal time provides the opportunity to recharge, relax, and recover. This will not only help prevent burnout but will also allow a

---

1 S. Schultz, personal communication, Sept. 2, 2023.

freelancer to maintain a high level of energy and motivation when it comes to work-related tasks, which will increase productivity.

Leaving time for personal and restorative activities outside of work will also positively impact focus and the ability to concentrate while at work. Taking breaks and engaging in activities that bring joy and relaxation can improve cognitive functioning, creativity, and problem-solving skills. Therefore, a freelancer is more likely to stay mentally refreshed when prioritizing personal time, which will increase the ability to tackle work-related tasks efficiently.

Regularly assess how well a work-life balance is being achieved. If current strategies for achieving harmony between work and non-work-related activities is not working, adjust those strategies. Be open to making changes and adapting as necessary. Maintaining a work-life balance is a personal journey, unique to each lawyer. It may require trial and error to find the right combination of strategies that work. Sometimes, it may be impossible. For example, a freelancer involved in preparing for and second chairing a three-week trial will probably have to put non-work-related personal activities on hold for a period of time. Similarly, a freelancer involved in due diligence work for a deal that is supposed to close the next week will probably not have time to focus on activities outside of work for a while.

That does not mean there is a lack of balance. Lawyering is not a nine to five job, which is what makes it so challenging to integrate work and personal time. Flexibility is vital. However, even just the process of working toward prioritizing personal time will create a positive cycle that improves overall well-being. Employing specific strategies for finding fulfillment outside of work will contribute to a more engaged and productive work life. One particular route to achieving balance that is becoming more and more popular is the practice of mindfulness.

CHAPTER 24

Mindfulness Matters
Cultivating Clarity and Calm in the Chaos

"Peace of mind is only a single breath away."

—Nate Macanian

According to the Mayo Clinic's website, mindfulness is a "focus on being intensely aware of what you're sensing and feeling in the moment, without interpretation or judgment."[1] The American Psychological Association's *Dictionary of Psychology* defines mindfulness as an awareness of your internal states where it is possible to observe thoughts, emotions, and other present-moment experiences without judging or reacting to them. An often-cited definition of mindfulness from John Kabat-Zinn, an author and founder of the Stress Reduction Clinic at the University of Massachusetts, is the "awareness that arises through paying attention, in purpose, in the present moment, and non-judgmentally."[2] In short, mindfulness means being fully present in the moment. There is a quote inscribed on the walls of Yad Vashem, the Holocaust Museum in Israel, which sums up what it means to be mindful even though it was meant as a commentary on the Holocaust. It roughly translates to:

Remember the past
Live the present
Trust the future

A growing body of research shows that mindfulness practices can reduce stress and anxiety, fostering a sense of well-being. By cultivating present moment awareness and nonjudgmental acceptance, mindfulness offers a powerful tool for mitigating stress, improving resilience, and enhancing emotional well-being.

---

1 *Mindfulness Exercises*, MAYO CLINIC (Oct. 11, 2022), https://www.mayoclinic.org/healthy-lifestyle/consumer-health/in-depth/mindfulness-exercises/art-20046356#:~:text=Mindfulness%20is%20a%20type%20of,mind%20and%20help%20reduce%20stress.
2 *Jon Kabat-Zinn: Defining Mindfulness*, MINDFUL (Jan. 11, 2017), https://www.mindful.org/jon-kabat-zinn-defining-mindfulness/.

Brain imaging shows that mindfulness practices cause changes in the grey matter of the brain, including the region of the brain that regulates emotions. Medical research has confirmed that a regular mindfulness practice leads to decreased levels in the body of cortisol, the stress hormone. The behavioral health field has incorporated mindfulness-based treatments into its therapies like mindfulness-based stress reduction (MBSR) and mindfulness-based cognitive therapy (MBCT) because of the success these treatments bring in helping people manage stress-related disorders.

In short, it is now scientifically proven that mindfulness enhances emotional well-being, improves cognitive functioning, and has physical health benefits as well. An accumulating body of research shows that mindfulness practices offer a holistic approach to cultivating a more balanced and fulfilling life. Therefore, incorporating mindfulness into daily routines can lead to greater peace and happiness amidst the chaos.

So, what are mindfulness practices? Mindfulness practices encompass a wide range of transformative techniques to allow the cultivation of present-moment awareness. Those who are new to mindfulness can use guided practices. There are many apps, podcasts, and other resources with free, guided mindfulness practices, like those found on https://natemacanian.com/meditate. They can be short practices that last for minutes or they can be much longer.

Many mindfulness practices focus on breathing. Nate Macanian from Boulder, Colorado, is a mindfulness teacher who has hosted numerous mindfulness workshops, interactive classes, and retreats for individuals, small groups, and world-class companies like Google, Twitter, Palantir, Wix, Kraft Heinz, and the Omega Institute. In working with mindfulness techniques, Nate emphasizes breath in his mindfulness meditations. In answering why the breath is the object of such attention, he notes that the breath is anchored in the present moment:

> [I]n order to feel more present, it makes sense to train our brains to develop a sharp focus on something that is inherently rooted in the present moment. Consider this—can you breathe in the past or future? The breath always offers an opportunity to establish a felt connection with what is happening right here and right now. If your mind is truly focused on breathing, it is impossible to simultaneously ruminate about the past or daydream about the future, which research has shown often leads to feelings of anxiety and unhappiness. A grounding into the present moment allows us to feel more joyful and in sync with the world around us, and the breath is the best tool to get there.[3]

From a scientific perspective, Nate points out that "[t]here is a direct and well-studied biochemical relationship between your breath and your brain.

---

3 N. Macanian, personal communication, Sept. 22, 2023.

By placing focus on your breath, you can manually hack your brain to create altered states of consciousness. Just by consciously choosing to direct your awareness to your inhales and exhales (which is always happening anyway), you can actually flip the switch of your brain's circuitry to shift from the Sympathetic Nervous System (Fight or Flight) to the Parasympathetic Nervous System (Rest and Digest)."[4]

Mindful breathing involves directing attention to the breath by observing its natural rhythm to focus on the present moment. Focusing on the sensations of inhaling and exhaling can cultivate a sense of deep calm and relaxation. Mindful breathing can be practiced anywhere, making it an accessible tool for stress reduction and emotional regulation. For example, a lawyer can have a special place to practice mindful breathing, such as a favorite chair, lying down in bed, or settling into an outdoor space. However, lawyers can also simply close their eyes while sitting in a chair at a desk while taking a short break from work to practice mindful breathing. The key is to find a comfortable and quiet space where there are no distractions.

To practice mindful breathing, gently close your eyes. Take a moment to bring your attention to the present moment. Notice the sensations of your body, such as the bed under you or the chair supporting your back. Start by taking a few deep breaths, inhaling through your nose and exhaling through your mouth. Let your breath return to its natural rhythm. Shift focus to the sensation of the breath as it enters and leaves the body. Notice where you feel your breath. It will be different for different people. Some people feel their breath in their nostrils, some in their chest, and some in their abdomen. As you inhale, bring your attention to the sensations of the breath entering the body. Does the air feel cool as it passes through your nose? Warm? Does your chest rise? Or does your abdomen expand? Can you feel the air pass through your body? Do the same as you exhale. Observe the physical sensations of the air leaving your body.

A more advanced mindful breathing practice involves trying to feel your breath in different parts of your body. For example, you might inhale and direct your breath into your arms or legs. If you have a point of pain in your body, you can breathe into that spot. Notice what happens to your discomfort when you focus your breath on a point of pain.

Continue mindful breathing for a few minutes or longer. Even just a few minutes of regular mindful breathing can have a positive impact. Perhaps start with a few minutes of mindful breathing a couple of times a week and slowly build up to longer, more frequent sessions. As with any other activity, mindfulness takes practice.

Your mind will undoubtedly wander as you engage in mindfulness practices. Whenever you notice it wandering, gently refocus attention on the breath

4 *Id.*

and the sensations in the body. Each time you notice your mind drifting, simply acknowledge it and guide your attention back to the present moment. As you conclude the practice, take a few moments to appreciate the stillness and peacefulness you have cultivated. Notice how your body feels and notice a sense of calm and relaxation. When you are ready, slowly open your eyes.

Nate Macanian commented on how our breath changes depending on our mental state because the mind and body are not separate, but one. For example, Nate teaches that if you find your breath shallow, fast, and uneasy, chances are you are feeling stressed, scared, or frustrated. However, the opposite is equally as true. When your breathing is slow, easy, and deliberate, your mind is probably settled. Nate proposed an experiment to try with your breath. The next time you are feeling anxious about an upcoming deadline or have a work conflict that you cannot get out of your mind, notice your breath. Is there asymmetry to its natural flow? Then pay attention to how fluidly your breath flows the next time you are very relaxed, like when reading a good book or listening to gentle music. "The point is, at any given moment, you can actually get a pretty clear signal on where your mind is just by observing how you're breathing. The mental space we occupy expresses itself in the form of breathing."[5] This is why breathing is such an important part of many mindfulness practices.

A body scan meditation is another kind of mindfulness practice that involves systemically bringing attention to different parts of the body. Usually, a body scan meditation starts from the toes and gradually moves upward. This mindfulness practice enhances body awareness and promotes a connection with physical sensations. Mindfully scanning the body allows for the identification of particular areas of tension or discomfort in the body and then allows those areas to release through relaxation.

Again, start like you would for a mindful breathing practice. Find a comfortable and quiet space free from distractions where you can lie down or recline. Close your eyes gently. Take a few deep breaths to allow yourself to relax and start letting go of tension in your body. Bring your attention to the present by focusing on the sensations in your body. When you are ready to start, begin by bringing your awareness to your feet, first one foot, then the other. Notice any sensations in your toes, the arches of your feet, your soles, and your heels. If you are wearing socks, observe how they feel on your feet. Are they tight? Do they bring warmth?

After scanning your feet, slowly move your attention up to your calves and lower legs. Keep moving upward, allowing your awareness to travel through your knees, thighs, and up to your hips, observing any physical sensations along the way.

More to your lower back and abdomen. Notice the rise and fall of your belly with each breath. Observe any areas of pain or tension. Direct your attention

5 *Id.*

up to your chest and upper back. Notice the expansion and contraction of your ribs, chest, and back when you inhale and exhale. Feel the sensation of your breath moving through your upper body. Shift your focus to your hands and arms and observe any sensations as your awareness travels through your fingers, hands, wrists, forearms, and up to your shoulders.

Bring your attention to your neck and throat. Notice any tension in this area. Observe your breath moving through your neck and throat. Move your attention to your face. Notice any sensations in your jaw, cheeks, eyes, and forehead. Many people unknowingly hold tension in their jaws. Part your lips, move your tongue off the roof of your mouth, and take a breath. Notice your entire face relax.

As you are engaged in a body scan meditation you can observe any sensations in your body without trying to change them. Simply sit with the sensations, even if those sensations are pain, tension, or other discomfort. Or, you can allow any areas of tension to soften in your mind, inviting relaxation to those areas. Focus specifically on the area of discomfort. Breathe into it. As you exhale, release the discomfort.

Once you have finished the body scan, expand your awareness to your whole body. Feel the sensation of your entire body. When you are ready, take a deep breath in and as you exhale, gently wiggle your fingers and toes. Slowly bring movement back to your entire body, allowing yourself to transition back to your surroundings.

You do not need to be still to practice mindfulness. Another foundational practice is mindful eating, which encourages people to bring full attention and awareness to the act of eating. Research has shown that mindful eating can be a powerful tool in helping with weight loss. Eating slowly and savoring each bite, noticing flavors, textures, heat, and other sensations enhances digestion and fosters gratitude for the nourishment food brings, something normally taken for granted, which helps to prevent overeating.

Begin at any meal by choosing a piece of food from your plate. Take a moment to observe its appearance. Notice its color and shape. If you can pick it up, feel its texture. Think about and appreciate the nourishment that the food provides. Before taking a bite, express gratitude either silently or out loud for the food. Then take a small bite, but do not chew immediately. Pause and hold the food in your mouth, noticing its flavors, texture, and temperature without rushing to chew or swallow. Begin chewing slowly. Notice the movements of your jaw and the sensations of chewing. Pay attention to the flavors that are released as you chew. When you swallow, feel the food traveling down your throat. Repeat this process with each bite, savoring the food and fully engaging your senses.

Mindfulness practices can also occur during exercise. One kind of mindfulness training is a walking meditation, which can be adapted to any kind of exercise. A walking meditation involves bringing awareness to the physical sensations and movements of walking. Whether a very slow walk or a more purposeful one, a walking meditation focuses attention on the sensations of each step, the contact of the feet with the ground, and the general experience of walking.

Finding a quiet and safe place to walk, free of distractions, is the first step for a walking mediation. Walking on a street or sidewalk with a lot of traffic and noises or walking in an area with safety issues will distract from the meditation. Begin by standing still and breathing deeply for a few seconds, becoming fully present in the moment. Start walking at a relaxed pace, paying attention to the sensation of your feet contacting the ground. Feel the weight shifting from one foot to the other as you take each step. Bring your attention to the physical sensation of your feet touching the ground—the pressure of pushing off one foot and landing on the other, how your feet feel on different surfaces, and what part of your foot is contacting the ground. Listen to the sound your feet make when they contact the ground. As you continue walking, tune into the movement of your legs and hips. Notice your arms swinging. Feel the flow of your body moving in its natural rhythm.

Expand your awareness past your body to your surroundings. Notice the colors, shapes, textures, sounds, smells, and feel of the environment around you. Try focusing on a particular sound, like a bird chirping, the sound of the wind rustling the leaves on the trees, a dog barking, or even the distant sound of traffic. Feel the temperature on your body. Is the sun warming your skin? Is the wind chilling your hands or face? Observe how your body adjusts to navigate changes on your path, like a curb, uneven surfaces, or a crack in the sidewalk.

As you are coming to the end of your walk, slow down your pace. Take a few moments to stand still and notice how your body feels. Close the walking meditation by expressing appreciation for the walk and for being able to connect with the outdoors. Practicing mindful walking is something you can do whenever you have the opportunity, even when simply walking around your house or walking from your car into an office.

Mindfulness can be practiced anywhere, anytime. When driving and listening to the radio, focus on one of the instruments you hear in a song that is playing. Then focus on a different instrument. Listen to the sound a drink makes when you pour it over ice cubes. Instead of rushing through a shower in the morning, observe how the warm water soothes and relaxes you. Noticing the feedback of the keyboard when typing, the sound of your smart phone when sending a text message, or the feeling of sinking into your pillow when you lay down to go to sleep are all forms of mindfulness. Shifting your attention to what is happening now, even if only momentarily, will allow you to focus on the present.

Incorporating mindfulness into daily routines can profoundly impact well-being, mental clarity, and overall quality of life in a positive way. Mindfulness practices offer easy, accessible, and effective tools for cultivating self-awareness and for being present in the moment, which is part of a transformative journey toward peace and fulfillment. Remember, though, that mindfulness is a practice so it takes practice. Each time you engage in mindfulness meditations, it will strengthen the ability to stay present for a longer period. Be patient. Be kind to yourself. As you become more comfortable with mindfulness practices, you will be able to increase the time spent to suit your needs. Experienced practitioners can spend hours on mindfulness exercises and feel like the time passes in minutes. There are mindfulness retreats where practitioners spend days on mindfulness meditations without conversing.

Mindfulness techniques can become a powerful source of grounding, rejuvenation, and connection with the world around you. They have scientifically and medically demonstrated benefits for those seeking to enhance their well-being. Mindfulness promotes physical, mental, and emotional health; reduces stress; enhances self-awareness; and improves cognitive functioning. By incorporating mindfulness into a daily routine, lawyers can experience a profound shift in their overall quality of life and happiness.

It is this improved quality of life that lawyers are seeking in exploring the freelancing landscape. Stepping away from a traditional work model can provide a lawyer with immeasurable rewards in terms of time, freedom, flexibility, and balance, all without giving up financial security. It is this that is the joy of freelancing.

Appendix A
Checklist for Starting a Freelance Law Practice

What follows, in no specific order, are factors to consider when starting a freelance law practice. Although comprehensive, the list is not wholly inclusive of everything a freelancer should think about. By contrast, depending on a freelancer's circumstances, not every item listed here will be necessary to start a freelance practice. Independent analysis of preferences and jurisdictional requirements is essential to make this checklist as specifically applicable to any individual's particular situation as possible.

I. Business Plan

    A. Formal or Informal
    B. Executive Summary
    C. Services Offered
    D. Pricing Model
    E. Target Market
    F. Marketing Strategy
    G. Revenue Projection
    H. Expense Projection

II. Office Space

    A. Brick and Mortar

        1. Purchase
        2. Lease (Month to Month or Term)
        3. Turnkey Office
        4. Shared Workspace
        5. Working from Client's Office

    B. Home Office

        1. Dedicated Workspace
        2. Insurance Requirements
        3. Technology Needs
        4. Physical Space for Equipment and Files

C. Virtual Office

    1. Technology Capabilities
    2. Access to Meeting Spaces

D. Hybrid

III. Billing Models or Fee Structure

    A. Hourly
    B. Flat or Fixed Fee
    C. Subscription
    D. Contingency
    E. Hybrid

IV. What Type of Corporate Entity

    A. Compliance with State Laws Regarding Type of Entity Available to Lawyers
    B. Sole Proprietorship, PC, PA, LLC, PLLC, LP, LLP, PLLP, C-Corp, S-Corp
    C. Liability Protection
    D. Tax Considerations
    E. Risk Tolerance
    F. Governance Obligations
    G. Operational Flexibility
    H. Administrative Requirements
    I. Expenses to Maintain Corporate Entity

V. Financial Considerations

    A. Starting Capital
    B. Self-finance or Incur Debt
    C. Furniture (Desk, Chair, Bookshelves, Filing Cabinets)
    D. Equipment (Computer, Monitors, Printer, Scanner, Telephone, Shredder)
    E. Supplies (Paper, Toner, File Folders)
    F. Letterhead/Business Cards
    G. High-Speed Internet
    H. Marketing and Advertising Costs
    I. Legal Software (Case Management and/or Document Management Software, Billing Software, Legal Research License)
    J. Professional Service Fees (CPA or Legal Consulting Expenses)
    K. Licensing or Bar Association Fees
    L. Business Licenses or Permits
    M. Continuing Education Costs
    N. Monthly Overhead Projection
    O. Revenue Structure
    P. Bank Accounts (Operating Accounts, IOLTA Accounts, Merchant Services Account, Line of Credit, Firm Credit Card)

Q. Retirement Account

R. Health Savings Account

VI. Insurance

    A. Professional Liability Insurance (Legal Malpractice Insurance)

    B. General Liability Insurance

    C. Premises and Property Coverage

    D. Cyber Liability Insurance

    E. Life Insurance

    F. Disability Insurance

    G. Health Insurance

    H. Business Interruption Coverage

    I. Workers Compensation

    J. Employment Related Practices Liability Insurance

VII. Technology

    A. Hardware

        1. Desktop

        2. Laptop

        3. Tablets

        4. Printer

        5. Monitors

        6. Servers

        7. Cell phone

    B. Software

        1. AI

        2. Word Processing

        3. PDF Document Reader/Creator/Handler

        4. Legal Research License

        5. Communications Technology

        6. Videoconferencing App

        7. Case Management Software

        8. Document Management Software

        9. Time, Billing, and Accounting Software

        10. Scheduling, Calendaring, or Docketing System Software

        11. Conflicts Checking Software

    C. Connectivity and IT Management

        1. Internet Service Provider

        2. IT Management (Fixed-Fee Service [Ongoing], Break and Fix Service Provider, Do-It-Yourself)

3. Cloud Workspace
4. File Organization, Storage, Backup (Cloud, On-site, Hybrid)
5. VPN

VIII.   Rainmaking (Generating Clients)

A. Developing a Niche
B. Marketing and Advertising

1. Website
2. Social Media Profiles
3. Social Media Advertising
4. Content Creation
5. Word-of-Mouth
6. Existing Contacts

C. Building Relationships
D. Providing Exceptional Services
E. Referrals through Professional Networking
F. Exposure through Community Involvement
G. Showcasing Expertise
H. Legal Service Platforms

IX.   Administering a Law Practice

A. Invoicing Clients
B. Accounts Receivable
C. Accounts Payable
D. Financial Reporting
E. Tax Compliance
F. Document Management
G. Managing Cashflow
H. Managing Workflow

X.   Avoiding Pitfalls

A. Ethical and Professional Obligations
B. The Engagement Letter
C. Conflicts of Interest
D. Attorney-Client Confidentiality
E. Managing the Client Relationship
F. Succession Planning

XI.   Work-Life Balance

A. Personal Well-Being
B. Mental Health
C. Mindfulness Practices

Appendix B
Sample Business Plan

Executive Summary: Law Firm of Carla Martino, LLC (Carla Martino, Esq.) is a start-up freelance law practice that aims to provide high-quality legal services to clients on an hourly basis, flat-fee basis, and subscription-fee basis. Martino Law Firm offers expertise in various areas of law, including contract law, business law, and real estate law. The business may also generate revenue through the sale of legal documents, such as templates for contracts or estate planning documents.

The primary goal of the Law Firm is to offer high-quality legal services to lawyers and law firms while maintaining low overhead costs so Carla Martino can offer her services at a competitive rate. Formerly part of the leadership team of Delta Construction as its Chief Operations Officer and one of the founding members of the Merion Real Estate Law Group, both in the Philadelphia, Pennsylvania, area, Carla Martino has both the real-world and legal experience to provide exceptional services in the area of business transactions and litigation, with a specialty in real estate matters.

Services and Pricing Model: The Law Firm will offer a range of legal services, including but not limited to, drafting contracts, providing legal advice, and doing appearance work for a law firm's clients in court. The primary focus will be on contract law, business law, and real estate law. Other legal services will be provided based on the needs of the hiring law firm.

The pricing model for the Law Firm will be on an hourly basis, flat-fee basis, and subscription-fee basis. The hourly rate will be $100 per hour. The flat-fee rate will depend on the complexity of the legal matter. This Business Plan assumes an average per project flat-fee rate of $500. The subscription-fee rate will be $500 per month, which will give law firms unlimited access to verbal legal advice. The business will also sell contract templates for $50 each.

Target Market: The target market for the Law Firm includes small law firms and solo practitioners in need of legal advice or representation whose clients cannot afford to pay big law firm prices. Because of low overhead, the Law Firm can provide legal services to smaller law firms and solo practitioners at more affordable rates. The Law Firm will primarily focus on law firms and solo practitioners in the local area, although services can be provided remotely to clients outside of the area.

Marketing Strategy: The marketing strategy for the Law Firm will be centered around building relationships and establishing a strong reputation in the local community. This will include attending networking events, speaking at seminars, and leveraging social media platforms to increase brand awareness.

Initial website design, development, and hosting is forecast to cost $2,000 in the first year. That cost is forecast to remain the same after the first year to account for website modification to add or change content. Social media marketing is forecast to cost $1,500 annually and includes social media content creation and management. Networking expenses are forecast at $1,000 annually and include ticket prices to attend industry events and hosting a workshop or seminar. Content marketing is forecast at $500 annually and includes the creation of a quarterly, online newsletter. Total marketing expenses are forecast at $5,000 annually.

Revenue: The Law Firm will generate revenue from legal services billed on an hourly basis, flat-fee basis, and subscription-fee basis. The business may also generate revenue through the sale of legal documents, such as templates for contracts. The following revenue projection assumes:

- Hourly rate of $100 with a minimum total of 60 hours monthly
- Average flat fee of $500 per project with a minimum of two projects per month
- Subscription fee for unlimited access to verbal legal advice of $500 monthly with a minimum of two clients
- Sales of a minimum of three contract templates per month

Total projected first year revenue:

Hourly:	$72,000
Flat fee:	$12,000
Subscription:	$12,000
Templates:	$ 1,800
Total	**$97,800**

Expenses: The primary expenses for the Law Firm will be legal software and research tools, professional liability insurance, office supplies, and marketing expenses. The business will operate out of a home office to reduce overhead costs and commercial liability insurance costs.

Total projected first year expenses:

Legal research license:	$2,500
Case management software:	$3,000
Marketing expenses:	$5,000
Malpractice insurance:	$3,000
Organizational memberships:	$ 500
Accounting fees:	$2,000
Equipment:	$4,000
Total	**$20,000**

Financial Projections: In its first year of operation, the Law Firm aims to generate revenue of $97,800, with a net profit of $77,800. Revenue is projected to grow by 10 percent annually. The business will only incur the initial equipment cost in the first year. Equipment maintenance cost for the second year is forecast at $1,500. Expenses are forecast to grow 5 percent annually. For the second year, expenses would be $1,500 for equipment maintenance plus a 5 percent growth over the $16,000 in non-equipment-related expenses ($800) for a total of $18,300. The following table shows the financial projections for the first three years of operation.

Year	Revenue	Expenses	Net Profit
1	$ 97,800	$20,000	$77,800
2	$107,580	$18,300	$89,280
3	$118,338	$19,215	$99,123

Conclusion: The Law Firm aims to provide high-quality legal services to small law firms and solo practitioners while maintaining low overhead costs. By targeting small law firms and solo practitioners in need of legal help, the business aims to establish itself as a trusted legal advisor in the local community. The pricing model offers clients flexibility at affordable rates, which will enable the business to capture different market segments. The marketing strategy will help to generate a consistent flow of clients. The financial projections show a profitable and sustainable business model.

Appendix C
Corporate Structures

Specific laws, regulations, and rules vary by jurisdiction and it is important to understand them when choosing the right corporate structure for a freelance law practice.

Corporate Structure	Number of Owners	Taxation	Corporate Formalities	Liability Protection	Other Factors
Sole Proprietorship	Single owner	Personal income tax (profits and losses reported on owner's tax return)	Minimal formalities; no separate legal entity from the owner	No limited liability protection (owner's personal assets at risk)	Simplest and most common business structure for individual entrepreneurs
S-Corporation (S-Corp)	Single or multiple shareholders (owners)	Pass-through taxation (profits and losses pass through to shareholders' personal tax returns)	Strict adherence to corporate formalities; must hold regular meetings, maintain detailed records, and follow bylaws	Limited liability protection for shareholders (personal assets generally protected)	Suitable for small businesses; subject to certain restrictions such as U.S. citizenship requirement for shareholders
C-Corporation (C-Corp)	Single or multiple shareholders (owners)	Double taxation (profits taxed at corporate level and then again on individual shareholders' tax returns)	Strict adherence to corporate formalities; must hold regular meetings, maintain detailed records, and follow bylaws	Limited liability protection for shareholders (personal assets generally protected)	Suitable for large businesses, ability to attract investors through stock offerings
Professional Association (PA)	Owned by licensed professionals	Generally taxed as a C-Corp or S-Corp	Similar formalities as regular corporations; specific to licensed professionals	Limited liability protection for shareholders (personal assets generally protected)	Provides liability protection to licensed professionals
Professional Corporation (PC)	Owned by licensed professionals	Generally taxed as a C-Corp or S-Corp	Similar formalities as regular corporations; specific to licensed professionals	Limited liability protection for shareholders (personal assets generally protected)	Provides liability protection to licensed professionals

Corporate Structure	Number of Owners	Taxation	Corporate Formalities	Liability Protection	Other Factors
Limited Liability Company (LLC)	Single or multiple members	Pass-through taxation (profits and losses pass through to members' personal tax returns)	Fewer formalities compared to corporations; flexible management structure	Limited liability protection for members (personal assets generally protected)	Flexible profit distribution
Professional Limited Liability Company (PLLC)	Typically owned by licensed professionals	Pass-through taxation	Follows similar formalities as regular LLC; specific to licensed professionals	Limited liability protection for members (personal assets generally protected)	Allows professionals to form an LLC while still maintaining liability protection
Limited Partnership (LP)	General partners (unlimited liability) and limited partners (limited liability)	Pass-through taxation for limited partners; general partners are personally taxed	Formal partnership agreement required; general partners manage the business	Limited liability protection for limited partners; general partners have unlimited liability	Limited partners have no management authority and are liable only up to their investment
Limited Liability Partnership (LLP)	Partners	Pass-through taxation (profits and losses pass through to partners' personal tax returns)	Formal partnership agreement required; all partners have equal management authority	Limited liability protection for partners (personal assets generally protected)	Commonly used by professional firms such as law firms
Professional Limited Liability Partnership (PP)	Owned by licensed professionals	Pass-through taxation	Follows similar formalities as regular LLP; specific to licensed professionals	Limited liability protection for partners (personal assets generally protected)	Provides liability protection to licensed professionals

Appendix D
Outlines of Sample Marketing Plans

Example 1: A Transactional Real Estate Freelancer Marketing Primarily through Online Channels

Summary: As a freelance lawyer specializing in real estate law, the goal is to target small, successful law firms who do not have enough lawyers to service all their clients. This marketing plan focuses primarily on online strategies, with supplementation by in-person marketing efforts.

Market Analysis: The target clients are small law firms specializing in real estate law. Those law firms could have individual or corporate real estate clients, as well as property management company and real estate agency clients. Lawyers practicing in the field of real estate law typically charge by the hour. An experienced lawyer practicing in this area will charge on average $200 per hour. By minimizing overhead, it is possible to offer freelance legal services at less than half that rate and still reach revenue goals.

Brand Development: Prior to engaging in any other marketing efforts, create a user-friendly website. Post relevant content. Capture email addresses for further marketing efforts.

Activate social media profiles on LinkedIn, Instagram, and Facebook. Generate at least 100 followers in the first month. Aim for 300 followers by year's end.

Attend at least two in-person events per quarter put on by specialized bar associations for real estate lawyers and industry conferences to establish personal connections with small law firm representatives.

Content Marketing: Create two informative blog posts monthly about recent real estate law changes that impact contract negotiation or property management issues, that discuss relevant local regulations, or that highlight case studies emphasizing expertise.

Create a monthly legal newsletter addressing common real estate legal issues to post online and to email.

Digital Marketing: Invest in targeted Google Ads focusing on keywords related to real estate law for small firms, aiming for a click rate of 5 percent in three months.

Engage with small law firms on social media platforms, sharing legal tips and industry news, with the objective to increase engagement by 25 percent in six months.

Client Testimonials and Referrals: Gather three client testimonials in first quarter, showcasing successful collaborations with small law firms and prominently feature them on website.

Solicit referrals from current clients and from lawyers attending in-person networking events. Ask for at least two referrals per month.

Client Engagement and Retention: Send monthly newsletters to existing clients, updating them on recent legal developments and offering insights.

Seek feedback from every client at least twice a year to assess client satisfaction.

Measuring Progress and Success: Acquire five new clients in the next six months, tracking the source of each client to evaluate the effectiveness of different marketing channels. Adjust marketing channels and efforts accordingly.

Increase website traffic by 10 percent in the next quarter through SEO optimization, content marketing, and Google Ads, measuring progress using tools like Google Analytics.

Achieve a 25 percent increase in social media engagement in six months, monitoring likes, shares, comments, and follower growth.

Establish connections with 10 small law firm representatives in the next year through in-personal events, fostering relationships that can lead to referrals.

Example 2: A Litigator Engaged Primarily in In-Person Marketing Efforts

Summary: As a freelance lawyer specializing in providing litigation services, marketing efforts are geared toward predominately an in-person approach, supplemented by a professional website and blog.

Market Analysis: Target law firms of all sizes engaged primarily in civil defense litigation involving governmental entities and officials. Identify those with contracts with the state risk management division and public insurance funds. These are the firms that will represent state and local public entities and officials. Avoid law firms that primarily provide plaintiffs' or private corporate representation.

In-Person Marketing: Attend at least two legal networking events monthly, aiming to establish connections with potential clients or referral sources.

Join at least one local and one national bar association focusing on litigation, participating actively to build reputation within the legal community.

Engage in community events, nonprofit work, or sponsor initiatives (seminars or webinars) to increase visibility and credibility.

Online Presence: Maintain a user-friendly website with service offerings, client testimonials, and a blog updated monthly to showcase successes and expertise.

Client Engagement and Retention: Provide personalized attention to every client, ensuring their satisfaction and encouraging positive, word-of-mouth referrals.

Follow up with clients after every case or project resolution, seeking feedback to assess satisfaction.

Measuring Progress and Success: Secure five new clients within the first year, tracking the source of each client to assess the effectiveness of different in-person marketing channels.

Monitor website traffic and blog to determine the number of unique visitors and engagement levels. If website traffic is significant or increases significantly, adjust marketing plan to focus more on online efforts.

Establish connections with at least two potential client law firms or referral sources at each networking event.

Appendix E
Sample Engagement Letter

[Freelancer Name]
[Address]
[City, State, Zip]
[Email Address]
[Phone Number]
[Hiring Law Firm Name]
[Contact Lawyer's Name]
[Address]
[City, State, Zip]

[Date]

Re: Engagement Letter—Appeal of Trial Verdict in [identify lawsuit]

Dear [Contact Person's Name]:

Thank you for asking me to handle the appeal in [identify lawsuit] on behalf of [Law Firm Name]. I am writing to confirm the terms of my engagement in this matter.

I will provide legal services to defend the appeal in [identify lawsuit]. I will conduct the necessary legal research, review the trial court record, prepare the appellate answer brief, and perform any other tasks related to the appeal process except for appearance work. If there are oral arguments or any other need to appear in court, [Law Firm Name] will be solely responsible.

My billing rate is $100 per hour, payable within 30 days from the date of invoice. I will maintain detailed records of the time spent on the appeal and provide monthly invoices for services rendered by the 10th day of the month following the month in which I provided legal services (e.g., for services provided in March, I will provide an invoice on or before April 10th). Late charges of [amount or percentage] will accrue for any balance that is outstanding for more than 30 days.

Any expenses incurred during my engagement, such as court filing fees or transcript costs, in addition to taxes on expenses, will be billed separately and reimbursed by [Law Firm Name]. I will not incur expenses without the prior consent of [Law Firm Name].

[Law Firm Name] understands that I am an independent contractor and that no attorney-client relationship is formed between me and [identify end client]. [Law Firm Name] shall have ultimate decision-making authority over any work product prior to it being filed or used in any manner. I will provide drafts and seek approval from [Law Firm Name] prior to filing any brief or document with the court.

This engagement does not extend to any services after the appellate decision is issued. Any legal work beyond the services described in this letter will require a new agreement.

Upon the conclusion of the engagement, I will retain copies of all relevant documents, files, and correspondence pertaining to this engagement for [number] years. After this period, I will securely dispose of the material in compliance with applicable laws and regulations.

After performing a conflict check, to the best of my knowledge, there are no conflicts of interest that would prevent me from providing representation in this matter. If any conflicts arise during the engagement, I will promptly notify [Law Firm Name] and discuss potential resolutions and/or a course of proceeding.

In the unfortunate event of an unexpected incapacity or untimely death, I have planned for [Successor Attorney's Name] to settle any outstanding invoices and to act for me regarding any other matter related to my law practice, not including performance of the work set forth in this agreement, which will be the responsibility of [Law Firm Name] to complete.

This engagement shall be governed by and construed in accordance with the laws of [State]. Any disputes arising out of or in connection with this engagement shall be subject to the exclusive jurisdiction of the courts in [County, State or Federal Jurisdiction].

The parties shall first try to resolve any disputes arising out of or relating to this engagement through mediation. If the parties cannot agree on a single mediator, each party shall select a lawyer and those two lawyers shall select a mediator, all three of whom will mediate the dispute.

Please review this engagement letter carefully and return a signed copy to indicate your agreement with and acceptance of its terms.

Thank you for the opportunity to work with [Law Firm Name] on this important matter. I look forward to helping you bring this matter to a successful conclusion.

Sincerely,

[Freelancer]

Accepted and agreed:

[Law Firm Name]

By:_____

[Authorized Signatory]

Date:_____

Index